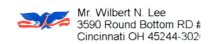

Mr. Wilbert N. Lee
3590 Round Bottom RD #
Cincinnati OH 45244-302

Windows NT™: The Next Generation

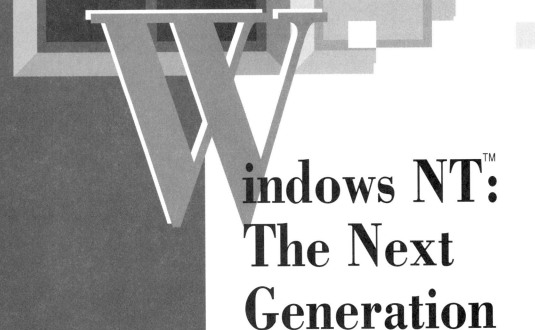

Windows NT™: The Next Generation

Len Feldman

SAMS
PUBLISHING

A Division of Prentice Hall Computer Publishing
11711 North College, Carmel, Indiana 46032 USA

To Susan, who always believed in me, and Karin, who helped me believe in myself.

© 1993 by Sams Publishing

FIRST EDITION
FIRST PRINTING—1993

All rights reserved. Printed in the United States of America. No part of this book may be used or reproduced in any form or by any means, or stored in a database or retrieval system, without prior written permission of the publisher except in the case of brief quotations embodied in critical articles and reviews. Making copies of any part of this book for any purpose other than your own personal use is a violation of United States copyright laws. For information, address Sams Publishing, 11711 N. College Ave., Carmel, IN 46032.

International Standard Book Number: 0-672-30298-5

Library of Congress Catalog Card Number: 92-82091

97 96 95 94 93   5 4 3 2 1

Interpretation of the printing code: the rightmost double-digit number is the year of the book's printing; the rightmost single-digit number, the number of the book's printing. For example, a printing code of 93-1 shows that the first printing of the book occurred in 1993.

Composed in Utopia and MCPdigital by Prentice Hall Computer Publishing.

Screen reproductions in this book were created by means of the program Collage Plus, from Inner Media, Inc., Hollis, NH.

All terms mentioned in this book that are known to be trademarks or service marks have been appropriately capitalized. Sams Publishing cannot attest to the accuracy of this information. Use of a term in this book should not be regarded as affecting the validity of any trademark or service mark.

Publisher
Richard K. Swadley

Acquisitions Manager
Jordan Gold

Acquisitions Editor
Gregg Bushyeager

Development Editor
Mark Taber

Technical Editor
Bruce Graves

Technical Consultants
Noel J. Bergman
David Kerr
Rick Segal

Contributing Author
Scott Wallace

Senior Editor
Grant Fairchild

Editorial Assistants
Rosemarie Graham
Sharon Cox

Editorial Coordinator
Becky Freeman

Formatter
Bill Whitmer

Production Director
Jeff Valler

Production Manager
Corinne Walls

Imprint Manager
Matthew Morrill

Proofreading/Indexing Coordinator
Joelynn Gifford

Production Analyst
Mary Beth Wakefield

Book Design
Michele Laseau

Cover Art
Tim Amrhein

Graphics Images Specialists
Tim Montgomery
Dennis Sheehan
Sue VandeWalle

Production
Katy Bodenmiller
Lisa Daugherty
Carol Johantges
John Kane
Sean Medlock
Roger S. Morgan
Caroline Roop
Michelle M. Self
Greg Simsic
Angie Trzepacz
Suzanne Tully
Alyssa Yesh

Indexer
Suzanne Snyder

Contents

Introduction   **xvii**

1 The Road to Windows NT   **1**
   Windows NT: Evolution and Revolution 2
   Is Bigger Better? MULTICS, Timesharing, and Security 4
   Bell Labs, Digital Equipment, and UNIX 6
      UNIX Goes to School 8
   Microsoft, MITS, and the Birth of the Personal Computer 10
      CP/M and the PC Tower of Babel 12
   IBM and PC DOS 14
   Xerox's Graphic and Networking Revolutions 16
      Graphical User Interfaces 16
      Local Area Networking 18
      Xerox PARC, Macintosh,
        and the Birth of Microsoft Windows 19
      MS-DOS Evolves Into OS/2 22
   The Microsoft/IBM Schism 25
   Windows 3.0 Takes Off 27
   The Challenges of Windows NT 29
      The UNIX Threat 29
   NT Responds to the UNIX Challenge 32
   Conclusion 33

2 Microsoft's Blueprint for the Nineties   **35**
   Operating Systems: New Applications, New Choices 37
      Networks and Client/Server Computing 38
      Pen Computing 39
      Personal Digital Assistants or PDAs 40
      Multimedia Computers 41
   Microsoft's Operating System Family 42
      Modular Windows: Lean and Mean 42
      Mobile Windows: One for the Road 46

Windows NT: The Next Generation

  DOS and 16-Bit Windows: The Big Middle 50
  Windows and Networking: All Together Now 55
  Windows NT: Top of the Heap 58
 Conclusion 60

3 Windows NT in Profile   63

 32-Bit Addressing 64
 Virtual Memory 68
 Preemptive Multitasking 72
 Symmetric Multiprocessing 76
  Asymmetric Versus Symmetric Multiprocessing 78
  Threads 80
 Client/Server Architecture 82
  The Client/Server Model Within NT 85
 Security and Enhanced System Integrity 88
  Access Control Security 89
  System Integrity 92
 Support for DOS, OS/2, 16-Bit Windows 3.X,
  and POSIX-Compliant Applications 94
  DOS Compatibility and the Virtual DOS Machine 95
  WOW: 16-Bit Windows Compatibility 96
  OS/2 Compatibility 97
  POSIX Compliance 97
 Platform Independence 98
 Networking 99
  Peer-to-Peer Networking 100
  Interoperabiliy 100
  Client/Server Networks with LAN Manager 101
 Conclusion 103

4 A Quick Walk Through Windows NT   105

 Starting from the Top: Logging On 106
 Control Panel 109
 Print Manager 114
 Administrative Tools 119
  User Manager 119
  Disk Manager 124
  Performance Monitor 126

Contents

    Backup 127
    Event Viewer 128
    Registry Editor 129
  File Manager 130
  Logging Off 135
  Conclusion 136

5 A Developer's View of Windows NT   139

  The NT System Architecture 140
    The NT Executive 142
    System Services 142
    Executive Components 143
    The Kernel 157
    Hardware Abstraction Layer 159
    Summary 160
  The NT Development Environment 161
    4G Virtual Address Space 161
    Multitasking Support:
      Several Paths to the Same Destination 162
    Object Security 165
    Multiprocessor Support 166
  The Win32 Application Programming Interface 168
    API Functionality 170
  Windows NT SDK Graphical Development Tools 173
    Dialog Editor 173
    Process Viewer 176
    Spy 178
  Conclusion 180

6 Networking with Windows NT   183

  Networking with Windows NT: Home Run or Strike Three? ... 184
    Microsoft's Networking History 184
    The Operating System Is the Network 187
  The OSI Reference Model and Windows NT 188
  NT's Network Driver Interface Specification 191
    NT Transport Protocols
      and the Network and Transport Layers 192
    Redirectors and the Session Layer 195

Windows NT: The Next Generation

    Providers and the Presentation Layer 196
    The Application Layer and Windows NT 198
NT's Key Networking Features: Peer-to-Peer Networking 200
    Client/Server Networking and Windows NT 204
    Network Security: A Matter of Trust 208
    Fault Tolerance 211
    Distributed Processing 213
Caveats and Conclusions 215

7 Windows NT Versus DOS and Windows   217

Why Look at Windows NT? 218
NT and the Windows Family 219
    MS-DOS 220
    The Windows Revolution 226
    Windows and Win32s 231
    Windows for Workgroups 232
    Windows NT 239
Conclusion 245

8 Windows NT Versus OS/2   247

OS/2 Explained 248
OS/2 2.1 Features 249
    Multitasking 250
    More Memory 251
    Application Compatibility: DOS, Windows, and OS/2 253
    Adobe Type Manager Font Support 256
    High Performance File System (HPFS) 257
    Application Protection 260
    REXX 262
    The Workplace Shell and the System Object Model 263
OS/2 Connectivity 266
    Networking 266
    Novell NetWare 267
    LAN Server 268
    LAN Manager 268
What Windows NT Has That OS/2 2.1 Doesn't 269
    Portability 269
    Symmetric Multiprocessing 270

Extensibility 270
　　　Security 271
　　　Fully 32-Bit Operating System 272
　　　NTFS 272
　Conclusion 273
　　　Summary of Features 274

9　Windows NT Versus UNIX　　　　　　　　　　277

　UNIX: Coming of Age on the Desktop 278
　A Quick Introduction to UNIX....................................280
　　　Sophisticated Process Management 283
　　　Multiprocessing 284
　　　The File Metaphor 284
　　　Device Drivers 285
　　　Interprocess Communications 286
　　　32-Bit Linear Memory Addressing
　　　　and Virtual Memory Management 287
　　　Spaces and Modes 287
　　　System Call Interface 288
　　　Shells, X Window, and APIs 288
　　　Security 289
　　　Networking 290
　UNIX and Windows NT: Differences 292
　　　UNIX Advantages 292
　　　UNIX Disadvantages 293
　　　NT Advantages 294
　　　NT Disadvantages 295
　The PC UNIX Contenders 296
　　　NeXTSTEP: Object-Oriented UNIX 296
　　　SCO UNIX 301
　　　SunSoft Solaris 304
　　　Univel UnixWare 308
　Decisions, Decisions 313
　　　NeXT NeXTSTEP 313
　　　SCO UNIX 313
　　　Sun Solaris 314
　　　Univel UnixWare 314

Windows NT: The Next Generation

10	**Making the Choice: Windows NT or Not?**	**319**
	The Decision Dilemma: Four Criteria for Action	320
	Functionality	321
	Reliability	328
	Interoperability	334
	Compatibility	338
	Some Final Thoughts	345
11	**The Future of Windows NT**	**347**
	Windows NT: Meeting the Market	348
	Application Availability	350
	Longevity	354
	Competition	358
	Forecasts	366
	Conclusion	368
A	**Glossary**	**371**
B	**Bibliography**	**391**
Index		**395**

Acknowledgments

My deepest thanks to my agent, Matt Wagner, and Waterside Productions. Matt's advice was invaluable throughout the project. When for a time it looked like the book might never be completed, his quick efforts helped to save the project. Thanks also to Scott Wallace, who cowrote the first drafts of Chapters 7, 8, and 9.

Special thanks to Gregg Bushyeager and Mark Taber, my editors at Sams, who kept the project on track and patiently taught me how to write a readable, informative book. It'll be easier the next time, I promise.

Thanks also to Bill Pitts and Toshiba America Information Systems, for the use of the Toshiba T4400SXC color notebook computer on which I ran Windows NT while writing this book. Bill supplied the computer on short notice, and he extended his loan of the equipment several times in order to give me the time I needed to finish my writing. I couldn't have completed this book without his help.

I'm extremely grateful for the cooperation of Dave De Puy and Jerry Dusa of Eagle Technology, my consulting clients during the time that I wrote this book. Dave and Jerry allowed me to set my own schedule, and they put up with me when I straggled in after late-night marathon writing sessions. I also learned a tremendous amount about local area networking and Novell NetWare from the Eagle organization.

I greatly appreciate the technical help and product information I received from Shelly Womack and the entire Microsoft author relations and technical support organizations. Thank you very much for permitting Sams to publish this book prior to Windows NT's final release.

To my friends, teachers, clients, employers, coworkers, and editors over the years, thank you. Your support gave me the knowledge and courage necessary to take on this project. Many thanks to Avram Grossman and Mark Vlach for their assistance in helping me understand the Windows NT architecture.

About the Author

Len Feldman is a marketing consultant with 13 years of computer industry experience. He has consulted for Borland, Eagle Technology, Hitachi, Radius, Toshiba, Western Digital, and other clients. Mr. Feldman served as an industry analyst covering the multimedia marketplace, and was chief sysop of the Multimedia Vendor Forum on CompuServe in 1991-92. He holds a B.S. degree from Robert Morris College and an M.M. degree from Northwestern University's Kellogg Graduate School of Management.

Introduction

Microsoft's Windows NT (which stands for *new technology*) operating system is one of the most important new software products in years. It's the first new "industrial-strength" operating system of the nineties, and it promises to have an enormous impact on the existing Windows, OS/2, and UNIX marketplaces. NT will ultimately affect thousands of computer software and hardware vendors, hundreds of thousands of software developers, and millions of computer users.

With the advent of Windows NT, some of the world's largest computer companies, including IBM, Microsoft, Novell, and Sun Microsystems, have cranked up their public relations machinery to tell you their "truth" about Windows NT and convince you that they have the best approach to operating system design. In an information war such as this between world-class competitors, it's often difficult to distinguish between promises and reality, and between useful information and obfuscation.

About This Book

Windows NT: The Next Generation is intended to provide an objective management-level introduction to the features and capabilities of Windows NT and comparative information designed to help you decide if, when, and how to adopt NT.

This book is not meant to be a programmer's reference, nor is it a user's guide—although it does provide plenty of useful information for both software developers and end users. It's intended to be a decision-making resource, a high-level introduction to the strengths and weaknesses of Windows NT that will help you evaluate your computing needs and determine the ability (or inability) of NT to meet those needs.

Windows NT: The Next Generation

This book is being published before the formal introduction of Windows NT in order to give you the information you need to objectively evaluate the claims and counterclaims made by the many vendors, researchers, industry analysts, and other opinion-makers with a stake in NT's success or failure.

No book written before the official shipment of any computer product can totally reflect its final features, capabilities, and performance. However, given testing of the beta-level developer versions of NT, interviews with industry insiders, extensive research, and the benefit of 13 years of computer industry experience, I'm confident that you'll find *Windows NT: The Next Generation* an accurate, informative guide to the present and potential future capabilities of NT and its closest competitors.

Who This Book Is For

Windows NT: The Next Generation is for anyone currently evaluating or planning to evaluate Windows NT as a platform for application development and delivery. This book was written with the assumption that the reader has a basic understanding of computer terminology and concepts, and some of the discussions also assume some familiarity with DOS and 16-bit Windows.

This book's primary focus is on PC-based computing environments, but it also discusses topics of interest to users of workstations, servers, minicomputers, and mainframes. Existing DOS, Windows 3.x, OS/2, and UNIX users will find discussions tailored to their needs and interests. This book compares Windows NT to each of these operating systems and provides a set of practical guidelines to help you decide whether NT is right for you.

Windows NT: The Next Generation is especially relevant to the following readers:

- End Users: Chapters 1 through 4 provide extensive information about the history of Windows NT's development, features, and capabilities. If you're currently using local-area networking, or plan to do so, read Chapter 6. Depending on your current operating system or the operating system with which you're comparing NT, read Chapters 7, 8, or 9, and conclude with Chapters 10 and 11 to

Introduction

round out your evaluation of NT and learn more about NT's future and competing operating systems.

- Software Developers: Chapter 2 describes how Windows NT fits into Microsoft's overall operating system strategy, and Chapter 3 details NT's features and capabilities. Skip to Chapter 5 for an extensive discussion of NT's architecture, differences between the Win32 API and the existing Windows 3.X API, and a look at the NT Software Developer's Kit. Depending upon your current development platform, or the platform that you're comparing NT against, read Chapters 7, 8, or 9. Conclude with Chapters 10 and 11 to round out your evaluation of NT and learn more about NT's future and competing operating systems.

- Administrators: Chapter 3 introduces NT's features, and Chapter 4 describes many of NT's system administration tools. Chapter 6 discusses NT's networking features and provides insight into how to integrate NT into existing networks and computing environments. If you're working in an existing DOS-based Windows, OS/2, or UNIX environment, read Chapters 7, 8, or 9, respectively, to learn more about the essential differences between NT and your current operating system. Chapter 11 is useful for learning more about the future of NT and competing operating systems.

- Information System Managers: Start with Chapter 2 to get an understanding of how NT fits into Microsoft's overall operating system strategy. Chapter 3 introduces NT's features, and Chapter 4 shows you what your end users and system administrators will see when they use NT. Chapter 5 provides in-house software developers with essential information about NT, and Chapter 6 explains NT's networking capabilities and interoperability with your existing systems. Depending on the operating system or systems that you're already using, Chapters 7, 8, and 9 compare NT and your existing operating system head-to-head. Finally, Chapters 10 and 11 give you some practical comparisons and advice that you can use to evaluate whether or not to adopt NT. Chapter 11 also forecasts the winners and losers of today's operating system wars and provides additional information about the future of NT and other operating systems.

Windows NT: The Next Generation

How This Book Is Organized

Windows NT: The Next Generation seeks to provide answers to the following questions:

- What features does Windows NT offer and how do they work?
- How does NT compare with other popular operating systems?
- What criteria can end users, software developers, system administrators, and MIS managers use to evaluate whether NT is right for their needs?

This book covers three major subject areas :

- Windows NT in depth
- Windows NT head-to-head
- Evaluating NT

Windows NT In Depth

This section introduces you to the history of NT and its place in Microsoft's overall operating system strategy. You'll get a solid understanding of NT's features and capabilities, and both a user's and developer's perspective on NT. In addition, you'll learn about NT's networking capabilities and interoperability with other computer systems.

Chapter 1, "The Road to Windows NT," offers a historical perspective of the key events, participants, and products that led to Windows NT.

Chapter 2, "Microsoft's Blueprint for the Nineties," outlines Microsoft's operating system strategy for the nineties, from software for consumer electronic products to enterprise-wide operating systems such as Windows NT. This chapter also briefly compares Microsoft's operating system family and those of its competitors.

Chapter 3, "Windows NT in Profile," contains a high-level, yet detailed introduction to Windows NT, focusing on the real-world value of its features.

Introduction

Chapter 4, "A Quick Walk Through Windows NT," focuses on a user's view of Windows NT. This chapter introduces you to the main features of the security subsystem, Program Manager, and File Manager. It reveals the secrets of NT's new system administration features.

Chapter 5, "A Developer's View of Windows NT," provides a detailed look at NT from a developer's point of view. The executive, which represents the heart and soul of the NT operating system, is examined. Key NT features of special significance to software developers, differences between the 16- and 32-bit Windows Application Programming Interfaces, and important tools from the NT Software Developers' Kit, are all discussed.

Chapter 6, "Networking with Windows NT," investigates NT's extensive networking support features. NT's capabilities are examined in the context of industry-standard networking architectures, and NT's compatibility with a variety of network protocols and network operating systems is examined. The features and value of LAN Manager for Windows NT are also discussed.

Windows NT Head-to-Head

This section compares Windows NT head-to-head with its three most popular desktop operating system rivals: DOS and 16-bit Windows, OS/2, and UNIX. You'll learn the similarities and differences between NT and its rivals, and you'll receive some practical advice on how to make the right operating system choice.

Chapter 7, "Windows NT Versus DOS and Windows," compares Windows NT's features and capabilities with the existing world of DOS and 16-bit Windows.

Chapter 8, "Windows NT Versus OS/2," explores the similarities and differences between OS/2 and Windows NT and provides some guidelines for comparing and choosing between the two operating systems.

Windows NT: The Next Generation

Chapter 9, "Windows NT Versus UNIX," examines and explores the differences between Windows NT and UNIX. The UNIX operating system's architecture, as represented by UNIX System V, is examined and compared to Windows NT. Four important PC-based UNIX variants (NeXT's NeXTSTEP, the Santa Cruz Operation's SCO UNIX, SunSoft's Solaris, and Univel/Novell's UnixWare) are described and compared. The chapter concludes with some additional guidelines for comparing and choosing among Windows NT and its UNIX competitors.

Evaluating NT

The final section of the book compares DOS and 16-bit Windows, OS/2, UNIX, and NT on seven critical criteria, chosen for their practicality and usefulness in evaluating your real-world needs. Because the operating system you choose will affect your computing environment for years to come, this section forecasts the future of NT and rival operating systems.

Chapter 10, "Making the Choice: Windows NT or Not?" compares DOS-based Windows, OS/2, UNIX, and Windows NT using a set of practical, time-tested criteria. The four operating systems are compared on functionality, reliability, interoperability, and compatibility.

Chapter 11, "The Future of Windows NT," continues the comparisons of Windows, OS/2, UNIX, and NT by focusing on issues related to the future of each operating system and its successors: application availability, longevity, and competition. Following this discussion, the chapter reveals the three operating system vendors whom I believe are the most likely to survive the forthcoming operating system wars and explains why those three companies were chosen. Finally, the chapter concludes with independent analysts' forecasts of NT's future market penetration.

The choice of an operating system for your current and future computer applications is one of the most important decisions you can make. As you'll see, there are many factors to consider before adopting any operating system. This book will help you understand the features and benefits, advantages and disadvantages of Windows NT and other popular operating systems so you can make an informed, insightful choice.

1

The Road to Windows NT

This chapter introduces the key features and capabilities of Windows NT and discusses the origins of concepts underlying NT's design. You'll also read about some of the strategic reasons behind Microsoft's development of Windows NT.

Windows NT, Microsoft's newest and most powerful operating system, has been in development for more than 4 years. The origins of many of its key technologies go back almost 30 years. The designs of Windows NT, UNIX, and even DOS can all trace their origins back to the same roots. In order to understand why Windows NT has the features and capabilities it does, and why NT's architects made the design decisions they did, it's important to understand the history—including the politics—of Windows NT.

For example, NT and OS/2 are described today as deadly competitors, but did you know that at one time NT was actually called OS/2 3.0 by Microsoft? Did you know that NT's architecture borrows heavily from UNIX, and that one of NT's chief architects also led the design of the UNIX derivative operating system at the heart of NeXT Computer's NeXTSTEP? As you read this chapter, and for that matter, the rest of this book, keep in mind that "industrial-strength" operating systems such as UNIX, OS/2, and Windows NT are more alike than their developers often would like to admit. Once you understand the roots of Windows NT, and thus the roots of modern operating system designs, you can begin to understand the real value of NT's innovations.

Windows NT: Evolution and Revolution

Windows NT is Microsoft's flagship operating system for high-end personal computers, high-performance workstations, and local area network servers.

Operating System

A program or set of programs that provides essential services required by all other programs running on a computer. The operating

1 • The Road to Windows NT

> system is, in effect, a "superprogram" that coordinates the activities of all other programs and provides uniform access to system resources. An operating system provides a common way of accessing system resources so that application developers can focus on writing the best possible applications without worrying about system management.

Windows NT's advanced features draw on almost thirty years of computer industry progress made at such seminal research organizations as MIT and Xerox's Palo Alto Research Center. A few of NT's features that have their roots in this early era of the personal computer include

- Software emulation
- Compatible file systems
- Multitasking and multiprocessing
- Security subsystem
- Device drivers
- Graphical user interface
- Local area networking support

Windows NT also draws design guidance from many other systems, including Digital Equipment Corporation's VMS operating system and Mach, a variant of the UNIX operating system developed at Carnegie-Mellon University. As you'll see, NT is based on some of the computer industry's most innovative operating system technology.

Windows NT is likely to be one of the most important new computer products of the nineties because it will affect virtually every computer user and every application in one way or another. Windows NT will impact

- Desktop Computing: Windows NT combines UNIX's power with Windows' ease of use in a package that runs on everything that fits on your desktop, from a notebook computer to a top-of-the-line, 3-D graphics workstation.

Windows NT: The Next Generation

- Network Computing: NT includes its own networking capabilities, interconnects with a variety of networks and network operating systems, and supports enterprise-wide client/server networks.

- Secure Computing: NT implements C2 (Controlled System Access) security, a U.S. government-defined level of security and integrity that helps protect the system from unauthorized access and faulty programs.

- Mission-Critical Applications: NT supports a variety of fault-tolerant features that, when combined with its security and system integrity, make it an excellent platform for running applications crucial to an entire organization.

Fault Tolerance

A computer design feature that enables the system to continue running in the event of a hardware or software failure. For example, a fault-tolerant storage system allows a computer to continue running, and to recover important data, in the event of a hard disk or disk controller failure.

Windows NT brings mainframe-level operating system concepts to the desktop and network level and into a price category that most small businesses can afford. To help you better understand Windows NT, I'll examine the origins of some of its most important design concepts. The story of Windows NT is in many ways the story of the personal computer industry.

Is Bigger Better?
MULTICS, Timesharing, and Security

In 1969, a decidedly small software development was created at Bell Laboratories—a development that, despite its size, has had an enormous

1 • *The Road to Windows NT*

impact on the computer industry. For many years prior to 1969, the trend in the computer industry had been to make systems bigger: faster processors, more memory, higher-capacity mass storage devices, faster printers, and so on. More powerful hardware required more powerful operating systems.

An excellent example of a massively powerful operating system was MULTICS. MULTICS was designed in the sixties at the Massachusetts Institute of Technology for use on General Electric mainframe computers. In the seventies, after Honeywell acquired General Electric's computer business, MULTICS was adapted to run on Honeywell computers.

MULTICS had two key goals. First, it was to be a massive timesharing operating system on which many users could simultaneously run programs. The operating system would parcel out tiny slices of the processor's time to each program, in a process called multitasking.

Timesharing

The capability of enabling several users to simultaneously run programs on a computer, via multitasking (see the following paragraph).

Multitasking

A process whereby a computer appears to run several tasks at once by giving each program a tiny slice of the computer's time and rapidly switches between each program.

Second, MULTICS was to be the first truly secure operating system, designed to be safe enough for U.S. government applications. MULTICS implemented a ring architecture that could be thought of as a series of concentric rings with the inner ring closest to the computer's hardware and thus the most protected and the outer ring closest to casual users, such as

students, and thus the most open. The computer on which MULTICS ran duplicated the ring architecture in hardware. MULTICS was therefore tightly coupled to its hardware platform. MULTICS achieved its goals, but at a price. It was enormous and unbelievably complex, with every conceivable feature included by the designers.

The multitasking and security features of MULTICS were so useful, however, that they found their way into many other operating systems. Windows NT implements multitasking and multilevel security features while maintaining an uncomplicated system architecture.

Bell Labs, Digital Equipment, and UNIX

Bell Labs was one of the earliest and largest customers for Digital Equipment Corporation (commonly known as Digital, or simply DEC). While MULTICS represented the ultimate in big systems shared by many users, DEC was the first company to make "one person, one computer" its core strategy. DEC downsized and downpriced its computers so that they could be dedicated to one or just a few users and coined the term minicomputer. DEC sold large systems, but compared to the mainframes that dominated the computer industry for the first two decades of its existence, it built its business and reputation on small computers.

DEC's minicomputers were ideal development systems for Bell Labs' researchers. They were inexpensive, could be moved from office to office, and could be experimented upon without endangering the work of tens or hundreds of other users (as was always the case with larger time-shared systems).

In 1969, Ken Thompson of Bell Labs decided to write a tiny time-shared operating system for his DEC PDP-7 minicomputer. This operating system had all the basic multitasking functionality necessary to simultaneously support several users, even when run on computers with very limited memory and storage, such as the early PDPs.

With the input of several of his colleagues, Thompson succeeded. He named the resulting operating system UNIX, as both a play on the name MULTICS and as an indication that his new, small operating system could

1 • The Road to Windows NT

do essentially everything the complex MULTICS operating system could do. In 1970, Thompson and his colleague Dennis Ritchie moved UNIX to DEC's popular PDP-11/20 computer.

Compiler

A computer program that translates other computer programs from a high-level language (such as C, FORTRAN, or Pascal) into the low-level machine language of the target computer's hardware.

One of UNIX's unique design features is that it is based on a very compact core of essential functions called a kernel. Operating system developers can layer new operating system functions and commands, support for new input/output devices, and other extensions on top of the UNIX kernel. In fact, new commands can be written by programmers, or even by users, as combinations of other commands and functions, and these commands, or scripts, can be executed just like any other UNIX command or program. Although UNIX comes from humble roots, it was designed to be almost infinitely extensible.

Kernel

The most essential, or core, functions of an operating system. Kernels commonly manage the essential program execution and low-level input/output functions of the operating system.

Extensibility

The capability of adding new features and functions to an operating system or application program without needing to modify the original software.

Windows NT: The Next Generation

In 1973, Thompson and Ritchie rewrote the UNIX kernel in C. Prior to that time, system software developers believed it was impossible to achieve adequate performance from an operating system written in a high-level language.

High-Level Language

A computer programming language with commands (code) that resemble human language, which are converted into machine language (see the following definition). Popular examples are BASIC, C, C++, COBOL, FORTRAN, and Pascal.

Machine Language

A very low-level computer programming language that uses the native instruction set of a specific processor, such as an Intel 486 or MIPS 4000. Computers convert programs written in high-level languages into machine language for execution.

High-level languages (like C) must be compiled into machine code, and the machine code created by a compiler can never be as efficient as code written and hand-tuned by expert programmers. Thompson and Ritchie paid a performance penalty for rewriting UNIX in C, but Ritchie's C compiler created very efficient code. The speed and ease of programming, support, and upgrading that C afforded more than made up for any losses in raw performance.

UNIX Goes to School

All these achievements, as important as they were, probably would be little more than footnotes in the history of the computer industry had AT&T not

1 • The Road to Windows NT

made a critical decision in 1974. AT&T was in the telephone business, not the computer business, yet the company knew that UNIX was an important product. Rather than shelve or abandon UNIX as a laboratory curiosity, the company decided to license it for use on DEC minicomputers at educational institutions, at virtually no charge.

DEC's computers had already made strong inroads into colleges and universities, due to their low prices. However, DEC licensed its operating systems to schools for an annual per-computer fee, which added up to a significant percentage of each computer system's total cost. DEC's primary time-sharing operating system (RSTS) was already becoming obsolete. By running UNIX on their computers, schools could support more users per system and channel some of the money they were saving on license fees into purchases of more computer hardware and software.

An explosion of UNIX usage throughout the academic world was the result of this situation. Thousands of students learned to use and program UNIX systems. As these students graduated, they took their knowledge of UNIX to the commercial world. When AT&T began licensing UNIX commercially in 1977, tens of thousands of experienced UNIX programmers and system administrators were already working in the business world.

UNIX was originally limited to DEC computers and AT&T's own internal systems, but UNIX's design concepts spread rapidly throughout the computer industry. Here was an operating system designed to take advantage of the most recent innovations in computer design. It was modular and written in a high-level language, so theoretically it could be moved to any computer capable of running a C language compiler.

Software developers quickly saw the appeal of UNIX. Until then, every computer manufacturer sold and supported its own operating systems, which were incompatible with software for competitive computers. Programmers had to rewrite popular programs for accounting, database management, and other applications, so that the programs would run on every operating system. UNIX, though, could run on a variety of computers from different manufacturers, so applications written for one UNIX system could quickly be moved to another system without massive redesign. UNIX became the first platform-independent operating system.

Windows NT: The Next Generation

> **Platform-independent**
>
> The capability of an operating system or application program to run on otherwise incompatible computers.

Windows NT adopts and improves upon UNIX's multitasking and security features. Like UNIX, Windows NT is also platform-independent; NT runs on PCs, workstations, and shared servers based on Intel and Intel-compatible, MIPS, DEC, and (in the near future) Hewlett-Packard and Integraph processors.

Microsoft, MITS, and the Birth of the Personal Computer

In 1975, two years before UNIX became commercially available, the personal computer age began when *Popular Electronics*, a monthly magazine for the do-it-yourself electronics experimenter, featured the world's first personal computer on the cover of its January issue. The Altair, manufactured by a tiny company named Micro Instrumentation & Telemetry Systems (MITS), headquartered in an Albuquerque, New Mexico storefront, was based on Intel's then-revolutionary 8080 8-bit microprocessor (revolutionary because it was the first general-purpose 8-bit computer on a single chip). The Altair came with 512 bytes of RAM standard (many of today's digital watches have more memory than the Altair) and could be expanded to a maximum of 4K of RAM. By comparison, even today's cheapest PCs have 640K of RAM.

The Altair was a bare-bones computer by any definition. It looked like a miniature version of DEC's PDP-8 minicomputer. Unlike today's PCs with their keyboards, displays, and printers, users communicated with the Altair via a row of tiny toggle switches and lights. A few lucky users could bypass the switches and lights with a teletype (a slow, clanking keyboard and printer with a paper tape reader and punch for data storage).

As with any computer, the Altair had to be programmed in order to make it do anything useful. Unfortunately, for most users, the only way to program the Altair was to flip tiny toggle switches on its front panel to enter 8080 machine language programs.

Most computer programmers preferred to work with high-level languages such as FORTRAN or COBOL, which were originally designed for use on mainframe computers. FORTRAN (Formula Translator) was used primarily for engineering, scientific, and mathematical applications; COBOL (Common Business-Oriented Language) was designed specifically for business applications. Compared to low-level assembly and machine languages, commands in these languages were similar to English, and programs written in them could be moved from one computer to another reasonably quickly and easily. For example, a FORTRAN program would first be compiled or converted to machine language, and then the computer would run the compiled program.

A high-level language that quickly gained popularity in the seventies was BASIC (beginner's all-purpose symbolic instruction code). Developed in the sixties at Dartmouth College, BASIC was a simplified version of FORTRAN designed for use by students. BASIC was interpreted instead of compiled, meaning that each line, or statement, in a program was interpreted on the fly into machine code and executed by the computer. If the programmer made a mistake, the BASIC interpreter would catch it, immediately indicate the error, and stop running the program. This made it easy for novice programmers to test and debug their programs interactively.

Debugging

The process of locating, identifying, and correcting errors in a software program or in the design of a hardware device. The "bugs" in debugging refer to the insects that occasionally crawled inside the ENIAC, the very first electronic computer, and caused electrical short-circuits which halted the computer.

Another advantage of BASIC interpreters was they could be made extremely compact and efficient. The popularity, ease of programming, and compact size of BASIC made it MITS' natural choice to be the Altair's high-level language. MITS, however, was a tiny computer hardware company

Windows NT: The Next Generation

with no in-house language developers, so the company sent an invitation to all comers: MITS would market BASIC from the first company to successfully demonstrate its software running on an Altair.

Among the many technology fans who fell in love with the Altair after reading the *Popular Electronics* article were two Harvard undergraduates, Bill Gates and Paul Allen. Gates and Allen set off to become the first to develop a working BASIC for the Altair. Neither Gates nor Allen owned an Altair, and only a handful of the computers were in existence. Using published information about the Intel 8080 processor, Allen wrote an emulator, or simulator, that would look exactly like an 8080 to software programs. The emulator ran on Harvard's PDP-10 mainframe computer. Gates used Allen's emulator to write and test the Altair BASIC interpreter. (As you'll see in Chapter 3, "Windows NT in Profile," this same emulator technology allows Windows NT to run DOS and 16-bit Windows programs.)

In February 1975, Allen flew to Albuquerque to demonstrate his and Gates' BASIC to MITS' founder Ed Roberts. Amazingly, their BASIC worked the first time, even though neither Gates nor Allen had ever seen an Altair, except on the cover of a magazine! Gates and Allen formed a company called Microsoft to market their BASIC, and MITS formally licensed Microsoft BASIC that summer. Microsoft was well on its way to setting its first de facto industry standards with BASIC and Disk BASIC. (Disk BASIC combined the BASIC langauge with a rudimentary disk-based operating system.) From that day forward, Microsoft has enjoyed a sustained growth path unparalled in the history of the computer industry.

CP/M and the PC Tower of Babel

UNIX suggested an elegant solution to a problem beginning to plague the nascent personal computer business in the late-seventies. Operating systems were not really an issue in the Altair days. The computers executed a tiny program called a bootstrap loader that would load a larger program, such as BASIC, into memory, and then run the larger program. BASIC could handle the operating system functions for such a small computer, but after personal computers began to add mass storage devices such as floppy disk drives, and as other languages such as FORTRAN, PASCAL, and C began to be used, operating systems became essential.

Every personal computer supplier developed its own operating system or bolted an operating system underneath BASIC. Overall sales of personal computers were growing by leaps and bounds, but only Apple (which introduced the Apple I in April 1976 and galvanized the industry the next year with the Apple II), Tandy, Commodore, and IMSAI were succeeding in their efforts to build large customer bases. Most of the remaining personal computer manufacturers were using 8080-compatible processors, yet software written for the Processor Technology SOL wouldn't run on Tandy's TRS-80, or vice versa.

Application developers had to write unique versions of their software for every computer and operating system, so to maximize sales and reduce development costs, they focused their attention on the most popular brands. Smaller computer companies without the resources of Apple or Tandy couldn't hope to attract major developers. Hardware companies also soon learned that their sales were directly related to the number of application programs available for their computers. More applications meant more sales. In short, hardware manufacturers built a "Tower of Babel" from dozens of incompatible operating systems. Computers without a library of applications were considered hobbyist's toys, so how could smaller manufacturers get the application software they needed for survival?

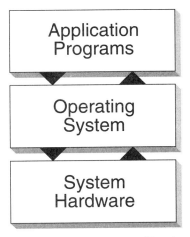

Figure 1.1. The interrelationships among application programs, operating systems, and computer system hardware.

Windows NT: The Next Generation

In 1978, Gary Kildall broke the logjam by devising a way to make dozens of personal computers from different manufacturers compatible with each other. He wrote an operating system called CP/M (control program for microcomputers) and founded the Digital Research Company to develop and market his software. CP/M was modeled after UNIX, and it provided a set of standardized calls, or routines, for disk storage and memory management, input/output, printer and display output, and other functions. By writing programs to use CP/M's routines instead of directly "talking" to specific hardware or using proprietary operating system features, application developers could make one program work on dozens of different manufacturers' computers. Like UNIX, CP/M was platform-independent.

CP/M was revolutionary in its own way because it was the precursor of the PC clone phenomenon that has overtaken the computer industry. By 1979, CP/M was the leading operating system for personal computers. By expanding the market for software developers, it caused the application software market to explode, which paved the way for major manufacturers like Xerox and Hewlett-Packard to introduce their own personal computers. CP/M was especially popular for business-oriented applications such as word processors and databases. Microsoft introduced its first hardware product in 1980, the CP/M SoftCard, which enabled Microsoft BASIC and the growing library of CP/M applications to run on the Apple II.

IBM and PC DOS

Throughout the seventies, IBM watched the personal computer industry from the sidelines. IBM's only contribution to the early PC industry was the 5100, a portable computer based on the obscure APL programming language. None of the companies in the personal computer business represented a direct threat to IBM's core business, which was mainframe computers, but IBM fought hard to be the sole supplier of computers to its customers. The company recognized that personal computers were efficient and cheap and were therefore becoming increasingly popular with its customers. After these small computers established a foothold in IBM's customer base, IBM was forced to devise ways to connect personal computers to its mainframes, and in some cases, even had to provide support for these systems.

1 • The Road to Windows NT

During the summer of 1980, IBM recognized marketplace demands and decided to introduce its own personal computer. IBM's customers would have no reason to purchase an Apple or Tandy computer after the IBM PC was available. The company's natural inclination was to follow its mainframe practices and design a proprietary computer, but advisors both inside and outside IBM convinced senior management to develop an open-architecture computer using off-the-shelf parts. In July 1980, IBM management gave the green light to the project, with the requirement that in order to beat other anticipated competitors to market, the entire system—hardware and software—had to be ready for introduction within one year.

IBM turned to Microsoft for help in developing an operating system for its new PC, and Microsoft called upon Seattle Computer Products and Tim Paterson. Paterson was the codeveloper of the CP/M SoftCard, and in 1979 his company was an early supplier of Intel 8086-based processor boards. Paterson hoped to run CP/M-86 on his boards by the end of the year, but as Digital Research's schedule continued to slip, he decided to write his own 16-bit operating system. The resulting operating system, QDOS, was completed in September 1979. QDOS provided many of the same system calls as CP/M and used some of the same names for system functions, but it also borrowed some additional conventions directly from UNIX and incorporated a unique disk file management system.

16-Bit Processor

A computer that can move and process two 8-bit bytes of data at a time, as compared to an 8-bit processor, which can handle only one byte at a time. A 16-bit processor generally is twice as efficient, and therefore twice as fast, as a comparable 8-bit processor because it can work on twice as much data at one time.

16-Bit Operating System

An operating system designed to take full advantage of a 16-bit processor.

Windows NT: The Next Generation

For CP/M users, QDOS was familiar enough that 8-bit programs could readily be ported by application developers to 16-bit QDOS systems. For Microsoft, QDOS was ready and could be delivered to IBM in time to meet the 12-month deadline. On August 12, 1981, as part of IBM's announcement of its Personal Computer, PC DOS (later also marketed by Microsoft as MS-DOS, and commonly called DOS), the most popular operating system in history, was born. More application software has been developed for DOS than for any other operating system in computing history. Windows NT was developed to both maintain compatibility with this huge library of software and overcome DOS's limitations.

Xerox's Graphic and Networking Revolutions

While the personal computer business was just a dream in 1973, Xerox's Palo Alto Research Center (PARC) was already completing the Alto, a personal computer that represented a radical departure from established computer design concepts. The Alto and its successor, the Bravo (neither of which Xerox ever put into production), laid the foundation for what a personal computer is today.

Graphical User Interfaces

Unlike virtually every other computer of its day, the Alto featured a display monitor capable of displaying sophisticated graphics. Xerox PARC designed a laser printer called Dover that could print the same sophisticated text and graphics, which led to the first what-you-see-is-what-you-get (WYSIWYG) computer system: what appeared on the display is identical to what prints on paper.

Instead of the arcane text listings of directories and subdirectories of files required to navigate through conventional computer operating systems, the Alto used its bitmapped display to provide a new way of working with computers: the desktop—a stylized representation of items found on a

1 • The Road to Windows NT

conventional office desktop, such as file folders, mail, and in-and-out baskets. The graphical symbols used to represent these items are called icons.

To execute commands and programs and to navigate between files and directories, the Alto used a mouse. Mice had been developed many years earlier at SRI International for use as a pointing and selecting device, but they had never been fully integrated into a computer's design prior to the Alto.

The combination of a graphical display, a desktop, and a mouse formed the foundation for the world's first graphical user interface, or GUI.

Graphical User Interface (GUI)

A software program that enables users to interact with a computer by using a mouse to manipulate graphical objects (files, printers, and so on) instead of typing commands.

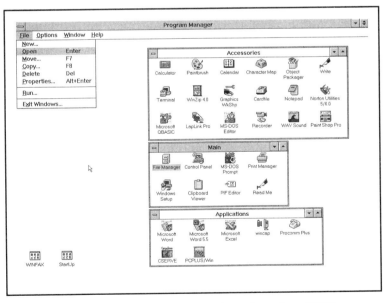

Figure 1.2. Typical elements of a graphical use interface (GUI).

Windows NT: The Next Generation

> **Icon**
>
> A graphical symbol that represents a file, program, or device within a GUI. For example, Windows NT application programs are represented as icons within the Windows Program Manager.

As you will see, the basic GUI concepts and designs first formulated at Xerox PARC in the seventies are an integral part of Windows NT today.

Local Area Networking

PARC also devised solutions to the problem of sharing resources between computers, such as files and printers. In the Alto and Bravo era, mass storage devices such as hard disk drives were extremely expensive, and floppy disk drives were unreliable. Dedicating a hard disk drive to every computer was simply too expensive, PARC's laser printers were still more expensive, and the cost of equipping even a few computers with both was prohibitive.

Computers needed a practical way to share resources. Many techniques existed to connect two computers together, but connecting several computers together so they can share resources and communicate with each other when necessary was impossible. PARC solved this problem by applying a technology first created for passing computer messages among sites via radio transmission. This technology, called carrier sense multiple access/collision detection, or CSMA/CD:

- Allowed multiple computers to monitor and access a single transmission link.
- Let every computer use the link when needed.
- Handled collisions, those times when two computers tried to access the link at the same time.

Instead of using a radio link, which is noisy, prone to failure, and slow, PARC researchers connected the computers with a special kind of low-noise coaxial cable used predominantly in the cable television industry. This cable link supported data transmission at 10 megabits per second. (To understand

1 • *The Road to Windows NT*

just how fast this link was, consider that the maximum speed of sending data across phone lines at that time was just 1,200 bits per second. PARC's new technique was almost 10,000 times faster.)

PARC's link between computers became known as a local area network, or LAN, and PARC's specific version was called EtherNet.

Local Area Network (LAN)

A high-speed communications link between two or more computers, which allows the computers to share data and system resources.

DEC, Intel, and Xerox adopted EtherNet as a local area networking standard. EtherNet is the most widely used LAN in the world today. The concepts of shared peripherals and high-speed computer-to-computer communications pioneered at Xerox PARC are a fundamental part of the communications and networking architecture of Windows NT.

Xerox PARC, Macintosh, and the Birth of Microsoft Windows

It's ironic that none of the PARC innovations from the seventies and early eighties ever became successful Xerox products, but PARC was extremely open with information about its technologies. In 1979, Xerox made a million-dollar investment in Apple and gave Steve Jobs, Apple's cofounder, a tour of PARC, where he saw all the Alto-related technologies. In that one day, he became a GUI convert.

Jobs redirected the efforts of the team developing Apple's Lisa (a desktop computer with a bitmapped display and mouse) toward a GUI model similar to the one he saw at PARC. At approximately the same time, Jef Raskin, a manager in Apple's technical publications department, was assigned to head a new project to develop a $500 home computer, which in Raskin's thoughts quickly became an information appliance—easy to set up, easy to use, and inexpensive. Raskin called his computer Macintosh.

Windows NT: The Next Generation

Initially, Jobs wanted nothing to do with the Macintosh, and Raskin felt the same way about the PARC GUI, although he liked the capabilities of a bitmapped display. However, Lisa was becoming more and more complex and expensive, and the Macintosh was quickly becoming a low-cost, barebones version of Lisa, compatible with the bigger machine but much less expensive. As Jobs would refer to it, the Macintosh was the people's computer. In the spring of 1981, Raskin was forced off the Macintosh project, and Jobs became the full-time project manager.

A few months later, Jobs gave Bill Gates a secret demonstration of a Macintosh prototype in an effort to convince him to port Microsoft's programming languages and spreadsheet program (Multiplan, which was then being tested) to the forthcoming Mac. Gates was well aware of Xerox PARC's research through published reports, but the Mac was his first opportunity to see a GUI running on an inexpensive personal computer. Like Jobs, Gates had his own revelation that GUIs represented the future of personal computer software. Gates initiated his own GUI development project (called Interface Manager) in the fall of 1981. Interface Manager was to be a standardized interface between application programs and MS-DOS. The generic term currently used for such software is an application programming interface, or API.

Application Programming Interface (API)

A standardized library of programming tools used by software developers to write applications that are compatible with a specific operating system or graphic user interface.

NOTE

In early 1982, Microsoft and Apple signed an agreement stating that Apple would license key portions of the Macintosh operating system to Microsoft in return for Microsoft's development of software for the Macintosh. This agreement enabled Bill Gates to participate in the

1 • The Road to Windows NT

> Macintosh introduction, but limitations on Microsoft's ability to use Apple's technology written into the contract laid the groundwork for subsequent look and feel lawsuits between Apple and Microsoft.

Several other companies were working on their own GUIs. VisiCorp, the publisher of the enormously successful VisiCalc spreadsheet, introduced its own GUI for IBM PCs, along with a suite of integrated business application programs, under the name VisiOn in November 1982. Two months later, Apple introduced Lisa, at a $10,000 price. Gates, fearing his competitors would establish an insurmountable market lead, called a press conference later that same month to announce that Microsoft would ship its own GUI before VisiCorp actually shipped VisiOn. Privately, Gates expected to ship Interface Manager, now renamed Windows, in January 1984.

Windows' development was much more complicated than Gates had anticipated, and in October 1983, when VisiCorp started shipping VisiOn, Windows was nowhere near completion. Further compounding the problem was IBM's refusal to market Windows, in favor of its own in-house developed GUI, TopView. Microsoft had signed up 24 PC-clone manufacturers to support Windows, but IBM declined. In fact, IBM licensed VisiOn as an addition to its product line. Finally, as a key Macintosh developer (and one of only three developers that Jobs chose to showcase at the Mac's introduction), Gates knew the Mac would be announced in January 1984 with a flurry of publicity.

In early November, Gates launched his own competitive strike by announcing Windows. The software was far from ready for customer shipment, so the announcement was more accurately a technology demonstration, but Microsoft succeeded in upstaging Apple and VisiCorp for a short time. Windows didn't actually ship to customers until November 1985, more than two years later than initially projected by Gates and almost three years after Microsoft's GUI plans were first revealed. By the time Windows 1.0 shipped, IBM's TopView had been abandoned, VisiOn was being sold off in an attempt to save the rapidly crumbling VisiCorp, and even the Apple Macintosh was struggling in the marketplace. Once Windows 1.0 shipped to customers, it was also dead on arrival, and many industry pundits wondered if PC GUIs really had a market.

Why did all the first-generation GUIs fail? Industry analysts came up with a few reasons.

- All the GUIs, with the exception of the Macintosh, were crude and unappealing, because the graphics capabilities of the PC hardware were very limited. The need to support character-mode PCs further crippled the DOS GUIs.

- The GUIs, including the Macintosh, were slow and unresponsive. Power PC users could accomplish more in less time by using DOS.

- The original Macintosh had very limited expansion options and was unappealing to PC and Apple II users who relied on their computers' expansion slots for additional functionality.

- VisiCorp's VisiOn was a closed system that took much longer to arrive at the market than expected. By the time VisiOn shipped, competitive products had surpassed its individual application modules (word processing, spreadsheet, and database).

MS-DOS Evolves Into OS/2

In late 1983, IBM committed itself to the production of its second generation PC, the PC/AT. Market success was essential; IBM was still reeling from the failure of its PCjr. home computer. IBM needed to choose between two Intel processors to form the core of the PC/AT, the 80286 and the 80386 (more commonly known in the abbreviated forms, 286 and 386). The 286, which was available immediately, was Intel's first attempt to correct some of the major design flaws in earlier processors, such as the memory segmentation design that was such a nightmare for DOS programmers. The 386, which was still under development, would be Intel's first 32-bit processor and promised both far better performance and fewer programming headaches than the 286.

The 286 processor ran in two modes, real and protected. Real mode was 100 percent compatible with the IBM PC's original processor, only faster. Protected mode eliminated some of the original PC's memory problems, but it was incompatible with DOS and couldn't run existing DOS applications. The forthcoming 386 offered even greater performance boosts for DOS

1 • *The Road to Windows NT*

applications without incompatibility, and the 386 ran everything in a single mode, which made system programming much easier.

Microsoft recognized that the advanced features of the 386 would enable it to develop a second-generation operating system with vastly superior performance and many new features, including multitasking and virtual memory.

Virtual Memory

A memory management technique that allows an operating system to run programs which exceed the amount of physical high-speed memory available by substituting hard disk storage space for random-access memory.

The 386 would also be an excellent processor for Windows and other graphics-intensive software. Therefore, Bill Gates lobbied IBM to base the PC/AT around Intel's 386 and begin a new project to jointly develop an advanced DOS product that would take advantage of the 386's capabilities. Windows development continued, and Gates hoped that Windows would become the standard user interface for Advanced DOS.

IBM management also understood the limitations of the 286, but they were under heavy pressure to release a new PC. The 286 was immediately available, while the 386 was as far as two years away from shipping in quantity. IBM also considered the 386 to be so powerful that it would be overkill for a single-user PC; a 386-based PC could be a threat to IBM's highly profitable line of small business computers. Therefore, IBM rejected Microsoft's proposal and designed the PC/AT around the 286. The first PC/ATs shipped to customers in October 1984.

In mid-1985, Microsoft and IBM agreed to begin joint development of Advanced DOS for the PC/AT. IBM's lackadaisical attitude toward the project and the 286's poorly-designed protected mode, which made programming almost impossible, bogged down development. The PC/AT was selling extremely well with DOS, and IBM saw no reason to rush a potentially confusing new operating system into the market.

Windows NT: The Next Generation

In 1986, two events caused IBM to change its game plan. First, Apple successfully promoted the desktop publishing concept with the Macintosh and the LaserWriter laser printer, which finally legitimized GUIs and forced IBM to improve the graphics capabilities of its PCs. Second, Compaq introduced the first 386-based PC in September, with enormous performance advantages over the PC/AT. Compaq, which had always been a supplier of reliable PC clones, took the mantle of technological leadership away from IBM and scored big sales gains at IBM's expense. IBM took eight months after the Compaq introduction to release its own 386-based PC.

To beat back Compaq and regain market leadership, IBM was forced to take Microsoft, and Advanced DOS, more seriously. IBM agreed to speed up development of this new operating system, now called OS/2, but still demanded that the operating system work on the 286-based PC/AT, as well as the new 286 and 386 computers under development as part of IBM's still-secret PS/2 line of PCs. Microsoft pushed IBM hard to adopt Windows as the GUI for OS/2. IBM agreed, but required Microsoft to develop a custom version of Windows, called the Presentation Manager, to IBM's specifications.

Microsoft and IBM agreed to begin full-scale development on what would become OS/2 1.0, but even as the two companies were beginning work, the seeds of their eventual divorce were sown. Microsoft had planned to allow application programs to use the same Windows API, regardless of whether they were running on top of DOS or OS/2; now, the two operating systems would have two different, and significantly incompatible, APIs. Before this time, Microsoft programmers, working under Microsoft supervisors, performed most development. Then, IBM developers in the United States and Europe would work hand-in-hand with their Microsoft counterparts, and Microsoft's programmers would often work under IBM supervision. IBM's bureaucracy and rules gnawed at the morale and productivity of Microsoft's more freewheeling developers.

IBM had its own concerns about Microsoft. On many occasions, IBM management tried to convince Gates to kill Windows because they saw it as a threat to OS/2. In their view, DOS's role was to continue to run the huge library of existing character-mode programs, whereas OS/2 would be used for new, graphics-intensive applications. IBM saw no need for a GUI like Windows on top of DOS, and worse, Windows might confuse developers about DOS's real role and delay their adoption of OS/2. Microsoft was committed to OS/2, but Bill Gates refused to bet the entire company on its success and continued funding Windows development.

When OS/2 was formally announced in April 1987, along with IBM's new PS/2 line of personal computers, many signs indicated all was not well. OS/2 1.0 wouldn't ship to customers until the end of the year, and the critical software development tools needed to create new applications were also delayed. OS/2 would be much more expensive than DOS, and it placed heavy demands on a PC: 8M of RAM were suggested for best performance, at a time when most PCs had only 1 or 2M. In addition, a high-capacity hard disk and new display controller were required for the best performance.

OS/2 1.0 started out badly and never really recovered. Few OS/2 applications were available for many months after OS/2 finally shipped, and graphical applications had to wait for the Presentation Manager, which didn't ship until fall 1988. For most developers and users, OS/2 didn't represent a viable alternative to DOS.

The Microsoft/IBM Schism

Microsoft's pivotal position as a supplier of core operating system technology to every PC manufacturer, and its parallel development of OS/2 and Windows, positioned the company to respond quickly to IBM's market and product problems.

Windows 2.0 was released in mid-1988. It was bare-bones, especially when compared to the Macintosh GUI, but it was an improvement over 1.0. For example, Version 1.0 didn't allow users to overlap multiple windows on the display; the windows had to be resized so that all of them could fit on a single screen. This display technique is called tiling. Version 2.0 supported overlapping, in addition to tiled, windows.

Microsoft aggressively solicited software developers to use 2.0, and it began leaking hints about its forthcoming Windows 3.0 that both excited and confused the development community. Developers were excited because

Windows NT: The Next Generation

Windows 3.0 promised to be a huge improvement over 2.0, and confused because they weren't sure how a "fortified" Windows 3.0 would be positioned alongside OS/2, or for that matter, which one was the best one for them to support.

Throughout 1988 and 1989, the relationship between Microsoft and IBM deteriorated. IBM management suspected Microsoft was losing interest in OS/2 and thus was diverting critical development resources to Windows, while Microsoft was frustrated with its inability to get IBM to take a more aggressive and creative product development path. Outside developers received mixed messages. IBM tried to convince them to put 100 percent of their efforts into OS/2, while (depending upon which Microsoft group they spoke with) they'd either get a somewhat diluted version of IBM's pitch, or they'd be told to defer their OS/2 development plans in favor of a new, killer version of Windows.

In November 1989, Jim Cannavino, who was responsible for IBM's entire personal computer business, and Gates made a joint presentation to a group of dealers in which they indicated that they had strengthened their companies' mutual commitments to OS/2. Windows was to be limited to entry-level applications on small PCs, such as portables and 286 systems. OS/2's application range was to be broadened. A bare-bones OS/2 system could run with only 4M of memory, instead of the 8M originally required. In short, Windows and MS-DOS would be relegated to simple, consumer-oriented tasks, while OS/2 would handle everything else.

According to an account in the book *Hard Drive*, written by James Wallace and Jim Erickson, at an IBM press conference a few days later Cannavino inadvertently gave the impression that Microsoft was planning to kill Windows altogether. The reporters and analysts at the conference picked up on Cannavino's comments, and Gates responded to the negative press coverage by increasing Windows 3.0's development budget and staff, in part by transferring several OS/2 developers to the Windows team. Microsoft staffers were instructed to ignore the comments made in the earlier joint presentation and to continue to follow Microsoft's original development plans. Gates' reaction confirmed IBM's worst fears.

Windows 3.0 Takes Off

From early December 1989 to May 1990, Microsoft ran a prerelease, promotional campaign and developer recruitment program for Windows 3.0, the likes of which had never before been seen in the computer industry. The company spent more than $3 million on the one-day announcement in May and a total of almost $15 million in the first month after the announcement. It was extremely risky. Over the years, Windows had developed a reputation as vaporware that didn't work very well when it was finally shipped. If Windows performed to Microsoft's expectations, however, its sales would rise as the price of memory and PCs spiraled downward.

Figure 1.3. Version 3.0 finally made Windows a serious contender.

Windows NT: The Next Generation

Windows 3.0 was incredibly successful, for the following reasons:

- For the first time, Windows 3.0 made the PC user interface truly comparable to that of the Macintosh.

- Microsoft promoted Windows 3.0 with the most expensive and extensive product launch in software industry history.

- The cost to upgrade to Windows 3.0 was very low, and hundreds of thousands of copies were virtually given away.

Windows 3.0's success was achieved, even though it still had some serious flaws and suffered from a shortage of application software until the first quarter of 1991. For the first time, the IBM PC could go head-to-head with the Macintosh in ease-of-use. While Windows 3.0 wouldn't win most of the contests, for the first time it was a serious contender. Customers no longer had to pay Apple's premium price in order to use a mouse and a friendly GUI. Apple was clearly concerned and worried by Microsoft's success. Apple's low-cost strategy, which has caused wrenching changes for Apple's employees, dealers, and developers, was primarily precipitated by the success of Windows 3.0.

Third-party developers jumped into the market in order to add functionality to Windows 3.0. Major application developers such as Lotus and WordPerfect jumped into the Windows market, either with released products or with announced commitments to supply Windows-compatible products. Other companies introduced utilities that improved or extended Windows' own features. For example, Symantec introduced Norton Desktop for Windows, a replacement for Windows' native Program and File Managers that offers an even more Mac-like user interface, as well as additional features for system maintenance and user programming.

The success of Windows 3.0 (and Microsoft's unabashed promotion of Windows at the expense of OS/2) brought the IBM/Microsoft relationship to an end. At first, the two companies announced that IBM would take over development of OS/2 Version 2.0, while Microsoft would focus its attention on a next-generation version for a variety of computers called Portable OS/2 or OS/2 3.0. In late 1991, however, Microsoft announced that Windows NT would replace OS/2 3.0 as its high-end operating system of the nineties.

IBM's 1992 launch of OS/2 2.0 was successful, with over one million copies shipped in six months. However, the company's microcomputer operating system plans for the mid-nineties and beyond are somewhat confusing. In addition to OS/2, IBM supports AIX (its UNIX derivative operating system) and is developing two new operating systems: a microkernel operating system based on AIX with OS/2 compatibility and a new object-oriented operating system with Apple as part of the two companies' Taligent joint venture. (See Chapter 11, "The Future of Windows NT," for more discussion of IBM's plans.)

The Challenges of Windows NT

When Microsoft abandoned OS/2, top management knew that the company had to come up with a replacement. IBM was now the only company marketing OS/2, but Microsoft had contributed most of the technology, so in a way, Microsoft was competing with itself. Microsoft also realized its new high-end software would take at least two years to release, so Microsoft knew OS/2 had a big head start with developers and end-users. (Today, two years is longer than the life expectancy of a single generation of application software.)

Consequently, Windows NT couldn't be just as good as OS/2. It had to offer the same, and more, features and capabilities that OS/2 would be offering when NT was ready to ship. OS/2 1.0 wasn't successful, but OS/2 2.0 would ship as early as a year before NT. If OS/2 2.0's sales took off, IBM would have market momentum and NT might become an also-ran, like the many UNIX variants fighting for tiny slivers of market share. Even worse, Microsoft might have to share or cede its domination of the PC operating system business.

The UNIX Threat

OS/2 wasn't the only competitive focus for the NT team. A new breed of desktop computer, called a workstation, was first introduced by Apollo Computer and Sun Microsystems in the mid-eighties for networked engineering and scientific applications. Workstations from companies such as Sun, Hewlett-Packard (which acquired Apollo in the late-eighties), IBM, DEC, and Silicon

Windows NT: The Next Generation

Graphics all used high-performance RISC (reduced instruction set computer) microprocessors, and all ran UNIX variants. These workstations once sold for tens of thousands of dollars, but by 1990, entry-level workstation prices fell well below $10,000. These systems could outperform even the fastest PCs, and UNIX's capabilities were far ahead of DOS. UNIX supported multitasking and multiuser systems with integrated networking support, while DOS clung to the one user, one computer model.

Reduced Instruction Set Computer (RISC)

A computer architecture that uses relatively few hardware-based machine language instructions, in return for significantly better performance. The instructions that were once executed in machine language are executed in software on a RISC processor.

As workstation prices fell, the high-end and network server PC markets would inevitably intersect with the entry-level workstation market. These low-end workstations could carry UNIX into the PC market. Several companies offered UNIX for 386- and 486-based PCs. The most successful version was XENIX, originally developed by Microsoft under license from AT&T and eventually taken over by the Santa Cruz Operation (SCO). For the most part, however, PC UNIX systems were relegated to specialized, niche applications. Microsoft's concern was that the advent of cheap RISC workstations could change that equation.

UNIX Strength 1: Platform Independence

One of UNIX's chief advantages (as I'll discuss in more detail in Chapter 9, "Windows NT Versus UNIX") is that it runs on many different computers from different manufacturers. This means that programs written for UNIX are portable: you can move them from one computer to another, and even from computers based on one processor design to others using a completely different processor. (This has always been simple in theory, but more complex and difficult in practice. The programs must be modified to accommodate the variations in different versions of UNIX and then recompiled to run on the target computer.)

In the mid-eighties the U.S. government began to require that many of its current and future computers run a standardized offspring of UNIX called POSIX. POSIX is a UNIX-like application programming interface that doesn't require software to be rewritten in order to move an application from one computer to another. UNIX's inherent portability, along with POSIX's adoption by the U.S. government, gave UNIX enormous momentum in the computer industry, from workstations to mainframes. Even such bastions of proprietary operating systems as DEC and IBM were forced by market pressure to offer their customers UNIX and POSIX.

UNIX Strength 2: Multitasking and Multiprocessing

UNIX users can take advantage of multitasking, multiprocessing (supporting programs running on more than one processor at a time), and built-in networking support. Furthermore, some UNIX workstations are powerful enough to run DOS and even Windows applications under UNIX at the same speed as a mid-range 386 PC. Microsoft's hegemony over the PC operating system business was at risk.

Multiprocessing

The ability of an operating system to support, and of applications to run on, computer systems with more than one processor.

UNIX Strength 3: Security

One key strength of UNIX, relative to operating systems such as DOS and even OS/2, is security, an area almost totally ignored by DOS and Windows. Even the very first release of UNIX was a multiuser system. Several people can simultaneously use the UNIX system from their individual computer terminals. Each user can store files on the computer. To keep one user from accidentally erasing or changing another user's files, each user has a directory in which they can store their own files. However, users can easily access other users' directories and files.

Windows NT: The Next Generation

It became clear to UNIX developers that directories alone couldn't keep bad things from happening. One user might inadvertently (or with malice aforethought) erase another user's files. An unauthorized user could read or even modify a file with sensitive information (for example, payroll records or employee evaluations). As more organizations adopted UNIX, the risks became much greater.

AT&T and its UNIX licensees responded with a multilevel security system, managed by a system administrator who has virtually unlimited power. Now, when a user accesses a UNIX system, the user may also be assigned to a group of users whose file access is controlled in the same way. When creating a file under UNIX, a user can limit access to that file to just the user, to the user's group, or to everyone using the computer. (You can protect directories in the same way.) Further, the user can place limits on how the file or directory can be accessed. Permission to read, write, rename, and delete a file can all be controlled by an individual user or user group.

For the most part, this security is not needed in a single-user system. If only one person uses the computer, why bother restricting access? Very few PCs are used as multiuser systems, and most of those are already running UNIX. Problems occur because of networks. The advent of PC networks and file servers changed everything. Suddenly, private files were accessible to coworkers or strangers. File servers provided shared storage for many users, and the first network users encountered all the security problems faced by UNIX's pioneers. Add the U.S. government's requirement for secure computer systems and security on the desktop becomes very important.

NT Responds to the UNIX Challenge

Microsoft responded by incorporating many of UNIX's features into Windows NT, including multitasking, multiprocessing, security, and networking.

Microsoft also made a move that marked a new direction in its operating system strategy. In late spring of 1991, MIPS Computer, DEC, Compaq, and several other computer companies formed a group to develop standards called ACE (advanced computing environment) for a new generation

1 • The Road to Windows NT

of personal computers. These computers would be a hybrid of workstation and PC design, using PC-like buses and hardware designs with a MIPS 4000 RISC processor.

At the ACE press conference, Microsoft announced that it would provide a version of Windows NT for the MIPS 4000. This marked the first time that Microsoft committed to write an operating system for a non-Intel processor. The ACE announcement was Microsoft's first step toward platform, and processor, independence. In 1992, Microsoft committed NT support for computers based on DEC's new Alpha, a high-performance 64-bit RISC processor.

> **NOTE**
>
> Although both DEC and Compaq eventually withdrew from the ACE initiative and most other work on ACE development stopped, Microsoft continues to support the MIPS 4000 and DEC Alpha.

With these announcements, the stage was set for Windows NT to be a world-class operating system that offered a simple upgrade path for existing DOS and Windows applications and users and could go head-to-head with OS/2 and UNIX.

Conclusion

The road to Windows NT was long and took many twists and turns. NT represents the best of 30 years of operating system design from the world's leading software supplier. Today, Microsoft's operating system family extends from Modular Windows (a DOS/Windows hybrid designed to be built into palmtop computers and personal organizers) to Windows NT (a state-of-the-art operating system for servers, networks, workstations, and high-end PCs). Chapter 2, "Microsoft's Blueprint for the Nineties," reveals the design and details of Microsoft's operating system blueprint for the nineties.

2

Microsoft's Blueprint for the Nineties

Windows NT: The Next Generation

This chapter explores how Windows NT fits into Microsoft's operating system plans for the nineties. The information in this chapter was obtained from published reports and discussions with industry analysts and other insiders. You'll read about Microsoft's plans to offer the Windows GUI on everything from the smallest palmtop computers and Personal Digital Assistants (PDAs) to the largest mission-critical distributed processing system. I'll also compare Microsoft's operating system plans to those of other software vendors.

Palmtop

A handheld computer that typically runs applications useful outside the office, such as personal schedulers, notetakers, and small spreadsheets. Virtually all palmtop computers are designed around the Intel X86 processor architecture and can run DOS and DOS applications; some are powerful enough to run Windows applications as well.

Personal Digital Assistant (PDA)

A device that integrates the functions of a computer and communications device, such as a modem or cellular telephone, into a single handheld package. Unlike a palmtop computer, a PDA is not a general-purpose PC and often does not use an X86-compatible processor. PDAs run customized versions of DOS and Windows, or specialized operating systems such as PenGEOS and Go PenPoint. PDA applications are usually written specifically for PDAs.

> **Mission-Critical Applications**
>
> Computer applications that are essential to the day-to-day operations of a business or governmental agency. Examples include reservation and plane scheduling systems for airlines, policy processing systems for insurance companies, and securities trading systems for brokerage firms.

Operating Systems: New Applications, New Choices

Throughout most of the 1980s, choosing an operating system was easy. Microsoft's DOS was really the only PC operating system. Early alternatives, such as CP/M-86 and the Softech P-System, never really took off. DOS clones, such as Digital Research's (now Novell's) Concurrent DOS and DR DOS, found a wider audience but still gained only a tiny share of the market. For PC networks, users overwhelmingly preferred Novell's NetWare LAN operating system. Competitors such as Microsoft's LAN Manager and Banyan's VINES were also-rans at best. Similarly, in the workstation and server marketplace, UNIX was the mainstay, and every hardware manufacturer offered its own UNIX variant.

The stability of the eighties has given way to confusion and volatility in the nineties. New computer designs and applications have led to a variety of new operating systems and new uses for existing operating systems. The choices are richer and more complex than ever before.

Windows NT: The Next Generation

Computer system manufacturers, software developers, and users are all wrestling with operating system choices in a way not seen since the early days of the personal computer industry. Where the options were once clear-cut—DOS for PCs, the Macintosh OS for Apple Macs, UNIX for workstations and multiuser systems, and proprietary operating systems for minicomputers and mainframes—the choices today are much more varied and depend on answers to the following questions:

- What are the applications?
- Who are the users?
- What's the computer (and network) architecture?

The following sections cover a few of the most recent trends and their impact on operating systems.

Networks and Client/Server Computing

As more organizations put their computers on network systems, the demand for shared files, printers, and communications connections expands. DOS simply can't provide the performance, flexibility, or security to support these new networks, so users have turned to LAN operating systems such as NetWare. However, even the DOS- and OS/2-based LAN operating systems have their limits, so an increasing number of large network users are exploring UNIX as a high-performance alternative. Client/server computing, in which many computers (clients) share the applications, data, and peripherals of one or more larger, faster computers (servers), is rapidly becoming the predominant computer architecture of the nineties.

SunSoft's Solaris 2.0 UNIX variant is moving to Intel 386, 486, and Pentium-based computers, as is NeXT Computer's NeXTSTEP. Novell and the UNIX Systems Laboratories (formerly owned by AT&T and several other computer companies, now wholly owned by Novell) formed a joint venture called Univel, which offers a NetWare-compatible UNIX variant for Intel-based computers called UnixWare. The Santa Cruz Operation (SCO) remains the biggest seller of UNIX for PCs, with SCO UNIX. These operating systems will battle Windows NT and OS/2 for market leadership.

2 • *Microsoft's Blueprint for the Nineties*

Pen Computing

Pen computing is a term for computer systems that use a stylus instead of a keyboard as their primary means of input (for selecting menu items and interacting with the computer like a mouse and for handwriting recognition). Pen systems are ideal for users who are uncomfortable with or unable to use conventional computers. Organizations with large field workforces, such as express delivery services, utilities, police departments, and companies with large sales forces, are adopting pen computing as a means of gathering data.

Pen-based applications are often quite different from keyboard-based tasks because the pen is the primary tool for data input and menu selection, replacing both the keyboard and mouse. Pen systems also require a lot of processing power to support graphic, paper-like displays and the capability to recognize handwriting. To meet the unique needs of pen systems, a variety of operating systems have been developed. Communication Intelligence Corporation's PenDOS is a DOS clone enhanced with pen support capabilities. GeoWorks' PenGEOS is a graphic pen operating system for very small computers. Go Corporation's PenPoint is an object-oriented operating system designed from the ground up for pen-based applications, and Microsoft's Windows for Pen Computing is an API layered on top of DOS-based Windows for pen applications.

Figure 2.1. *The Toshiba Dynapad T100X pen computer. It runs Windows for Pen Computing or Go Corporation's PenPoint.*

Windows NT: The Next Generation

Personal Digital Assistants or PDAs

Personal digital assistants is a new class of pocket-sized computer, designed for personal data management in the field. PDAs typically run applications targeted to field user needs. For example, instead of full-featured word processors such as WordPerfect or Microsoft Word, PDAs offer simpler note-taking applications. PDAs run personal schedule managers, libraries of city maps, and other applications targeted to the needs of professionals on the go. PDAs also require extensive wired and wireless communications options, including connections to electronic mail systems, networks, and remote computers.

Figure 2.2. *The Hewlett-Packard 95LX palmtop PC is a forerunner of the coming PDAs.*

PDA developers have chosen several operating system paths. Hewlett-Packard adopted DOS and Windows for its PDAs. Apple developed a new operating system for its Newton PDA and licensed both its hardware and software designs to Sharp. AT&T, Matsushita, NEC, Toshiba, and Eo have all adopted Go's PenPoint for their PDAs, whereas other manufacturers are planning to adopt GeoWorks' GeoWorks OS and PenGEOS. IBM is planning to run a version of OS/2 on its PDAs and may support other operating systems as well. Microsoft has proposed a stripped-down version of 16-bit Windows and DOS called Modular Windows for PDAs. (See the "Modular Windows: Lean and Mean" section for more information.)

Multimedia Computers

In addition to text and graphics, multimedia computers can support audio, video, and animation. Most multimedia systems are based on Apple's Macintosh System 7 or Microsoft's Windows, but low-cost home multimedia players generally don't have the power or data storage necessary to run these full-featured operating systems. For example, Philips' Compact Disc-Interactive, or CD-I (also called the Imagination Machine) uses OS/9, a small, fast operating system for Motorola 680X0-family computers. Commodore's CDTV player uses a compact version of AmigaDOS (not to be confused with Microsoft DOS), and the Tandy Video Information System (VIS) uses Modular Windows.

When it comes to operating systems, one size doesn't fit all. Different applications, computer architectures, and users often require different operating systems. Most operating system suppliers have chosen to focus on a handful of platforms or applications. For example, PenPoint is focused on pen applications and runs on Intel 386 (or greater) processors, as well as on AT&T's Hobbit RISC processor. SunSoft's Solaris focuses on networked client/server systems and runs on Sun's SPARC and Intel's 32-bit processors.

The current mix of operating systems and applications looks something like Figure 2.3.

Windows NT: The Next Generation

Enterprise-Wide Systems	IBM OS/2	NeXT NeXT STEP	Novell UnixWare	OSF OSF/1	Sun Solaris	USL UNIX System V
Client/Server Networks	Banyan VINES		IBM LAN Server			Novell NetWare
Peer-to-Peer Networks	Artisoft LANtastic		Novell Personal NetWare			WEBcorp WEB
Desktop PCs	IBM OS/2		IBM PC-DOS		Novell DR DOS	Apple System 7
Pen, Notebook and Subnotebook Computers	CIC PenDOS	GeoWorks PenGEOS		GO PenPoint	GRiD PenRight!	IBM OS/2 Pen Extensions
PDAs, Organizers and Home Multimedia Systems	GeoWorks GEOS		Novell ROM DOS		Apple Newton OS	General Magic TeleScript

Figure 2.3. The principal microcomputer-based operating systems and their platforms.

Microsoft's Operating System Family

Microsoft is committed to being the first vendor to supply operating systems for every application and most popular computer architectures, from the smallest PDA to the largest enterprise-wide network. Microsoft's strategy is to offer Windows for every application and at every performance level. The Microsoft operating system landscape looks like Figure 2.4.

Starting from the simplest dedicated systems, here's a look at Microsoft's operating system blueprint for the nineties.

Modular Windows: Lean and Mean

PDAs and consumer multimedia players are very different products, yet they share several characteristics.

2 • Microsoft's Blueprint for the Nineties

- They both have limited memory and little or no rewritable mass storage. PDAs are limited because of their small physical size; multimedia players are limited because of cost.
- They both use inexpensive, low-powered processors, to keep costs down, and in the case of PDAs, to extend battery life.
- They don't look or act much like conventional PCs. PDAs commonly use a pen or miniaturized keyboard for input and an odd-sized liquid crystal display (LCD) for output. Multimedia players use a button similar to a video game controller button and a joystick controller for input, and a common color TV set for display.

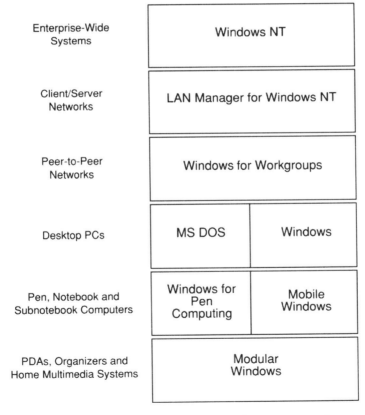

Figure 2.4. Microsoft's operating systems or environments and their platforms.

Windows NT: The Next Generation

The similar nature of these two very different families of devices led Microsoft to develop a stripped-down version of Windows and DOS called Modular Windows. Modular Windows contains MS-DOS and the essential features of Windows, but to save space, the familiar Window, File, and Program Managers are not included. Modular Windows fits in 1M of read-only memory (ROM), and unlike conventional Windows, Modular Windows can run directly from ROM. (Such software is often called "ROMmable" code.) Thus, Modular Windows can run on systems without floppy or hard disk drives. In addition, Modular Windows requires only 1M of RAM, of which almost three-fourths, or 700K, is available for application programs. This enables small or inexpensive systems to run Windows applications.

Random-Access Memory (RAM)

The high-speed semiconductor memory used by computers for program execution. In general, RAM is short-term, or volatile, storage; when the computer's power is turned off, all the data and programs stored in RAM are lost.

Read-Only Memory (ROM)

A form of memory that can be read from but not written to or otherwise modified by the computer.

The big advantage of Modular Windows is compatibility with bigger desktop PCs running Windows. Developers can create applications for PDAs and multimedia players using existing Windows development tools, then move these applications to Modular Windows systems. However, Modular Windows has two major drawbacks.

2 • *Microsoft's Blueprint for the Nineties*

Figure 2.5. *Microsoft's Modular Windows.*

The first drawback pertains to the omission of many standard Windows capabilities in an effort to hold down size and power requirements. Perhaps the most important feature omitted from Modular Windows is the Window Manager. This is the portion of Windows that provides what most people think of as the Windows user interface, such as pulldown menus, icons, and scroll bars within windows. Without the Window Manager, application developers must define, design, and implement their own user interfaces. Developers must spend more time and effort reinventing the GUI wheel, and each application is likely to have its own unique, and potentially confusing, look and feel.

A second major drawback to Modular Windows is that it runs on Intel X86 and compatible processors only. PDAs are often based on RISC processors, such as the ARM processor used in Apple's Newton and the AT&T Hobbit CPU used in Eo's Personal Communicators. Of the current crop of home multimedia players, only the Tandy/Zenith VIS uses an X86-compatible processor. Intel and compatible manufacturers are stalking the PDA and multimedia player marketplaces for customers, but acceptance of Modular Windows is, by design, limited to manufacturers who choose the Intel architecture.

Modular Windows represents Microsoft's attempt to participate in the PDA and consumer computing markets, but its success is far from certain. The proliferation of non-X86 processors and the growth of strong competitors may ensure that Microsoft will not be able to dominate the operating system market for these new products as it has for desktop PCs.

Mobile Windows: One for the Road

Palmtop, subnotebook, notebook, and pen-based PCs present a unique set of needs to operating system and application software developers. All these computers are purchased for portability, so they must be physically small and lightweight. The smallest of these devices can easily fit into a suit or coat pocket. Pen-based computers must be especially lightweight, because they are commonly used in field data-gathering applications, such as recording police accident reports and interviewing/questionnaire data capture, where the computer must be carried and used for several hours every day. Subnotebook computers often sacrifice built-in floppy drives (and sometimes even hard disks) to achieve a smaller, lighter, less power-hungry computer design. Small computers simply don't have the room to carry huge hard disks or tens of megabytes of RAM, so application programs for portable computers, and the operating systems they run on, must be compact and efficient.

Microsoft is developing a version of Windows called Mobile Windows to meet the special requirements of portable computers and their users. Industry analysts forecast that the portable computer segment will be the fastest-growing portion of the PC industry in the next five years, so it's clearly in Microsoft's best interest to address the needs of this market. The Mobile Windows effort is an outgrowth of Microsoft's Windows for Pen Computing development efforts, which originally focused exclusively on the special needs of pen-based applications. Mobile Windows incorporates Microsoft's pen developments and adds additional power management, communications, file, and storage space management features.

> **NOTE**
>
> At the time of this writing, Microsoft had not decided whether to release Mobile Windows as a separate product or to incorporate its features into Windows. Some time this year, the company will make its decision and release products that incorporate the features discussed in the following paragraphs.

Mobile Windows will enhance Windows for Pen Computing, also called Pen Windows, which is a pen-compatible application programming interface that runs under DOS-based Windows. Pen Windows enables users to do anything with a pen that they can currently do with a mouse under conventional Windows, and it allows any conventional Windows application to work with a pen. In addition, Pen Windows incorporates software for handprint recognition (the ability to convert handprinted letters, numbers, and symbols into character codes recognized by the computer). It also offers special data entry features, including a pop-up keyboard that displays on-screen and works like a conventional keyboard when the pen touches keys.

Figure 2.6. *Microsoft's Windows for Pen Computing.*

Some existing Pen Windows users, software developers, and industry analysts have complained that Microsoft's product isn't as easy to use or as well integrated as Go's PenPoint, an operating system designed specifically for pen computing. All pen computer users are also generally disappointed with the lack of quality and usefulness of handprint recognition, not just in Pen Windows but in every pen operating system. The Mobile Windows team is addressing these concerns by more smoothly integrating pen support into Windows itself, by improving the system's handprint character recognition, and by encouraging third-party developers to extend and improve Mobile Windows as they've already done for Windows in general.

Mobile Windows goes further than pen computing and deals directly with the problems inherent in all portable computers. One such problem is power

Windows NT: The Next Generation

consumption. Portability implies battery power, and in general, battery capacity is directly related to the battery's physical size. Portable computers must use small, lightweight batteries, yet the batteries must last long enough to provide a reasonable amount of work between recharges. A typical notebook PC operates two to three hours on a single battery charge, whereas a palmtop can operate for weeks on a set of disposable batteries. To conserve energy, portable computers employ sophisticated power management systems that automatically turn off power-hungry devices such as disk drives and display backlights when they're not in use, and can even slow down or stop the main processor.

Unfortunately, applications that regularly access the hard disk, modem, or other devices can easily defeat these hardware power management features. A word processor, for example, might swap program modules such as spelling and grammar checkers in and out of RAM from the hard disk of a desktop PC as needed, but a portable computer presents special problems. This constant swapping of program modules and data forces the hard disk to stay on all the time, sapping the battery's power and shortening its life. If the user tries to save power by lowering the amount of time the disk drive must be idle before the computer turns it off, performance suffers. Every time the disk drive is accessed, the user must wait while the drive comes up to speed, which takes several seconds.

An operating system that constantly shuffles programs and data to and from the hard disk can cause the same power consumption and performance problems which plague conventional Windows applications. Mobile Windows' designers are modifying Windows to support power management by:

- Reducing Windows' demands for hard disk access.

- Intelligently controlling application demands for hard disk and peripheral device access to reduce power requirements.

- Providing a set of power management guidelines for Windows application developers to follow.

Communications capabilities will also be enhanced in Mobile Windows. Portable computers often need to transfer data gathered in the field to a central computer site or receive data and programs for use outside the office. Current desktop Windows users know that modem communications under 16-bit Windows can often be painfully slow, especially when using inexpensive and commonly available 2400 and 9600 bps modems.

Mobile Windows will improve 16-bit Windows' communications performance over slow phone line links.

> **Bits Per Second (bps)**
>
> A measure of the speed of data transfer between two devices, generally over a communications line such as a phone line. To roughly measure the speed of data transfer in characters per second (each character being one byte long, with additional bits needed for the communications process), divide the bps figure by 10, so a 2400 bps modem transfers 240 characters per second.

> **Modem (modulator/demodulator)**
>
> A device that converts the digital (binary) signals used internally by computers for data storage, transmission, and processing into analog (sound) signals that can be transmitted over a phone line, cellular phone, or other device and back again.

Mobile Windows will also address a problem unique to portable computers, called file synchronization. The best way to illustrate this problem is with an example. A sales manager is often away from the office, making customer visits and working with other salespeople in the field. Suppose the sales manager develops a monthly sales forecast spreadsheet on the office PC and then copies the forecast to a portable computer in order to continue working on it. When the manager returns to the office, the revised forecast on the portable should be copied back to the office PC so that everyone has the most current information. If the manager must copy the forecast manually, however, mistakes may occur. A slip of the fingers could cause the manager to copy the old forecast over the newer, revised version, thus wiping out the changes. The revised forecast could be copied to the office PC under a different name that the sales manager doesn't recognize and can't find, or someone in the office could further modify the original version.

Windows NT: The Next Generation

File synchronization eliminates most of these mistakes by ensuring that the most current versions of files are always kept on both computers. In the forecasting example, when the office and portable PCs are connected the first time, Mobile Windows will ensure that the latest version (on the office PC) overwrites any older version of the same file on the portable. Similarly, when the manager returns to the office and reconnects the computers, Mobile Windows will determine that the portable now has the most recent version of the file and overwrites the older version on the office PC. Safeguards will be included to protect files that should not be updated or overwritten.

The final new feature of Mobile Windows will be storage space management. Currently, DOS-based Windows relies on DOS utilities such as Stac Electronics' Stacker and Addstor's SuperStor for compression/decompression. Mobile Windows will move some of the storage space management features into Windows itself, possibly including the capability for developers and users to reduce the size of Windows itself by mixing and matching Windows modules to create smaller versions of the GUI.

Mobile Windows, whether it appears in 1993 as a separate product or is incorporated into the conventional DOS/Windows products, will go a long way toward making Windows practical for small, easily portable computers, from palmtops to laptops. Together, Mobile Windows and Modular Windows will bring the Windows environment into entirely new applications and markets.

DOS and 16-Bit Windows: The Big Middle

Microsoft's operating system solution for most new and existing PCs remains DOS and 16-bit Windows (as well as Win32s, an API that gives 16-bit Windows the capability to run many 32-bit applications). The inclusion of DOS may be surprising, given Microsoft's huge investment in software development, advertising, and promotion—all designed to entice DOS users to migrate to Windows—but DOS is still important for a number of reasons.

First, over 100 million PCs worldwide still use DOS, with a little more than 10 million copies of Windows installed. Many, if not most, of these PCs are based on 8088, 8086, and 80286 processors that don't have the speed and features required by Windows. Often, these systems have only a megabyte or two of RAM and a small hard disk. These systems are still perfectly capable of running DOS applications, but can't always handle Windows' requirements. These systems may be upgraded or discarded in favor of faster, more powerful systems, but that is very expensive for users with tens, hundreds, or even thousands of PCs.

Another issue helping DOS remain viable is the cost and availability of Windows applications. To take full advantage of Windows, you need to run Windows applications. While most major software vendors provide upgrades for their users to switch to Windows, software upgrades are often as expensive, or even more expensive, than hardware upgrades. This is especially true when users with large numbers of PCs try to upgrade a whole suite of applications to Windows. As a further complication, even today, only a small percentage of the tens of thousands of DOS applications and utilities have been moved to Windows. For many PC users running specialized applications outside the typical office automation, desktop publishing, spreadsheet, and financial management categories, few or no Windows products are available still.

The third reason why DOS is still a linchpin of Microsoft's operating system strategy is the small but vocal and very influential group of PC experts called power users. Most power users first entered the ranks of PC users via DOS, and these users became comfortable and extremely familiar with DOS commands. They learned all the tricks and secrets for performing DOS tasks with minimum effort. For much the same reason that most Windows commands can be accessed both through menus and with keyboard commands, DOS commands represent a power user's shortcut. These users get lost in the menus, dialog boxes, and alerts of Windows, and they see Windows as an impediment to productivity. Of course, these users know that DOS, as a stand-alone operating system, will disappear eventually, but for now, they prefer to stick with what they know.

Windows NT: The Next Generation

Another reason DOS remains important to Microsoft is that serious, fully compatible competitors are now available. IBM has taken over development of its own PC DOS from Microsoft, and Novell acquired Digital Research primarily for access to DR DOS. Microsoft cannot afford to abandon the DOS segment of the operating system marketplace to either IBM or Novell, as both companies have or are developing competitors to Windows, and both will work hard to move their DOS-compatible users to their own 32-bit environments instead of Windows NT. Microsoft wants to keep control over the majority of DOS users and transfer them to Windows, and hence must continue to market and upgrade DOS.

Finally, 16-bit Windows runs on top of DOS and can't run without it. Over time, Microsoft plans to develop 16- and 32-bit versions of Windows that incorporate DOS functionality directly, but these versions are not yet available and won't be ready for some time. Microsoft needs a robust, powerful DOS backbone for Windows.

Microsoft's new MS-DOS 6.0 includes expanded memory management features, a built-in disk compression/expansion utility similar to Stacker, and client networking support for Windows for Workgroups. DOS will continue to evolve, adding more features and functionality, but it's reasonable to expect that sometime within the next few years Microsoft will merge DOS and Windows into a single product and end further product development for stand-alone DOS.

Over the same period of time, 16-bit Windows will grow to encompass a wider range of applications and platforms. At the low end, Windows will incorporate some design elements from Modular and Mobile Windows and be able to support smaller subnotebook and palmtop systems with limited memory and mass storage capacities. These systems will support the standard Windows user interface, but elements that require a lot of storage space, such as multiple device drivers, fonts, and sounds, will be limited.

Industry analysts, Windows developers, and press reports indicate that Windows' Program and File Managers (described in more detail in Chapter 4, "A Quick Walk Through Windows NT") will likely be unified into a single program, not unlike Macintosh's Finder. The standard user interface might then look much more like the Macintosh Desktop or Symantec's Norton Desktop for Windows. As an example of the possible changes to the Windows user interface, I'll first look at the existing Windows 3.1 Program and File Managers, and then view the unified desktop from Norton Desktop for Windows Version 2.0.

2 • Microsoft's Blueprint for the Nineties

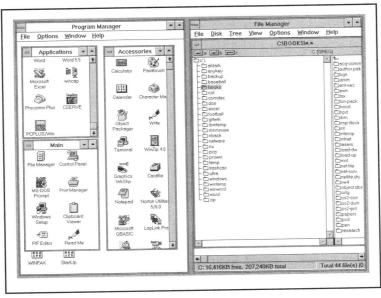

Figure 2.7. *The Program Manager and File Manager in Windows 3.1.*

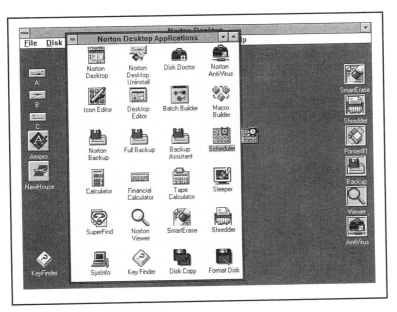

Figure 2.8. *Norton Desktop for Windows.*

Windows NT: The Next Generation

In addition to providing significantly greater ease of use, a unified Program and File Manager could be more space-efficient than the two current separate programs. This would help Windows run on smaller systems.

Other new features will also enhance Windows' usefulness. In current versions of 16-bit Windows, the Program Manager supports a limited drag and drop capability. For example, the user can drag the icon representing a spreadsheet file on top of the icon representing Borland Quattro Pro for Windows. When the user releases the mouse button, the file drops onto the Quattro Pro icon, which launches the program using the spreadsheet file for input. In future versions, the drag and drop capability may be greatly expanded. For example, a user who has access to more than one printer (for example, both a black-and-white laser printer and a color ink jet) could drop the same spreadsheet file onto an icon representing the desired printer, which would automatically launch the correct application and tell the Print Manager to print the selected file to the correct printer. This capability is available in add-on products for Windows today but will be directly incorporated into future versions of Windows.

In the past, Microsoft has incorporated the most popular functions of third-party additions and utilities into future releases of its applications and operating systems. For example, DOS memory management was pioneered by companies such as Quarterdeck with QEMM, and shells (for easier access to DOS functions and commands) were first introduced in products such as Norton Commander. All these functions are now incorporated into DOS. The same thing is likely to happen with Windows. The most important and powerful features of popular third-party enhancers such as Norton Desktop for Windows and Central Point PC Tools for Windows are likely to show up as integral parts of future versions of Windows.

Perhaps the most important evolution of 16-bit Windows will incorporate more of DOS' core functionality into Windows itself. Intel's 486 processor and clones are becoming the minimum standard CPU for all but the least expensive home and office computers, and the remaining installed 8088/8086/80286-based PCs will finally be retired in huge numbers. The widespread availability of powerful, low-cost 386- and 486-based PCs, combined with versions of Windows for virtually every size and shape of computer, will finally edge DOS out of the spotlight and into retirement. Ultimately, DOS

will likely be totally absorbed into Windows and cease to be a stand-alone product. Windows will continue to offer DOS compatibility with a DOS prompt window, but 16-bit Windows will become a full-fledged operating system similar to Windows NT by mid-decade.

In short, 16-bit Windows and DOS will continue to form the core of Microsoft's operating system strategy. Windows will evolve by adopting the best features of third-party utilities and programs. New, targeted versions of Windows for consumer entertainment/education systems, low-end portable computers, and high-end networks will expand Microsoft's market opportunities and provide a common development platform for a huge array of systems.

Windows and Networking: All Together Now

Over 125 million PCs have been sold worldwide since the introduction of the original IBM PC. Most of these computers have been sold to customers who own more than one PC. As the average number of PCs per site has grown, so has the demand for shared data and printers. This demand has fed the explosive growth of PC-based local area networks.

Originally, DOS was designed strictly as a single-user operating system with no provisions whatsoever for sharing files, printers, or other resources. Developers of the earliest popular networks, such as Corvus' Omninet and Datapoint's ARCnet, needed to develop their own DOS extensions to support file and printer sharing between PCs. These bare-bones networking schemes were not standardized and were consequently incompatible with each other. Although sales were brisk, none of the early rudimentary schemes ever really caught on.

Several companies developed more formal, sophisticated networking extensions to DOS called network operating systems, or NOS. An NOS is not a fully functional operating system like DOS. Rather, it is designed for extending DOS to support networks. The most popular NOS was, and remains, Novell's NetWare. NetWare implements a client/server network, which I describe in detail in Chapter 3, "Windows NT in Profile."

Windows NT: The Next Generation

> **Client/Server Networking**
>
> A form of networking in which programs and data files shared between several computers reside on a larger computer called a server, and the PCs using the shared data and programs are called clients. Clients can both share the resources of and execute applications on a server. Peripherals, such as printers and modems, can also be shared. A shared printer with memory for storing files waiting to be printed or connected to a computer with file storage is called a print server; a shared modem or set of modems is called a communications server.

NetWare is popular because it combines performance, data security, and high reliability into a package that works well with DOS and is relatively easy to learn. Competitors, including Microsoft's MS-NET, have tried to challenge Novell's success but failed. Microsoft tried again with a more advanced competitor called LAN Manager, which was based on OS/2, but NetWare continues to dominate the market with more than a 70 percent market share.

Although NetWare is the most popular NOS by far, it also has some problems. NetWare is a fairly expensive software package, and it requires a dedicated high-performance PC to act as a file server. NetWare networks, like most sophisticated local area networks, are difficult to set up and maintain. Special networking software and network interface cards must be installed in every PC on the network. The central file server is the nerve center of the network; if it fails, no one can access any data on the server and work usually grinds to a halt. This means NetWare networks require specialized, trained (and often expensive) technicians to install and manage them.

In spite of the effort and expense required to maintain NetWare networks, popularity indicates that the market wanted this kind of product. If someone could make a less-expensive alternative, one that's simpler to install and maintain, and that doesn't require a dedicated file server, it might be even more popular. A number of companies developed (and are continuing to develop) this kind of low-cost networking product, referred to as a peer-to-peer network.

> **Peer-to-Peer Networking**
>
> A network operating system that allows any computer on the network to share its data and peripherals with any other connected computer, eliminating the need for dedicated servers. Peer-to-peer networks tend to be less expensive and easier to install than client/server networks, but they are also less secure, support fewer users, and present more file management problems than client/server systems.

The most popular peer-to-peer networking product for PCs is Artisoft's LANtastic, which has grown to dominate the peer-to-peer networking market almost as completely as Novell dominates the PC client/server market. Novell has tried, and failed, to derail LANtastic with its own peer-to-peer product called NetWare Lite.

Windows for Workgroups: Microsoft's Peer-to-Peer Solution

Microsoft's Windows for Workgroups, or WFW, is the latest entrant into the peer-to-peer networking market. WFW combines an enhanced version of 16-bit Windows with:

- Peer-to-peer networking.
- Microsoft Mail (an electronic mail application).
- Microsoft Schedule+ (a group meeting and calendar scheduling application).
- File security.
- Features for sharing and linking data documents between applications across the network.

WFW networks are fully compatible with LAN Manager and have limited capability to share data and peripherals with PCs on NetWare-based networks. Microsoft's primary targets for WFW are the hundreds of thousands of small PC workgroups not currently connected by networks. For

Windows NT: The Next Generation

existing Windows users, WFW is often easier to understand and use than other network operating systems because its networking features are directly integrated into Windows, not added on. DOS-only PCs can be connected as clients to WFW networks (meaning the DOS systems can access files and peripherals on connected Windows systems, but Windows users cannot access the DOS systems) with a software package called the Workgroup Connection for MS-DOS.

Microsoft has aggressively priced WFW (starting at under $100) to encourage as many Windows users as possible to try it. Like its competitors, Microsoft also offers plug and play bundles including copies of WFW, network interface cards, and cable. These prices are comparable to or lower than the combined prices for competitive NOS software and Windows. When combined with Microsoft's excellent distribution, sales, marketing, and promotion, WFW's low price makes it a strong contender for peer-to-peer market leadership, even though Microsoft initially appears to have underestimated both the market strength of LANtastic and other competitors, as well as the technical and organizational problems involved with installing even simple peer-to-peer networks.

Windows for Workgroups' peer-to-peer networking features pave the way for the far more sophisticated networking features of Windows NT. In the next few years, mixed peer-to-peer and client/server networks in which Windows NT systems act as servers and WFW systems act as clients will be commonplace. These mixed networks, with their ever-changing workgroups sharing information between members and accessing enterprise-wide information from servers, will offer unprecedented flexibility and total compatibility with Windows.

Windows NT: Top of the Heap

Chapter 3 provides an extensive introduction to Windows NT's features and capabilities, so this discussion primarily examines how NT fits into Microsoft's overall Windows strategy. Windows NT is Microsoft's flagship operating system, the culmination of the company's experience with DOS, OS/2, and its XENIX version of UNIX. Windows NT is designed to take full

2 • Microsoft's Blueprint for the Nineties

advantage of the power of today's most advanced Intel processors, as well as several of the leading RISC processors. It's Microsoft's first operating system since XENIX that is designed for use on non-Intel based computers.

NT runs many existing DOS programs and most 16-bit Windows applications (except those that write directly to low-level 16-bit Windows software routines), as well as POSIX applications and character-based OS/2 applications. Its true power, though, won't be fully realized until applications written specifically for NT are released. Applications that take full advantage of NT's multitasking and multiprocessor support, running on computer systems similarly tuned for NT, will demonstrate significant performance gains over conventional uniprocessor Windows applications.

Though no operating system is bulletproof, NT's technique of completely isolating applications from each other and from the operating system itself dramatically improves overall reliability. The 16-bit Windows system crashes due to "general protection faults" will largely become a thing of the past. NT's enhanced reliability, combined with its extensive security features, built-in peer-to-peer networking, and support for client/server networks via LAN Manager, will make it suitable for mission-critical applications.

Windows NT is Microsoft's answer to UNIX. NT offers the same basic functionality as UNIX and interoperates with UNIX-based networks, but it replaces UNIX's cryptic commands, arcane file structure, and jumble of incompatible graphical user interfaces with a single, standardized user interface instantly familiar to more than ten million Windows users. Windows NT is also the OS/2 that Bill Gates originally wanted: an advanced, 32-bit operating system that's totally compatible with the Windows GUI. It supports DOS applications but finally breaks away from DOS's limitations.

Whether Windows NT will be accepted as a mission-critical operating system by key customers in industry, government, and education remains to be seen. NT is still largely untested, and only a handful of applications will take full advantage of its power. Competitors such as IBM, Sun Microsystems, SCO, Univel, and others are working hard to prevent Microsoft from encroaching on their turf.

NT is by far the most complex product ever developed by Microsoft, and even sophisticated customers probably won't be able to purchase it from a

Windows NT: The Next Generation

computer dealer, install it, and configure a network without outside help. The level of technical support required by NT dwarfs that of any other Microsoft product except LAN Manager. The computer software dealers, distributors, and direct sales force that form the backbone of Microsoft's channels of distribution will be hard-pressed to offer the level of service and support required by NT, whereas competitors such as IBM, Sun, and Novell are far more experienced in providing the required level of technical support for complex operating systems, both directly and through specialized resellers.

Nevertheless, there's every reason to expect that Windows NT will be a successful product. If only 10 percent of the existing 16-bit Windows installed base upgrades to NT, its market share will be close to that of all UNIX variants combined. NT's inherent power as a network server will make LAN Manager a much more attractive alternative to Novell NetWare than it currently is and may help Microsoft grab the network operating system market share away from Novell, Banyan, and other competitors.

With NT, Microsoft will offer a compatible range of operating environments for everything from the smallest palmtop and PDA to enterprise-wide networks. No other environment will support such a wide range of computers and systems as Windows (although IBM is working on a similar family of operating environments based on Carnegie-Mellon University's Mach UNIX-variant operating system). Microsoft may not succeed in its attempt to dominate both the operating system and application software businesses for all segments of the computer industry, but with NT and the rest of the Windows family, it has an excellent chance.

Conclusion

Microsoft has identified the largest, most important, and fastest growing segments of the computer industry and has fashioned an operating system blueprint for the nineties to capitalize on these opportunities. Modular Windows, the entry-level Windows product, will be tailored for small, specialized, often low-cost consumer and business products such as Personal

Digital Assistants and home multimedia players. Mobile Windows will focus on meeting the special needs of pen-based, palmtop, subnotebook, notebook, and laptop portable computers.

DOS and 16-bit Windows will continue to serve the broad computing needs of desktop PC users, but most or all of DOS's functionality will eventually migrate directly into Windows. Windows for Workgroups will offer low-cost, peer-to-peer local area networking support, full compatibility with LAN Manager networks, and limited compatibility with competitive network operating systems such as NetWare.

Windows NT will support multitasking and multiprocessing and will be an excellent file server platform. With LAN Manager, NT will become a full client/server network operating system, directly competitive with NetWare and UNIX. Windows NT will support DOS, 16-bit Windows, OS/2, and POSIX applications in addition to native 32-bit NT applications. In short, Windows NT is designed to support enterprise-wide, mission-critical applications. Microsoft's suite of Windows operating environments will support the broadest range of applications and computer platforms in the industry.

3

Windows NT in Profile

Windows NT: The Next Generation

The Windows NT operating system ups the ante on its competition, including OS/2, UNIX, and Microsoft's own 16-bit Windows. Most of NT's features and capabilities are already available under one or more operating systems, but none has everything that Windows NT brings to the table. This chapter defines and explains NT's most important features so that you can have much of the information you need to determine whether NT is right for you.

This chapter examines the key features of NT in detail. The following list itemizes these features, starting with those that were specified in the product definition from the beginning:

- 32-bit addressing
- Virtual memory support
- Preemptive multitasking
- Multiprocessing support
- Client/server architecture
- System security and enhanced system integrity
- Platform independence
- Peer-to-peer networking, coexistence with other network servers, and support for LAN Manager

32-Bit Addressing

I'll first define some terms to help you understand what 32-bit addressing means and why it's important, then I'll briefly discuss how DOS and 16-bit Windows perform addressing.

3 • *Windows NT in Profile*

> **Address**
>
> The location of a single byte of information in the computer's memory or mass storage. An address can be *physical*—point to a specific byte of data in a specific physical location in memory or on disk—or *virtual*—point to a logical (software-based) address that the operating system then maps to a specific physical address. Windows NT uses virtual addressing to provide each application with 4 gigabytes of address space (of which 2 gigabytes are reserved for the operating system).

Chapter 1, "The Road to Windows NT," examined the history of Microsoft's operating system developments and explained that DOS was designed around the memory management capabilities (and limitations) of Intel's 16-bit 8086 and 8088 microprocessors. The 8086 and 8088 offered a 20-bit address space, which means they could physically address one megabyte of memory. Twenty bits didn't fit extremely well into a 16-bit word size, so Intel's engineers came up with a scheme for accessing any address, called *memory segmentation*.

The engineers divided the megabyte of memory into sixteen 64K *segments*, or chunks. They chose 64K because programmers are familiar with 64K addressing from the old 8-bit processors, such as the Intel 8085 and Zilog Z80. In order to calculate a physical memory address, the segment number is multiplied by 16, and then a 16-bit offset is added. The result points to the selected byte of memory. In this way, programmers could get to any address within the 1M address space. (Other 16-bit processors of the same era, such as the Motorola 68000, used a linear addressing scheme that could address any byte in memory directly, without segments or offsets. IBM chose the Intel processor instead, and the rest is history.)

If this sounds convoluted and slightly stupid, that's because it was. IBM engineers made matters worse by further dividing up the 1M space. The first 640K of memory was accessible to programmers, but the upper 360K was

Windows NT: The Next Generation

reserved for system software and functions. The result was a programming nightmare that has haunted DOS programmers ever since, because to maintain backward compatibility, this addressing scheme still persists years after the Intel 386 first made it obsolete.

Over the years, developers have formulated a variety of schemes for addressing more than 640K of memory. In addition to utilities included in MS-DOS 5.0 and Windows 3.1, several third-party software developers have devised their own schemes. Two of the most popular examples are Quarterdeck's QEMM and Qualitas' 386Max. All these tools extend usable memory far beyond the 640K limit, but as any user of these memory managers will tell you, getting them to work with a specific PC configuration and suite of applications and utility software is often a time-consuming and frustrating process. It always seems at least one critical application or utility is incompatible with your memory manager.

The Intel 386 was the first DOS-compatible processor that implemented a linear address space and theoretically should have eliminated memory segmentation, and along with it, the need for third-party memory managers. In reality, the 386's 32-bit linear address space was incompatible with programs written for older Intel processors.

Incompatible programs included DOS and all programs written to run under DOS. To maintain compatibility with the huge installed base of DOS and DOS applications, Intel included an addressing mode, called *real mode*, that is 100 percent backward-compatible with earlier processors and software. Unfortunately, when running in real mode, the 386 (and 486) looks and acts like nothing more than a very fast 8086. DOS, which was written around the limitations of the 8086/8088 and the original IBM PC, still looks and works very much like an extremely fast version of its 1981 ancestor, including all the addressing limitations.

Real Mode

A memory addressing mode that uses the same memory segmentation model (segment:offset addresses) as the original Intel 8086 processor.

3 • *Windows NT in Profile*

> **Protected Mode**
>
> A memory addressing mode that uses linear addressing, instead of segments and offsets, to access any byte within memory. Protected mode also implements hardware memory protection features used by Windows and Windows NT.

Windows NT takes advantage of the linear address space of the 386, 486, and Pentium (Intel's 586) processors, as well as RISC processors such as the MIPS 4000 and Digital Alpha, to provide true 32-bit addressing. In doing so, NT forgoes backward compatibility with DOS and 16-bit Windows, but offers a feature called a *virtual DOS machine* (VDM)—described in more detail later in this chapter—that allows NT to run DOS and 16-bit Windows applications.

A 32-bit addressing scheme has several advantages. First, by eliminating memory segmentation, software development is easier and faster. Programmers no longer need to be intimately familiar with the memory requirements of their applications. Next, 32-bit addressing improves system performance by eliminating the processing overhead that software memory managers require. In fact, Windows NT doesn't need any third-party memory managers. Getting rid of the memory managers also eliminates their various software and hardware incompatibilities, which means NT's software configuration and installation can be simpler and easier than that of DOS or 16-bit Windows.

The final advantage of 32-bit addressing is a vast increase in available program and data sizes, illustrated in Figure 3.1. As I mentioned previously, Windows NT supports a maximum combined program and system size of 4 gigabytes, which is hundreds of times larger than the practical limits on DOS and 16-bit Windows program sizes. Complex applications that process extremely large files (such as image processing programs) or mission-critical transaction-oriented applications (such as reservation, financial trading, and insurance claims processing systems) are difficult or impossible to implement under DOS and Windows. All these applications are well within Windows NT's capabilities, due in large part to its 32-bit addressing.

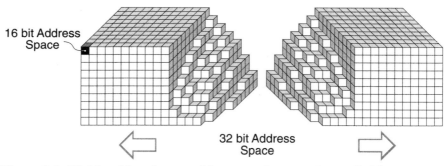

Figure 3.1. 32-bit addressing provides a vast increase in available program and data sizes.

Virtual Memory

Windows NT's 32-bit address space gives applications access to 4 gigabytes of memory (of which 2G are reserved for use by the operating system), which is more than sufficient for almost any conceivable application. The two primary types of computer memory are random access memory (RAM) and mass storage, which is usually contained on a hard disk.

RAM is fast; today's PCs typically use RAM that can retrieve or store a byte of data in 70 nanoseconds, or 70 billionths of a second. RAM's second advantage is that programs can go directly to any memory address and retrieve a single byte, rather than needing to first skip to the block, or area, on the disk in which the byte is located, and then scan through the block one byte at a time until the requested information is located. Hard disks, on the other hand, are many times slower than RAM and require at least one additional step. It obviously makes sense to use as much RAM as possible.

Unfortunately, technical and economic limitations make it impractical to use RAM for 100 percent of a computer's memory requirements. First, when the computer's power is turned off, anything stored in RAM is lost; this kind of memory is called *volatile* storage. (Many portable computers apply a small amount of power to their RAM, even when the computer is turned off, to temporarily retain the stored data. When the computer's battery runs out, the contents of memory are lost.)

The second disadvantage is price. RAM costs a tiny fraction of what it did at the start of the PC era, but it's still relatively expensive. Currently, 1M of RAM for PCs is selling for approximately $35. This cost limits the amount of RAM that can economically be installed in a PC. Typically, high-end PCs are shipped with 8M of RAM; most can be expanded to at least 20M, and some can hold 64M or more, but to get these high capacities, users must switch to higher-density RAM, which costs more per megabyte but occupies less physical space in the computer.

By comparison, hard disks start at 40M of storage capacity and can be as large as 2 gigabytes or more. At current prices, a 200M PC hard disk sells for approximately $400, or $2 per megabyte, less than one-fifteenth the price per megabyte of RAM. Hard disks also retain their memory's contents when the power is shut off; this kind of memory is *nonvolatile* storage.

The trade-offs of volatility versus nonvolatility are performance versus cost. Using both kinds of memory in a PC makes sense. Use RAM for executing programs and storing critical data when performance is essential, and use the hard disk for long-term storage when nonvolatility and cost per byte are important. If you had your choice and money was no object, you'd want lots of RAM and lots of hard disk space, for maximum performance and versatility. Reality dictates that you'll almost always have more hard disk space than available RAM.

What happens when you want to run a program that requires more RAM than you have available? Suppose you have a spreadsheet program that requires 2M of RAM and a spreadsheet file that requires another 2M, but you have only 4M? The operating system requires its own big chunk of RAM, so you won't have enough RAM space to run the operating system and process the spreadsheet at the same time.

With DOS, if you don't have enough RAM to load your program and data, you're out of luck. You'll need to buy additional RAM and install it in your PC. However, Windows NT offers a way to convert a portion of your hard disk into an extension of your RAM, so that you can run much bigger applications than could fit into RAM alone. This feature is *virtual memory*.

Windows NT: The Next Generation

Virtual memory, illustrated in Figure 3.2, extends the amount of high-speed RAM in a computer with slower but less expensive and more available hard-disk mass storage by fooling application programs into thinking a portion of the hard disk is simply part of the RAM address space. The following paragraphs describe how virtual memory works under Windows NT.

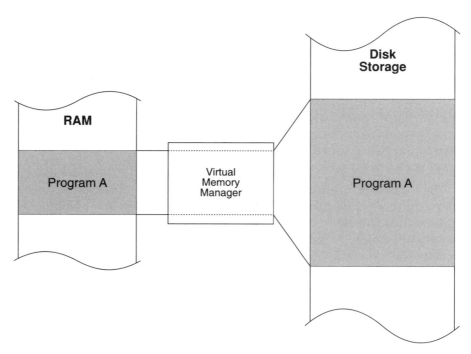

Figure 3.2. *Virtual memory allows programs to take up less space in RAM by temporarily storing parts of the program on disk.*

When the user or system administrator first installs Windows NT, the NT setup program checks to see how much RAM and hard disk space are available in the system. Based on the amount of available disk space, NT creates a *swap file,* which must be at least the same size as the amount of RAM installed in the system. The user can modify the swap file size during installation. The bigger the swap file, the larger the size of virtual memory, but this comes at the expense of permanent file storage disk space. This trade-off and the disk's total capacity determine the final swap file size.

> **Swap File**
>
> A section of a hard disk used by virtual memory managers to temporarily hold a portion of the RAM's contents in order to allow the system to run programs that are larger than the size of available RAM alone.

After Windows NT is installed and running, the swap file is used as temporary storage for RAM contents. NT's virtual memory manager performs two key tasks. First, it manages the stored data on disk and maps the addresses of the disk-based data into NT's 32-bit linear address space. The application can perform operations on the data in this virtual address space, no matter where the data physically resides (either in RAM or temporarily swapped to hard disk).

Second, the virtual memory manager temporarily moves some portions of RAM to the swap file when NT processes try to use more RAM than is available. In this case, inactive RAM contents are temporarily moved to the swap file space to make room for the needed data and are then swapped back into RAM when needed. To save time, instead of moving data byte by byte from RAM to disk and back again, RAM contents are swapped in and out as 4K pages.

The application program doesn't need to know anything about the swapping process. Frequent swapping results in heavy disk activity, however, and system response deteriorates. Likewise, a program processing a file in NT's virtual address space on the hard disk runs much more slowly than a program using data totally contained within RAM. NT's virtual memory manager is designed to minimize unnecessary swapping, but clearly—for large programs, very large data files, or systems running several programs at the same time—performance is directly related to the amount of RAM available; the more RAM available, the better the overall performance.

Windows NT: The Next Generation

The 16-bit version of Windows also supports virtual memory, but Windows NT's implementation is considerably more sophisticated. Under 16-bit Windows, the virtual memory swap space must be at least as large as available RAM, but is limited to approximately 30M. (If the user chooses to turn virtual memory off, in order to eliminate swapping and thus achieve greater performance, albeit with fewer—and smaller—applications running simultaneously, no swap file is needed.) These limits are fine for desktop PCs. They may cause problems, however, in server applications. If you have lots of RAM (say, 32M or more), the minimum swap space would take up a big chunk of disk space, while 30M of swap space is too little space for many RAM-intensive applications. Windows NT, on the other hand, enables you to assign as much or as little swap space as you need.

Virtual memory is not a panacea. It enables you to run big programs or process big files with a limited amount of RAM, but processing speed might be unacceptably slow. Microsoft suggests that end users probably need only 8M of RAM, but more RAM always provides better performance. If you use NT and the virtual memory manager is constantly swapping data between RAM and hard disk (thus bogging down the system), first try adding more RAM. You might also get some improvement from a faster hard disk, but the benefits of upgrading your existing disk or adding a faster one is small compared to the performance boost that adding RAM provides.

Preemptive Multitasking

Multitasking is the capability of a computer system to carry out more than one operation at a time. This operation might be to run a program, perform a process, or accomplish a task; they're all essentially the same. (In the NT architecture, programs or processes are broken down into smaller components called *threads*, which I will describe in more detail in the next section. NT can multitask these individual threads.)

> **Thread**
>
> The portion of a process that the operating system actually executes. All processes have at least one thread, but no thread can belong to more than one process. A multithreaded process has more than one thread and is designed so that more than one thread can be executed simultaneously.

What's so important about multitasking? Consider just one example: printing a document is a simple task that computer users face all the time. If you use DOS, when you tell your word processor to print a page, it must first convert the formats, fonts, special codes, and so on, into code that your printer understands. Then the operating system transmits as much of the file as the printer can handle at one time. The printer and operating system continue to trade information until the entire file is transmitted.

While all this happens, you can't do anything else; your computer's processor is dedicated to printing your file. A multitasking system can eliminate this bottleneck by printing the file while enabling you to perform other functions with the computer at the same time. In fact, the processor is performing just one task at any time, but it switches so quickly between tasks that it seems like you're performing more than one task at a time. (A computer with more than one processor can actually perform more than one task at a time. Each processor runs one task, and potentially, each processor can also multitask.)

A good analogy is the appearance of a continuous loop of motion picture film and what occurs when you run the film through a projector. When you hold the film to the light, you see that it contains a series of still pictures, or frames. When you run that same film through a projector at 24 frames per second, the images appear to move naturally; it's not apparent that you are looking at individual still pictures. Multitasking appears smooth and continuous, as does a running motion picture. While each thread is running, it has total control of the computer, but at some point, the operating system swaps out the thread and essential system information to a holding area, in a similar fashion to the swapping described under virtual memory. Another thread is swapped in, it runs for a given amount of time, and then it's frozen and swapped out. This happens fast enough that several threads appear to be running at the same time.

Two kinds of multitasking exist, *preemptive* and *nonpreemptive*, illustrated in Figure 3.3. With nonpreemptive multitasking, each thread determines how long it stays active before it's replaced with another thread. With preemptive multitasking, each thread is assigned a fixed amount of time, called a *time slice*, in which to run. At the end of the time slice, the thread is swapped out, no matter what the thread is doing at the time. Each thread process is also assigned a priority level, and execution of a thread can be suspended, or preempted, by a thread with a higher priority.

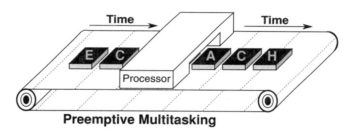

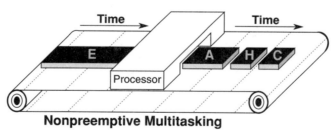

Figure 3.3. *In preemptive multitasking, each process is allowed a certain fixed time slice. In nonpreemptive multitasking, each process decides for itself how long it wants to take.*

3 • *Windows NT in Profile*

> **Preemptive Multitasking**
>
> A form of multitasking in which the execution of one thread can be suspended by the operating system in order to allow another thread to execute. On the other hand, under nonpreemptive multitasking, it is the threads themselves, rather than the operating system, which determine when one thread will relinquish control of the system in order to allow other threads to run.

Windows NT, as well as OS/2 and UNIX, uses preemptive multitasking to support multiple simultaneous processes. By comparison, 16-bit Windows uses a form of nonpreemptive multitasking called *cooperative multitasking*. In a cooperative multitasking system, each application must be written specifically to support multitasking. Each application must relinquish control of the processor to allow other applications to run. Preemptive multitasking doesn't require applications to be written to relinquish control; the operating system automatically suspends and restarts applications as it needs to in order to service every task.

Think of the processor as a toll road with a single toll booth. In a preemptive system such as Windows NT, each car takes exactly the same amount of time to enter the toll gate, pay the toll, and exit. If you happen to be the fourth car waiting in line, you can calculate exactly how long it will take you to reach the toll gate and exactly how much time you'll have to drive away.

In a nonpreemptive system such as 16-bit Windows, drivers determine how much time they will take after they reach the toll booth. If a driver fumbles for change, asks directions, or strikes up a conversation with the booth attendant, it takes longer for the next car to enter the toll gate, and all the following cars are delayed. It's impossible to determine exactly how long it will take for the fourth car to reach the gate.

In a nonpreemptive system, a thread can hog the computer for itself; while it's running, no other thread can get any computer time at all. By comparison, you can easily predict the performance of a preemptive system; if it takes your computer X amount of time to perform a task when one thread is

Windows NT: The Next Generation

running, it will take twice that much time when two threads are running, and so on. In addition, critical threads can preempt other, less important ones, just as an ambulance or police car can drive around a toll gate to bypass the queue.

Here's a familiar example of the failings of a nonpreemptive multitasking system. 16-bit Windows uses the Print Manager to route documents to a printer. If the printer is busy, the Print Manager is supposed to temporarily store each document on the hard disk and then pass it to the printer. While the Print Manager communicates with the printer and saves the document to disk, it has control of the system, so the user can't do anything else. In theory, this happens so quickly that the user regains control almost immediately, but in reality it takes seconds, and sometimes minutes, for the Print Manager to return control of the system to the user. The vastly improved Windows NT Print Manager supports preemptive multitasking so that the user really does regain control almost immediately. The user's activities have a higher priority and thus temporarily preempt the Print Manager so that the user doesn't perceive a delay.

Symmetric Multiprocessing

Virtually all desktop computers, whether they are PCs or workstations, have a single central processor unit, or CPU. The Intel 80386 is a CPU; so is the MIPS 4000. As described previously, a single CPU or processor executes one thread at a time, but it switches them so quickly that it appears as though it's running several at one time. However, how much one processor can do is limited. Switching between threads is a process in itself and takes a certain amount of time. As more and more threads contend for processor time, the processing resources involved in switching between the threads take up a greater portion of the available time. Either the processor stops accepting any new threads, or the threads each get so little processor time that everything grinds to a halt.

Starting in the late-seventies, computer designers opened the bottleneck with *multiprocessing*, or adding more processors for more performance. With two processors, you should get twice the performance; three processors should achieve three times the performance, and so on. Also, a computer system with more than one processor can run more than one thread at a time, without task switching. In reality, of course, performance gains obtained by adding more processors are never exactly linear; a significant amount of processing power is spent just managing the activities of multiple processors.

> **Multiprocessing**
>
> The usage of more than one processor in a computer system. The processors are connected by shared memory or high-speed links.

These computers, called *multiprocessor systems*, had even more potential advantages. If one processor was bogged down, tasks could be reassigned to other processors to improve performance; this capability is called *load balancing*. Tasks could be assigned to processors by priority; the highest priority tasks could be assigned to the processors with the lightest loads, while lower-priority tasks could wait their turn on busier CPUs.

Multiprocessor systems looked like a remedy for performance bottlenecks, but several problems quickly cropped up. For example, it's preferable to have only one copy of a database, no matter how many processors you have. If you're running an image processing program, you want to work on only one copy of the image, instead of one copy for each processor. Keeping multiple copies of the same data for multiple processors is inefficient.

It can also be dangerous, even with a single copy of the data. Consider a database manipulated by tasks running on two processors. Processor A reads a record from the database and prepares to make some changes. Processor B reads the same record from the database and also makes some (different) changes. Then, Processors A and B both write the changed record back to the database. Processor A gets to the disk first and writes the record, then Processor B rewrites the record, overwriting A's changes with its own. Without adequate safeguards, it's impossible to ensure the integrity of the database or even to know that you're reading the most current version of a record.

Asymmetric Versus Symmetric Multiprocessing

The operating system must be designed to support multiple processors. It must know how to parcel out tasks to the processors, and it must provide safeguards to ensure data integrity at all times. The two primary types of multiprocessing operating systems are *asymmetric* and *symmetric*, illustrated in Figures 3.4 and 3.5. Asymmetric systems run the operating system on one dedicated processor and run other tasks (user programs) on the remaining processor(s). All the input/output, or I/O (display, keyboard, printer, disk drives, and so on) is managed by the processor running the operating system. Symmetric systems run the operating system—or a large portion of it—on any one or all of the processors. All the processors share I/O, although specific devices might be assigned to specific processors. Windows NT implements a symmetric multiprocessing model.

> **Symmetric Multiprocessing**
>
> A multiprocessing system that runs the computer's operating system on more than one processor. Compared to *asymmetric multiprocessor* systems that dedicate one processor to running the operating system, symmetric systems are more reliable because the failure of a single processor is unlikely to crash the entire system.

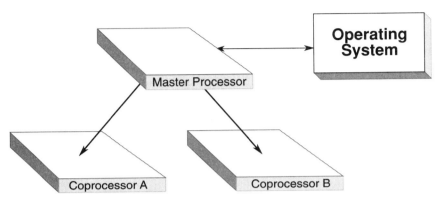

Figure 3.4. In an asymmetric multiprocessing system, one master processor runs the operating system.

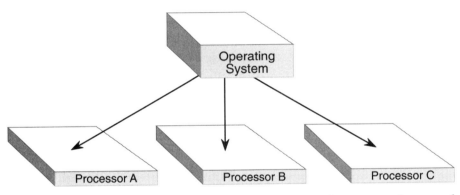

Figure 3.5. In a symmetric multiprocessing system each processor has equal access to the operating system.

The primary advantage of asymmetric multiprocessing systems is they're fairly easy to implement. To add more users or improve performance, you add more slave processors. In general, these systems dedicate RAM to each processor, which eliminates many data integrity problems. The underlying single-processor operating system may require only minor modifications to support additional processors.

Windows NT: The Next Generation

The biggest problem with asymmetric systems is their vulnerability to failure. If one of the slave processors fails or locks up, the master processor running the operating system can shift tasks to the remaining processors and keep the system going. If the master processor fails, however, everything shuts down because the only copy of the operating system stops, and all the I/O devices controlled by the operating system become inaccessible. In addition, even when the system is running normally, the master processor can bog down as demands on the operating system increase. When that happens, requests for I/O access from the slave processors are delayed, and the entire system slows down, even when some of the slaves have little or no load.

Symmetric multiprocessing systems are more difficult to implement, because they share a large portion of system memory and require many more safeguards for data integrity. The operating system must be able to run simultaneously on multiple processors also without tripping over itself, and it must be able to switch out any failed or halted processor while running on any other processor.

Symmetric systems have several advantages over asymmetric systems. First, they tend to be more efficient, because both operating system and user program tasks can be balanced between the processors. Operating system demands are spread across all processors, so the possibility of idle time on one processor while another is overworked is far less. Second, they're more reliable because a single processor failure is unlikely to bring down the entire system. Finally, they're not closely tied to a specific master/slave architecture, which makes symmetric operating systems more easily portable between processor architectures.

Threads

In the previous section, I introduced the term *threads*. Now, I'll discuss threads in a little more detail. In Windows NT, processes consist of a series of instructions, the virtual address space needed to hold the program and data, and the operating system resources required by the program as it executes. Within each process lies at least one thread, which is the component that NT actually schedules for execution. Without a thread, nothing happens.

That's the official version of things, but that's really splitting hairs—a process always implies a thread because a process without a thread is useless. In most cases, a process has only one thread. When the thread is executed, so is the process. However, many programs running under NT can in fact be written to do more than one thing at once, meaning that their processes could have more than one thread.

Consider a database program for travel agents. The program keeps track of the agency's client records, such as credit cards, memberships in frequent flyer programs, hotel preferences, accumulated mileage, and so on, on a local computer. It also connects to a reservation system via a network or modem to obtain flight information, fares, seat availability, and so on. The travel agent can request flight information for a client and call up the client's travel profile. The network connection to the reservation system will probably take considerably more time to establish and complete than retrieving the client profile from a local hard disk.

If this application is written as a single thread, the agent must wait until the reservation connection is made and the requested information is transferred before accessing the travel profile. As a multithreaded application, however, the program can begin accessing the client profile as soon as the travel agent sets up the network connection to the reservation system; while one thread awaits an answer to the reservation query, another is retrieving and displaying the client profile.

Windows NT can not only multitask these separate threads, but it can parcel out the threads to different processors in a multiprocessor system, with dramatic performance improvements. These multiple threads can truly be executed simultaneously, instead of the pseudosimultaneous execution provided by multitasking.

Remember that a program must be written to incorporate multiple threads. When most programs running on a multiprocessor system are single-threaded, many of the potential performance advantages of the system are lost. In some cases, one single-threaded process can slow down every processor in the system. This is especially true in networked systems where processes running on all the processors require the same resource, such as a network manager. If the network manager is multithreaded, the

Windows NT: The Next Generation

load can be balanced between threads running on multiple processors as demand for the manager's resources increases. If a single-threaded design is used, however, the network manager can run on only one processor; as demand increases, the processor bogs down and becomes a bottleneck for the entire system.

Windows NT's designers are encouraging application developers to take advantage of NT's support for multithreading. NT's architects practice what they preach. NT itself is multithreaded, and between user applications and system processes, it's not uncommon for ten or more threads to be active at any one time in an NT system.

Client/Server Architecture

In the last few years, the term *client/server computing* has become one of the computer industry's most popular buzzwords. People most often discuss client/server computing in conjunction with local area networks, or LANs. I'll first define it in terms of networks, and then look at Windows NT's architecture, which moves the client/server design from the network to the operating system.

For example, assume you work in a small business, and you have a single PC in the office. You have a hard disk in that PC for data storage. Additionally, you probably have a printer connected to the computer and possibly even a modem for data communications. That PC system works just fine for one person at a time.

Eventually, your business grows, and you hire more people. Each person has a PC. Now, you need to make some decisions. You can give each person a printer and modem, but that's expensive. Your own printer is idle most of the time, so why buy more printers? I'll add another problem. Your PC's hard disk contains some files that are absolutely essential to running your business, but from time to time, your coworkers also need access to those files.

As one way to save money and give everyone access to your resources, use floppy disks to copy files to and from your system. When coworkers need to print a report, they copy the report file onto a floppy, carry it over to your

3 • *Windows NT in Profile*

PC, read it in, and print it on your printer. When they need access to your files, they come over to your PC, copy the needed files onto a floppy, transfer them to their system, make changes, bring the floppy back to your PC, and copy the changed files onto your hard disk.

Many organizations work this way today (the slang term for such a scheme is *sneakernet*) but the problems are obvious:

- Lost productivity
- Lack of security
- Needless data redundancy
- Potential data corruption

Local area networking is an obvious way around these problems. In a LAN system, each PC is connected, or networked, together with all the others. Data and I/O devices such as printers and modems can be shared (these are often grouped under the term *resources*). With a LAN, all PCs in the office can share the same printer. Everyone in the office can access your files without interrupting your work. This kind of simple network is called a *peer-to-peer network*.

Sharing resources exacts a performance penalty. Your PC slows down when someone on the network wants to print a file because your computer must process that request while it's also working for you. Similarly, when someone is accessing a file on your hard disk, it takes longer for you to retrieve your own files.

In a small network, the performance impact of sharing resources usually isn't severe. If everyone is located in the same small area, it doesn't really matter whose PC physically contains the shared database or whose PC is connected to the printer. As the network grows and more computers are attached, however, delays begin to mount. Your PC slows down to a crawl because so many people are trying to access the group's shared data files. Your office begins to look like Grand Central Station because coworkers are constantly retrieving reports from your printer.

In this situation, simple peer-to-peer networking just won't cut it anymore. Now you need to dedicate a computer to managing the shared files. You may also need to remove the printer from your office and connect it to

Windows NT: The Next Generation

its own computer. That's when you enter the realm of client/server computing. The shared data files are transferred from your PC to a file server. The *file server* is a dedicated computer that does nothing but provide all users with equal access to a centralized file system. Anyone on the network who has files that other users need can transfer their files to the server. Your PC's performance improves because you no longer need to share your hard disk with the outside world. Figures 3.6 and 3.7 show client/server and peer-to-peer networking schemes.

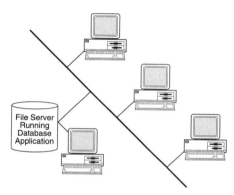

Figure 3.6. *A client/server network.*

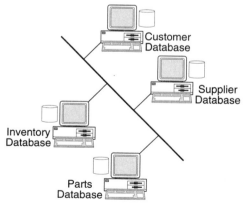

Figure 3.7. *A peer-to-peer network.*

> **File Server**
>
> A computer, with a large-capacity hard disk, that is attached to a local area network and stores files used by other computers attached to the same network.

In network-talk, your PC and the PC of every other user become clients to the file server. The *client* requests resources from a server—such as data files or access to a printer. The *server* responds by supplying the resources. As with your shared data files, you can move your printer out of the office and connect it to the network, either directly—with a special network interface—or through a computer. The printer becomes a shared resource, and it provides printing services to clients throughout the network.

The key point to remember about client/server computing is that servers provide client access to shared resources. Clients and servers communicate by passing messages between each other. As I discuss in the "Networking" section in this chapter and in more detail in Chapter 6, "Networking with Windows NT," Windows NT supports peer-to-peer networking directly. It can be a server on Microsoft's LAN Manager networks or UNIX-compatible TCP/IP networks, and it can be a client to many different network operating systems, including LAN Manager, IBM's LAN Server, and Novell NetWare. However, NT also applies the client/server model to the NT operating system itself with its own internal clients and servers. This topic requires a more technical discussion of NT.

The Client/Server Model Within NT

Windows NT has two modes in which it operates, *user mode* and *privileged* or *kernel mode*, as shown in Figure 3.8. Application programs, like a database, spreadsheet, or hotel reservation system, always run in user mode. The NT executive is the heart of Windows NT. The NT executive performs such tasks as managing input and output, virtual memory, and all processes, and controls the links between NT and the actual computer hardware. The executive runs in kernel mode, which is a special, high-security mode that is safe from interference by user processes.

Windows NT: The Next Generation

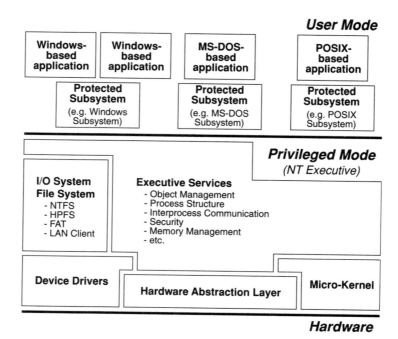

Figure 3.8. *Windows NT's layered architecture.*

Within user mode, you also find what are called *protected subsystems.* Windows NT provides a variety of protected subsystems. One example is the *Win32 application programming interface* (API). The Win32 API is the specification that software developers follow to access the user interface and other features of Windows NT. By using this API, developers don't need to be concerned about the hardware differences of various NT systems; the same application runs on many different computers. As a protected subsystem, the Win32 API is protected from user applications that try to steal or modify its memory, and therefore could crash NT. In addition, the Win32 API has safeguards that protect other subsystems from interference.

Another protected subsystem is the *security subsystem*, which provides password-protection and other security measures. DOS and 16-bit Windows applications run in their own area within user mode called a virtual DOS machine. The virtual DOS machine, in turn, communicates with the Win32 subsystem. OS/2 and POSIX applications have their own API subsystems; I'll discuss them later.

In the Windows NT environment, application programs are clients, and the protected subsystems are servers. The application program clients send messages to the protected subsystem servers through the NT executive, which provides a set of shared services for all the servers. The servers reply through the NT executive.

Just as with the networking example, the client/server model streamlines the operating system by eliminating duplicate resources. If the NT executive contained the APIs for all the operating systems that Windows NT supports, it would be unbelievably complicated. This architecture also allows other APIs to be added to NT without requiring a new executive. Additionally, each subsystem is a separate process in its own protected memory. If one subsystem crashes, it doesn't bring the entire NT system down. The subsystem processes are written to support multiple threads, and this enhances NT's multiprocessor capabilities.

In client/server systems, a process running on a client can access local resources as well as server resources, and the client application doesn't need to know where the resources are physically located. In Windows NT, servers running on a local processor can pass messages from their clients to servers running on remote processors without requiring the clients to know anything about the remote servers.

The client/server model simplifies Windows NT's design, makes it easier to add new APIs, and enhances the operating system's multiprocessor and networking support. NT's protected subsystem servers also communicate with other servers on the same processor for even greater operating efficiencies.

Windows NT: The Next Generation

Security and Enhanced System Integrity

Security, in relation to Windows NT, refers to two things:

- Control over access to the NT system and to files and subdirectories within the system.

- Protection of individual processes and the operating system, so that buggy or deliberately destructive programs can't crash other programs or the entire system.

In the first case, the need for security depends on the type of system and the applications. Control over system access refers to the requirement for unique user identification—user names and passwords—to access the operating system. This form of access control is a first-line defense designed to keep unauthorized users off the system altogether.

After a user has passed through system access security, the second level of defense becomes active. File and subdirectory security limits access to individual users, groups of users, or all users. For example, access to NT system files can be strictly limited to authorized system administrators, whereas common applications like word processors and spreadsheets can be made available to any user.

The second type of security implemented under Windows NT concerns system integrity. DOS and 16-bit Windows users know that it's very easy for an application or utility to crash other applications or the entire operating system. In a single-user system, such a crash can be painful but usually isn't devastating. Any open files that haven't been saved when the crash occurs are lost, but generally, the system can be restarted and work can proceed quickly.

In networked systems, however, an application or system crash can be a catastrophe, especially when a server crashes, because all the users and applications running on the server are affected. Many open files may be lost,

3 • *Windows NT in Profile*

and with mission-critical applications where hundreds of transactions may be in progress at any time, even a small amount of downtime can disrupt business in a big way. Windows NT has extensive facilities for ensuring system integrity to keep NT systems running under difficult conditions and to recover from system failures quickly and easily.

Windows NT's access control and system integrity features are discussed in the following two sections.

Access Control Security

Single-user operating systems such as DOS and 16-bit Windows have no built-in security features because most PCs are used by only one person, and it makes little sense for the sole user of a PC to have to keep track of passwords, file access permissions, and so on. For PCs that are shared by several users, third-party utilities are available to password-protect and encrypt individual files and whole subdirectories so that private files remain private.

Network operating systems such as Novell NetWare and Microsoft LAN Manager, which run on top of conventional operating systems such as DOS and OS/2, as well as network-oriented, general-purpose operating systems like Apple's Macintosh System 7 and the host of UNIX variants, are designed for environments where a single computer or file system is shared by many users. These operating systems implement a range of security features to allow data to be shared among users and applications while restricting access to sensitive and personal files.

As befits its primary role as a network-oriented, general-purpose operating system, Windows NT provides an extensive access control security system. The purposes of Windows NT security are to ensure that only authorized users gain access to the system (authentication) and to control access to files, directories, and system resources. If you're already familiar with UNIX or network operating systems, Windows NT's security features are easy to understand.

Windows NT: The Next Generation

NT's security subsystem is configured by a system administrator. All NT systems, even single-user machines, have an administrator. The sole user is also the administrator of single-user NT systems. The administrator establishes user names, creates user groups and assigns users to groups, controls passwords, locks out individual users and controls access to system functions. In short, the administrator controls all access to the system.

Before a new user can log on to a Windows NT system for the first time, the administrator must create a new user account with the user manager. The user account consists of a user name, password, and other user-related information. The administrator can assign individual users to groups. User groups are a convenient means for controlling system and file access for many users at a time. Access to directories, subdirectories, and individual files is usually controlled by group, although access can also be controlled by user. NT automatically assigns new users to a default user group specified by the administrator. User membership in a group can be changed by the administrator at any time, and any user can be a member of more than one group. Everyone in a group has the same level of access.

A comprehensive set of access levels is provided for directories, subdirectories, and files. When access permissions are set for a directory, they can be applied automatically to the directory itself and all existing subdirectories and files, or only to the directory and new subdirectories and files.

The administrator also controls access to specific system functions, especially those functions that affect system operations, security, and reliability (such as the ability to shut down the system, and to back up and restore hard disk volumes). This control mechanism is called the *user rights policy*. Because of the sensitivity of many of these functions, access is controlled on a user basis only. Rights to do everything from executing file and directory backups to shutting down the system remotely can be controlled by the administrator. In this way, users can be prohibited from taking actions that might disrupt or disable the system.

The access control system works hand-in-hand with the Windows NT file system. NT supports a variety of file systems, including:

3 • *Windows NT in Profile*

- FAT (file allocation table): DOS and 16-bit Windows use the FAT file system. The maximum size of a FAT volume under DOS 5, or any version of Windows running under DOS, is 2G. FAT supports filenames with a maximum length of eight characters as well as an optional one- to three-character extension—for example, COMMAND.COM and AUTOEXEC.BAT. Windows NT can use FAT file systems, but FAT file systems don't allow for access control on files or subdirectories and cannot be managed with NT's security features.

- HPFS (high performance file system): HPFS is OS/2's native file system. The maximum size of an HPFS volume is 4G. HPFS supports 255-character filenames. HPFS allows for limited access control features when used with LAN Server, but Windows NT cannot provide file- or subdirectory-level access control for HPFS volumes.

- NTFS (NT File System): NTFS is Windows NT's native file system. NTFS volumes can be as large as 17 billion gigabytes. Because filenames can be up to 255 characters long, files can be given more descriptive names instead of the cryptic names forced upon DOS and 16-bit Windows users. NTFS uses the Unicode character-encoding standard, which allows characters from virtually any international language, including Japanese, Chinese, Korean, and Arabic, and most European languages, to be used in filenames. Extensions are also provided for POSIX compatibility.

    NTFS includes a variety of features that enable quick recovery of disk-based files after a system failure. For example, NTFS can recover from many hard disk crashes on-the-fly, without requiring a complete system shutdown. Most important, NTFS supports all of NT's access control features. For maximum system security and reliability, Microsoft strongly recommends that all NT systems adopt NTFS.

Windows NT's access control security features are overkill for single-user stand-alone systems, but they are essential for networks and mission-critical applications. Users migrating from DOS and 16-bit Windows systems might be confused initially by all the user and file security settings, whereas UNIX users will appreciate the ease and friendliness of NT's User and File Managers. Either way, system security quickly becomes a part of everyday life for Windows NT users.

Windows NT: The Next Generation

System Integrity

The other half of the security equation is *system integrity*. System integrity refers to the ability of Windows NT applications and NT itself to continue running even when an application crashes or a process tries to modify a portion of memory that it shouldn't touch. To see why this is important, consider how DOS applications run. When any application runs, it grabs the space it needs from free memory. This works well as long as the application doesn't try to steal or modify another application's memory.

DOS doesn't support multitasking or multiprocessing, so its programs don't expect to share memory with other applications. When Windows 3.0 came along, Microsoft implemented a limited multitasking scheme on top of DOS. It enabled more than one application to concurrently use system memory. Windows 3.0 applications needed to be written very carefully to conform to this multitasking system.

Think of Windows 3.0's memory as a series of single-car garages: A running application is like a car parked in the garage. The same garage can be used by more than one car, but not at the same time. Each car's driver is supposed to check to be sure that the garage is empty before parking the car in the garage. Every once in a while, a driver doesn't bother to look first and hits a parked car. Both cars are damaged and might not run after the collision.

Some Windows 3.0 applications had a nasty tendency to modify memory and system resources already in use by another program. When this happened, one or both applications could crash and take Windows with them. The result of such a collision was the dreaded *unrecoverable application error* (UAE). The only way to recover from a UAE was to reboot the system. Any files being written at the time of the UAE could be corrupted. With Windows 3.1, the system's ability to detect and stop attempts by errant programs to mess up memory was improved, but problems remained. Windows 3.1 made it easier to recover from errors, but it was still possible for rogue programs to make the system so unstable that it had to be rebooted. In network server and mission-critical applications, where the cost of system failure is very high, Windows 3.1's improvements didn't go far enough.

3 • Windows NT in Profile

Windows NT is designed to prevent the kinds of catastrophic system failures so common under Windows 3.0 and still possible with current 16-bit Windows. NT does this by shielding the memory for each process from that of all other processes and by ensuring that one client doesn't interfere with another client's access to subsystem resources. To return to the garage analogy: When a car is parked in a garage, the garage door instantly closes. Any other car that tries to enter the same garage runs into the door, leaving the car inside unscathed.

NT uses four mechanisms for protecting memory:

- Separate address spaces: each process has its own virtual address space, and NT prohibits any process from accessing the virtual address space of any other process.

- Separate user and kernel modes: all applications run in user mode and are thus prohibited from accessing or modifying system code or data, which reside in kernel mode.

- Page flags: each page of virtual memory has flags that determine how it can be accessed in user and kernel modes.

- Object security: the virtual memory manager creates a special type of object called a section object, which is a window on a section of virtual memory. Every time a process accesses a section object, NT's security manager determines if the process has permission to perform the requested operation on the object, such as reading or writing it.

Resource Access Protection

Resource access protection offers similar safeguards. More than one process might need the same resource at the same time. Windows NT arbitrates between the competing processes to ensure they don't interfere with each other. Consider a database access program and a communications program, each of which is a process. Both need to send and receive information across the network. Because NT supports multitasking and multiprocessing, both processes could try to send requests for data across the network at the same

Windows NT: The Next Generation

time. NT controls access to the network resources so that data flowing to and from the network from both processes don't collide. NT also makes sure that data are routed to the correct process.

Most memory and resource collisions are accidents caused by faulty software. In some cases, however, the intrusions are deliberate. Under some multitasking operating systems, it is possible to write a program that reads and writes the memory of another process or temporarily seizes control of mass storage, network interfaces, or communication ports. These programs can be used to thwart security measures and modify or destroy sensitive data. No operating system is completely secure from penetration by a skilled programmer, but Windows NT's features for system integrity effectively guard against accidental and deliberate intrusion attempts.

Windows NT's combination of security and system integrity features answers the real-world threats to networked and mission-critical systems from unauthorized users and errant programs. They place a moderate burden on single-user systems while supporting the needs of very large enterprise-wide systems with hundreds or thousands of users. Finally, NT's security features are easy to understand and use. They require very little system knowledge.

Support for DOS, OS/2, 16-Bit Windows 3.X, and POSIX-Compliant Applications

One of Windows NT's greatest strengths is its capability to support multiple operating systems. An NT system can simultaneously run most DOS and 16-bit Windows, as well as many character-based OS/2 Version 1.X and POSIX-compliant applications. NT isn't compatible with every application, and its performance may suffer compared to computers running only DOS-based Windows, OS/2, or UNIX. Windows NT, however, offers a good blend of compatibility and performance for multiple-OS networks and applications.

DOS Compatibility and the Virtual DOS Machine

As you read in Chapter 1, one of Microsoft's highest operating system design priorities has always been to provide backward compatibility with previous versions of DOS and (to a lesser extent) with Windows. You saw the benefits of this strategy, and you also examined the costs—in programming complexity and in the inability to take full advantage of Intel's 386 and 486 processors.

First with OS/2 and then with Windows NT, Microsoft's operating system architects wanted to maintain backward compatibility with DOS and 16-bit Windows, while leaving behind the limitations of DOS. They needed to find a way for these older applications to run as compliant Windows NT applications. They settled on the same approach that Bill Gates and Paul Allen used to write BASIC for the MITS Altair without having access to an Altair—an *emulator*.

Windows NT runs DOS programs within a virtual DOS machine (VDM). One VDM process is created for each DOS program running under NT. Each VDM has its own private memory address space, a copy of 16- and 32-bit DOS emulators (which are fully compatible with MS-DOS 5.0), and all the DOS drivers required to execute the application. A 16M segmented address space is provided within the VDM for programs and data, and most DOS memory managers are supported. The VDM supports well-behaved DOS applications—that is, DOS applications that use system calls for all I/O. Applications that attempt to bypass DOS to directly access hard disks or other mass storage devices don't run. Standard DOS I/O requests are intercepted by the VDM and executed by either the Win32 API or the NT executive. Therefore, DOS I/O doesn't violate NT's system integrity features, and multiple DOS processes can share devices.

To DOS programs, the VDM looks and acts just like a DOS PC. The DOS window under Windows NT looks and acts just like the DOS window under 16-bit Windows with one important difference. Both 32-bit Windows NT programs and 16-bit DOS programs can be launched in the DOS window and routed to the correct protected subsystem, either the Win32 API or the VDM.

WOW: 16-Bit Windows Compatibility

You can run 16-bit Windows applications under Windows NT. From the user's point of view, 16- and 32-bit Windows applications look identical. They can be intermixed freely within program groups. They can be launched by clicking with the mouse or running the File|Run command in either the File or Program Manager. Launching the first 16-bit Windows program starts a new VDM. The VDM, in turn, loads an environment called *Windows on Win32* (*WOW*). The WOW VDM is based on the DOS VDM. It includes a "simulated" version of Windows 3.1 (with multitasking removed) in addition to the 16-bit Windows application and DOS.

Within the WOW VDM, the 16-bit Windows API is replaced by a combination of calls to the Win32 API, NT executive functions, and internal WOW routines. The result is a Windows API that's compatible at the function call level with the existing 16-bit Windows API, but whose internal design is radically different. The result is that some existing 16-bit Windows programs which bypass the API and go directly into the Windows window manager for better graphics display performance won't run under WOW.

Again, as with DOS, the 16-bit Windows application believes it's running on its own dedicated PC. Unlike DOS, however, additional 16-bit Windows applications don't require additional VDMs. Each additional 16-bit Windows application becomes a thread within WOW, and WOW takes care of multitasking. The Windows NT 32-bit window manager and *graphical device interface* (*GDI*) are used in place of the 16-bit Windows equivalents.

Therefore, all well-behaved 16-bit Windows applications run under WOW, but programs that access the internal code of the old 16-bit window manager or GDI might not work. For example, some paint, draw, and desktop publishing programs that could not provide adequate screen redraw performance under Windows 3.0 without accessing internal GDI code don't work under WOW. As applications are rewritten to be well-behaved under Windows 3.1 and future 16-bit Windows incarnations, incompatibilities with WOW will eventually disappear.

OS/2 Compatibility

OS/2 applications are designed to run in a multitasking, 32-bit environment, so Microsoft didn't have to build a virtual machine environment to safeguard Windows NT's system integrity. Instead, OS/2 applications are clients to the OS/2 API-protected environment. Because the OS/2 API supports only character mode applications, Presentation Manager-based applications are not compatible with NT's first release.

Many OS/2 server applications are character-based, but most applications written or updated for OS/2 2.0 use the Presentation Manager. If you're currently an OS/2 2.0 user, check your applications carefully before converting to Windows NT. Chapter 8, "Windows NT Versus OS/2," provides an extensive analysis of OS/2 2.0 versus Windows NT.

POSIX Compliance

As described earlier, POSIX is a standardized UNIX variant designed to ensure software source code portability and facilitate program maintenance. Instead of a unique program for every UNIX variant, only one version of the program's source code is required for any POSIX system. Like the OS/2 API, the first release of the POSIX API supports only character mode applications. This limitation is not as serious for POSIX as it is for OS/2, because most UNIX applications are character-oriented, as well as the standard UNIX user interface.

The introduction of standardized GUIs in the UNIX marketplace is a recent development. In the future, Windows NT's POSIX API may support the X Window graphics toolkit. This would enable popular UNIX GUIs such as Sun Microsystems' OPEN LOOK and the Open Systems Foundation's OSF/Motif to run in a POSIX window under Windows NT. As with OS/2, UNIX/POSIX users should study their application requirements very carefully before adopting Windows NT. See Chapter 9 "Windows NT Versus UNIX," for a comparison of Windows NT versus several of the most popular UNIX variants.

Windows NT: The Next Generation

Platform Independence

For years, UNIX held the distinction of being the only commercially-popular operating system that ran on otherwise incompatible computers. Workstations from Sun, Hewlett-Packard, DEC, Silicon Graphics, and IBM all use different, and incompatible, RISC processors, yet all run a variant of UNIX. The same version of UNIX that IBM supports on its RS/6000 workstations is also available for IBM mainframes. This platform independence is one of UNIX's biggest advantages. Usually, applications written for one version of UNIX can be modified easily to run under other versions. With UNIX, customers can move from one hardware vendor to another as their needs and budgets change and as technologies improve.

DOS users have enormous flexibility in choosing computers, but their selection is limited to computers based on the Intel x86 architecture that use processors from Intel, Advanced Micro Devices, Cyrix, Texas Instruments, and others. DOS applications don't run on RISC processors or on the Motorola 680x0 family of processors used by Apple and NeXT, unless there is an emulator like the Windows NT VDM.

Windows NT is Microsoft's first all-out effort to develop an operating system designed to run on multiple platforms. (Microsoft's version of UNIX, *XENIX*, ran on both x86 and 680x0 processors in the early eighties, but Microsoft eventually dropped the Motorola version.) The first sign that Microsoft was serious about supporting other platforms with NT was the ACE announcement, in which Microsoft committed its support for both Intel x86 and MIPS 4000 processor families. In 1992, Microsoft extended support to DEC's new Alpha RISC processor, and began development on a version for Hewlett-Packard's HP-PA processors.

By the end of 1993, Windows NT applications will run on computers based on all of these processors. The programs will need to be recompiled for each processor. DOS, 16-bit Windows, and OS/2 applications will run on all these computers under NT without modification or recompilation thanks to NT's built-in emulators. Many of the RISC processors supported by Windows NT are so powerful that DOS and 16-bit Windows applications will run faster than they do on all but the most powerful x86 family of processors, even when using an emulator.

Windows NT still has a long way to go until it has the same level of broad industry acceptance as UNIX. Microsoft has not published plans to port NT to Sun's SPARC RISC processor; IBM's RS/6000; IBM, Apple, and Motorola's forthcoming jointly developed PowerPC RISC processor; the Apple Macintosh; or any mainframe computer. However, nothing inherent in NT's design limits its portability to any of these environments. The key question is whether there will be a demand for NT. If customers ask for it, other computer manufacturers will be forced to support Windows NT eventually.

For now, users and applications demanding the greatest vendor and system flexibility probably should stick with UNIX. Over the next few years, Windows NT's market success will determine whether it becomes a viable alternative to UNIX.

Networking

This section briefly discusses Windows NT's networking capabilities. You will find a more detailed discussion in Chapter 6. NT offers a hybrid of the networking capabilities of Microsoft's Windows for Workgroups and LAN Manager. Like Windows for Workgroups, NT offers easily configurable, serverless, peer-to-peer networking for small groups of users, but for sophisticated users and applications, NT is also a powerful server operating system that includes powerful security features and the ability to work with multiple network operating systems.

Windows NT offers four types of network support:

- Peer-to-peer networking with other Windows NT systems and with Windows for Workgroups-based systems.

- Interoperability with other network operating systems, including DEC Pathworks, Novell NetWare, and Banyan VINES through the Windows Open Systems Architecture (WOSA). NT can also connect with UNIX TCP/IP-based networks.

Windows NT: The Next Generation

- Host (mainframe) network SNA connectivity through an NT version of the DCA/Microsoft Communications Server.

- Support for Microsoft's own LAN Manager network operating system for enterprise-wide client/server networks.

Peer-to-Peer Networking

Peer-to-peer networking is the capability of all systems on a network to share data and resources, without installing special server software on any of the systems. Networked NT systems can support electronic mail, access files on remote systems, and share printers. Just as with existing DOS-based networks, remote file systems look like additional disk drives to NT users and applications. All of Windows NT's security features are available over the network. File and resource access on any system can be controlled down to the individual user level, and only those directories and files that a user chooses to make public are available to remote systems.

Windows NT includes an intelligent network-setup capability that looks for installed network adapters and software. It automatically configures NT with the correct drivers. Although Microsoft claims that users who don't have extensive networking knowledge can use this tool to configure most simple peer-to-peer networks, early user experience with the related Windows for Workgroups product indicates that network installation may be difficult for novices.

Interoperability

Windows NT can interconnect with a variety of network operating systems to share files and resources. For example, NT systems can be connected to a Novell NetWare-based LAN and access data that is resident on NetWare servers.

Proprietary transport protocols such as Microsoft's NetBEUI, used by LAN Manager and IBM's LAN Server; Novell's IPX/SPX, used by NetWare; and the industry-standard TCP/IP transport protocol, used by UNIX and many peer-to-peer networks, can be installed by the user at any time with NT's networks control panel. Refer to Chapter 6 for more information.

As an example, simply by installing the appropriate network drivers, you can make an NT system a client or server on a UNIX TCP/IP network. NT can send and receive UNIX mail and support all the most popular UNIX networking protocols for file interchange without running UNIX utilities or forcing the user to learn UNIX commands.

Mainframe and minicomputer-based systems, as well as the Apple Macintosh, are supported as part of Windows NT's networking capabilities. For mainframes, Microsoft provides access to IBM's SNA through the DCA/Microsoft Communications Server. DEC VAX minicomputers are accessible through DEC Pathworks. LAN Manager for UNIX supports interconnection with most UNIX systems. Microsoft has pledged its support for interconnection with Apple Macintosh networks. Apple offers peer-to-peer networking as a standard part of the System 7 operating system; it also offers a more complex client/server networking scheme called AppleShare. Windows NT systems eventually will be able to share data and resources with any Apple network.

Client/Server Networks with LAN Manager

LAN Manager for Windows NT is Microsoft's solution for enterprise-wide networking and mission-critical systems. LAN Manager, Microsoft's network operating system, grew out of OS/2. OS/2 wasn't originally designed for server applications and client/server networks; it was a powerful single-user operating system with limited connectivity. Microsoft and IBM subsequently designed LAN Manager as a network server extension for OS/2 and added network support and connectivity features that OS/2 lacked. LAN Manager competed directly with Novell NetWare and targeted the same kinds of enterprise-wide PC-based networks. Though Microsoft eventually abandoned OS/2 to IBM, LAN Manager still requires OS/2 in order to run. However, Microsoft is porting LAN Manager to Windows NT. All future versions of LAN Manager will require NT in order to run.

Windows NT: The Next Generation

Much of the functionality of LAN Manager for OS/2 is built into Windows NT. LAN Manager for NT adds server support features while taking advantage of NT's extensive access control security. LAN Manager for NT provides controlled access to multiple domains on a network, where each domain consists of one server or a group of servers. The NT security system is extended under LAN Manager to control access to domains down to the individual user level. To reduce network overhead, users need to be validated by the security subsystem only once—in their local domain—to have controlled access to any domain and server on the network.

For mission-critical systems, Windows NT supports fault-tolerant features such as RAID (redundant array of independent disks) disk arrays, disk mirroring, drive duplexing, and striping with parity (writing a data partition, or virtual disk drive, across two or more physical drives for improved performance and enhanced data recovery). Windows NT includes a control panel for an *uninterruptible power supply* (UPS) in the event of a power failure. LAN Manager enables server UPS systems to be controlled across the network. LAN Manager supports remote network administration and problem diagnosis. Windows NT systems can be restarted from the network, and applications can be installed remotely.

Existing network sites, especially mixed systems supporting a variety of different computers, can utilize Windows NT's interoperability features. Windows for Workgroups-based networks can take advantage of Windows NT systems' performance for quasi-server applications without abandoning the simplicity of peer-to-peer networking. LAN Manager for Windows NT provides a solution for enterprise-wide networks, but LAN Manager has been poorly accepted to date. It's unlikely that Windows NT alone can change LAN Manager from a market also-ran into a market leader. If Microsoft and Novell can settle their differences, however, Windows NT most likely will find wide acceptance as a server for NetWare and UNIX networks.

Conclusion

This chapter discussed the specific features that make Windows NT one of the most powerful and flexible operating systems around. NT's configuration options are considerably more complex than those of 16-bit Windows, but they are much easier to understand and use than UNIX's. In short, Windows NT provides UNIX's multitasking, multiprocessing, security, and networking horsepower as well as backward compatibility with DOS, 16-bit Windows, and OS/2 applications, in a friendly Windows package. NT represents a new era in operating system design.

4

A Quick Walk Through Windows NT

Windows NT: The Next Generation

This chapter gives you a guided tour of Windows NT from a user's viewpoint. For most readers, this will be your first real look at NT. You'll see NT through the eyes of a user and an administrator, from logon to logoff. You'll view NT's security features from the user's perspective and examine the administrative tools used to manage system access and operations. I'll also discuss how the existing Windows Program, File, and Print Managers have been enhanced to incorporate some of NT's many new features.

> **NOTE**
>
> The illustrations and descriptions in this and subsequent chapters are based on the October 1992 beta release of the Windows NT Software Developer's Kit. The "look and feel" and actual contents of the released version of Windows NT may differ from what is presented in this book. Keep in mind that many of the features discussed in this chapter are available only to NT system administrators. Typical users won't have access to these features.

Starting from the Top: Logging On

Every time Windows NT is loaded on a desktop PC or server, the monitor displays the message box illustrated in Figure 4.1.

Figure 4.1. *Windows NT Welcome message.*

106

The Welcome message is displayed by the security subsystem, one of the protected subsystems in NT. As described in Chapter 3, "Windows NT in Profile," the security subsystem limits system, directory, and file access to authorized users only. Users are identified by unique user names and passwords.

The Welcome message tells users to press Ctrl+Alt+Del to log on. Any DOS or 16-bit Windows user knows that this key combination reboots a PC, and it is most often used in the event of an unrecoverable system crash. So why did Microsoft choose to use this sequence for logging on to NT? Security.

A programmer determined to defeat NT's security might write a program that displays a fake Welcome screen to learn user names and passwords of unsuspecting users. Any fake login application is halted, however, when Ctrl+Alt+Del is pressed. This ensures that only NT's Welcome window is displayed. For the sake of safety, users should always press Ctrl+Alt+Del when they start an NT system to ensure that no one can steal their user name and password.

Pressing these three keys together changes the Welcome window to appear like the window in Figure 4.2.

Figure 4.2. Welcome window ready to accept user authentication.

Each user is identified by a unique user name and password. The system administrator assigns the user name when a user is added to the system. The user selects the password. The domain is the server on which the user's account resides. The default domain is the local server or PC running Windows NT. Users can log on to any Windows NT system on the network to which they have access privileges.

Windows NT: The Next Generation

In the Windows NT system, the default user is the system administrator. For this section, if you have Windows NT installed, you need to log on as the administrator so that you can see the administrative tools, which are normally invisible to all users except the administrator. After you enter your password and either click OK or press Enter, the security subsystem verifies your user name and password. If you make a mistake, or if someone masquerades as the administrator with a phony password, NT displays the window in Figure 4.3.

Figure 4.3. *Logon Message warning of an incorrect user name or password.*

Click OK or press Enter, and type in a correct user name and password. Then, NT launches the Program Manager, which appears like the window illustrated in Figure 4.4.

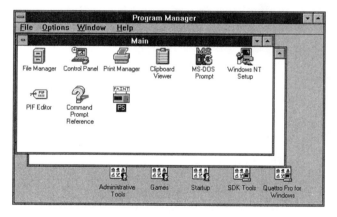

Figure 4.4. *The Program Manager with typical program groups.*

Experienced Windows 3.1 users will notice that the Windows NT Program Manager is identical to the 16-bit Windows version, with just a few exceptions. One difference is in the File menu, where in addition to the familiar file and program management choices, you can also select Logon or Shutdown.

Control Panel

I'll next examine some of the other new features and capabilities of Windows NT from the Main program group. When the Control Panel is open, the familiar Windows control options are available as well as a few new selections. The Color option enables users to set the color scheme for Windows NT's windows, menus, and dialog boxes. A variety of predefined schemes are available. Users may also define their own unique color combinations.

The Fonts option enables users to add, delete, and view the fonts available. TrueType fonts supported under Windows NT can be resized and scaled as desired for the user's display and printer.

The Ports option enables physical communications ports (serial and parallel interfaces) to be mapped to typical Windows NT device names, such as COM1, COM2, and LPT1. Windows NT can handle more than the COM1 through COM4 serial port assignments that are available under Windows 3.1. This means that NT can control intelligent serial multiport boards that support eight or more serial ports. This enables NT to be used for bulletin board systems (BBS) and other communications-intensive applications.

The Mouse option sets mouse tracking speed and double-click speed for selecting menu items. In addition, it enables users to swap the right and left buttons on the mouse for right-handed or left-handed use. The Desktop option controls the appearance of the Windows desktop. The background pattern can be selected and edited, and a predesigned wallpaper can also be chosen. Other options include screen savers, which automatically replace the desktop display after a user-defined delay. Users can also control window and icon spacing and select the cursor blink rate.

Windows NT: The Next Generation

The Keyboard option defines the length of time the computer waits to repeat a keystroke after the user presses a key and holds it down, as well as the repeat rate. The International option defines the user's home country, language, keyboard layout, and system of measurement. This option sets the language for all NT windows, menus, and dialog boxes, and it passes these settings along to Windows application programs that are written to incorporate multilingual capabilities.

The System option is a feature incorporated in Windows NT that is not available in Windows 3.x. If more than one operating system is installed on a computer, it enables users to specify the default operating system for startup. It also enables viewing (but not changing) system environment variables, which specify where Windows NT expects to find key system files. Users can, however, view, create, change, and delete user environment variables (which set key directories locations) from within the System dialog box, shown in Figure 4.5.

Figure 4.5. *The System dialog box.*

The availability and size of paging files for virtual memory can be set through the System control panel also. The paging file size controls the maximum number of programs and amount of data that Windows NT can handle at any one time. Figure 4.6 illustrates the Virtual Memory dialog box. In this case, 31M of hard disk space is allocated for virtual memory paging. Paging files can reside on one or more disks or disk volumes. A single paging file on logical drive D provides the entire 31M of paging space in this example.

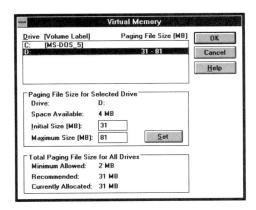

Figure 4.6. The Virtual Memory dialog box.

The Date/Time option in the Control Panel sets the PC's clock and calendar to the correct local time. Time Zone, another new Windows NT control panel option, specifies the local time zone (relative to Greenwich Mean Time—GMT) and determines how and if the system handles Daylight Savings Time. The Time Zone dialog box is shown in Figure 4.7.

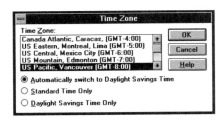

Figure 4.7. The Time Zone dialog box.

Three control panels support multimedia devices under Windows NT. The Drivers control panel displays the device drivers currently installed. It is used primarily for multimedia devices; it enables users to install new drivers or remove existing drivers. The MIDI Mapper is used in multimedia Windows NT systems to map MIDI instrument setups, instrument voice patches, and keys to the features of an installed sound board compatible with a Multimedia PC (MPC), such as AdLib Gold or Creative Labs Sound Blaster. If an NT system includes a sound board, users can assign sounds to key system events with the Sound control panel. For example, logging off from Windows NT can cause the computer to make a "ding" sound.

Networks is an enhanced version of the same control panel in Windows 3.1 and Windows for Workgroups. Figure 4.8 illustrates the default dialog box, which displays the current computer and domain names.

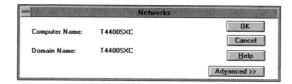

Figure 4.8. The Networks dialog box showing the computer and domain names.

By clicking the Advanced button, users can install or remove network software and drivers for adapter cards, configure or update an existing system, and add or remove the NT system from a specific work group or domain. Figure 4.9 illustrates the Networks Advanced options dialog box.

If the local NT system operates as a print, file, or communications server, the Server control panel enables these tasks to be started and managed. The Services control panel, another option in Windows NT that is not available in Windows, provides control over the tasks of system management, communications, or control installed in your NT system. In Figure 4.10, several services are available, but only the EventLog service is actually running. Each service can be started automatically at system start-up, at a specific time, or manually on user request. The services that are running in this example are as follows:

4 • *A Quick Walk Through Windows NT*

- EventLog: A process that logs administrator-specified events, such as logons and logoffs, process failures, missing drivers and other exceptions. The Event Log is viewed through the NT Administrator Tools' Event Viewer.

- Nbt, Tcpip, and Telnet: Processes for installing drivers, running the transport protocol software, and connecting to TCP/IP-based (primarily, UNIX) computers across the network. See Chapter 6, "Networking with Windows NT," for a detailed explanation of NT's networking features.

- Ups: The process for monitoring and management of an uninterruptible power supply, controlled by the UPS control panel.

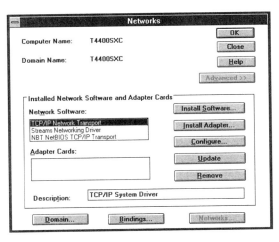

Figure 4.9. The Networks dialog box showing Advanced options.

The final new control panel option in NT is UPS, which enables an uninterruptible power supply to be monitored and controlled by a connection to one of the PC's communications ports. If a power failure occurs, Windows NT monitors the status of, and signals from, the UPS. NT alerts users to log off the system and complete a safe system shutdown before battery power runs out. Figure 4.11 is an example UPS dialog box.

Windows NT: The Next Generation

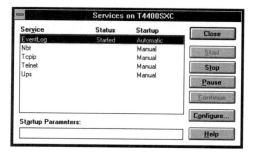

Figure 4.10. *The Services dialog box.*

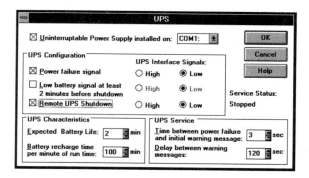

Figure 4.11. *The UPS dialog box.*

Print Manager

Windows NT offers a Print Manager that provides far more control over printer access and functions than 16-bit Windows. The 16-bit Windows Print Manager is little more than a simple print queue manager, and it's not a very useful one at that. Typically, 16-bit Windows applications send printing requests to the Print Manager. The Print Manager spools those files to the hard disk until the selected printer is available and then sends the files to the

4 • A Quick Walk Through Windows NT

printer. Some graphics-oriented applications, such as page layout programs for desktop publishing, need more control over the printer than the Print Manager provides. Those applications bypass the Print Manager and use their own printer control and queuing routines.

All Windows NT printing control is centralized in the Print Manager instead of scattered among windows and various applications. The top of the NT Print Manager window is shown in Figure 4.12.

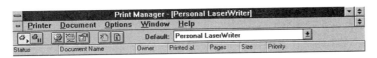

Figure 4.12. *The Print Manager window controls.*

Notice that NT's Print Manager window has a toolbar just below the menu bar. It is used to select common printer functions. The tools are described and illustrated in the following section.

Printer-Play/Printer-Pause: The first button looks like a combination of a printer and play button from a tape recorder. When it is selected, it turns the designated printer queue on and enables printing. The second button has a pause button like a tape recorder. It pauses the printer; print jobs accumulate in the printer queue until the first button is pressed.

Connect Printer/Disconnect Printer: If the first button is selected, the Connect to Printer dialog box is displayed (see Figure 4.13). Both local and remote printers across the network can be accessed. Status and printer queue information for each printer is available. This is especially useful in a multiprinter system when you want to print on the first available network printer. If the user clicks the second button, the current printer is disconnected from the computer.

Windows NT: The Next Generation

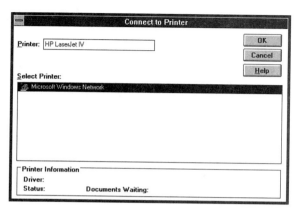

Figure 4.13. *The Connect to Printer dialog box.*

Printer Properties: This button enables you to configure the characteristics of your printer, including the name, software driver, and communications port. Figure 4.14 illustrates the Printer Properties dialog box that displays when the user clicks on this icon.

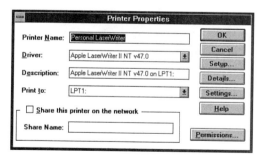

Figure 4.14. *The Printer Properties dialog box.*

The user can control many other printer properties by selecting other options shown in this dialog box. For example, Setup controls paper tray assignments, font downloading and substitution, and halftone printing.

4 • *A Quick Walk Through Windows NT*

These properties are specific to each printer. A PostScript printer like the one used in this example, illustrated in Figure 4.15, has different properties than an HP LaserJet-compatible printer.

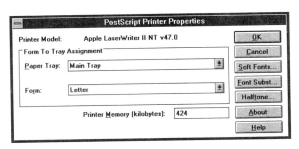

Figure 4.15. *The PostScript Printer Properties dialog box.*

The Printer Details dialog box, shown in Figure 4.16, controls configuration options that are normally set when a printer is first installed and subsequently rarely changed. These settings include the actual network that a printer is on, a printer's physical location, the times when a printer is available, print job priority for files sent to a printer, and the use of separator files (files that are automatically printed to physically separate one print job from another).

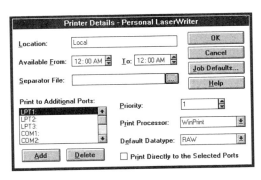

Figure 4.16. *The Printer Details dialog box.*

Windows NT: The Next Generation

The Permissions button opens a dialog box, Figure 4.17, that enables the system administrator to control access to the printer by group and user. (Refer to the "Administrative Tools" section in this chapter for more information.)

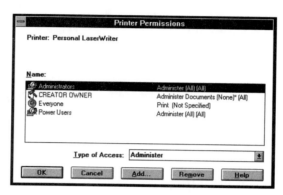

Figure 4.17. *The Printer Permissions dialog box.*

Stop Printing: This button aborts whatever print job is currently running on the selected printer, or at the user's option, any selected job(s) in the printer's queue.

Information: This button displays information about the currently selected printer.

The NT Print Manager improves and extends the capabilities of Windows 3.1's Print Manager, especially for networks with multiple printers. An NT administrator can check the status of and manage all the printers on the network from any system. NT users don't need to fiddle with settings for the LPTx: printer port. In fact, the user no longer needs to know anything about the printer's physical location or communications connection. The system administrator sets up the printers once, and NT makes them available to all authorized users.

Administrative Tools

Windows NT system administrators are responsible for initial system configuration, as well as normal day-to-day operations, such as system security and maintenance, disk management, and file backup. Windows NT provides a set of tools, called Administrative Tools, for performing these functions. Because unauthorized or novice users can disable system security and corrupt the system with some of these tools, NT restricts access to authorized administrator-level users. In fact, unauthorized users can't even view the Administrative Tools program group.

The basic NT system configuration includes five tools:

- User manager
- Disk manager
- Performance monitor
- Backup
- Event viewer

In addition, many NT system administrators choose to add the Registry Editor to the Administrative Tools program group. The following sections briefly discuss each of these tools.

User Manager

The User Manager is the administrative tool used to create and manage Windows NT user accounts. When the administrator opens the User Manager, the window in Figure 4.18 displays.

Notice that the top part of the window lists all the user accounts on this system. A scroll bar appears on the window if more users are defined than would fit on a single screen. For each user name—the name used during the logon process that uniquely identifies the user on the network—the system

Windows NT: The Next Generation

administrator may enter the user's full name and a description. This information is optional and isn't used by Windows NT, but it can help the administrator distinguish two or more users with confusingly similar user names.

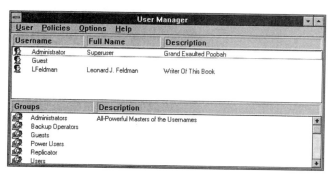

Figure 4.18. *The User Manager window showing users and user groups.*

The bottom half of the window lists all the defined user groups. As explained in the last chapter, user groups consist of one or more users with similar file and network access permissions. All the user groups on this system are default groups created by Windows NT, but it is easy to add, modify, or delete user groups to suit your needs.

To look at a user account entry, the administrator double-clicks on a user name and the User Properties dialog box displays. Figure 4.19 is an example of this dialog box.

A system administrator can freely change the Full Name and Description entries. The password, however, is always encrypted, and the administrator can't view it. However, in the event that there's no password on the account, or the existing password has expired, the administrator can create a new password by typing a new password in the Password field and then typing the identical password in the Confirm Password field. The User Manager doesn't change the password unless both match.

4 • A Quick Walk Through Windows NT

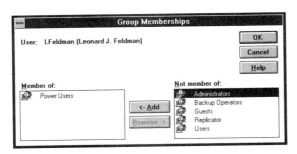

Figure 4.19. The User Properties dialog box.

Typically, an administrator creates a password only to enable a new user to log on to the system for the first time. For convenience, an administrator often chooses the user's last name or telephone extension number as the password, but these passwords can be guessed easily by system intruders and thus afford little protection. Therefore, when an administrator creates or changes a password, the "User Must Change Password at Next Logon" option is automatically selected. This forces the user to select a new, and preferably more secure, password immediately after logging on to the system.

A user can be assigned to one or more user groups. Clicking the Groups button at the bottom of the dialog box shown in Figure 4.19 brings up the dialog box to view these assignments, Figure 4.20.

Figure 4.20. The Group Memberships dialog box.

Windows NT: The Next Generation

The Group Memberships dialog box shows the groups that a user belongs to, if any, and enables the system administrator to assign a user to additional groups by selecting a group and clicking the Add button. To delete a user from a group, select a group in the Member Of list, and click Remove.

If the administrator clicks the Profile button in the User Properties dialog box, the User Environment Profile dialog box comes up. An example of this dialog box is shown in Figure 4.21.

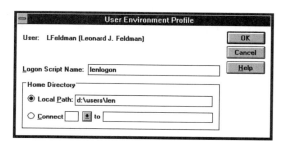

Figure 4.21. *The User Environment Profile dialog box.*

When a user logs on to the system, a logon script (written in NT's command prompt language, which is a mix of DOS, LAN Manager, and NT-specific commands) can automatically be executed. This script customizes the Windows NT environment for the user. For example, a user can choose to launch the POSIX subsystem or a customized Program Manager desktop, or even replace the standard Windows NT Program and File Managers with something like the soon to be released Norton Desktop for Windows NT. These and other choices can be specified in a logon script.

A user can specify the home directory in which to store personal files. The home directory can be on the local system, or the user can connect to a directory residing on a networked drive.

Now to return to the User Manager window and look at the defined groups. Double-clicking a group name displays the Local Group Properties dialog box, Figure 4.22.

4 • *A Quick Walk Through Windows NT*

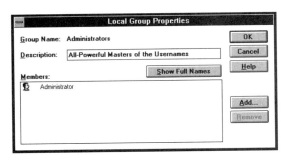

Figure 4.22. *The Local Group Properties dialog box.*

As with users, groups can have their own descriptions, too. The Members list shows all the group members. New members can be added by clicking the Add button, and existing members can be deleted from the group with the Remove button.

To add a user at the main User Manager window, the administrator selects User and then New User from the User menu, and the New User dialog box appears, Figure 4.23. The New User dialog box is similar to the User Properties dialog box. The administrator just has to fill in the user name and a password must be added. Fill in the blanks, click OK, and the user is ready to log on.

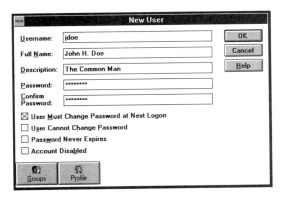

Figure 4.23. *The New User dialog box.*

Windows NT: The Next Generation

The New Local Group dialog box is accessed similarly, but through the User menu New Local Group option. It is virtually identical to the Local Group Properties dialog box illustrated in Figure 4.22.

The Policies menu on the User Manager window enables an administrator to control Account policies. For example, an administrator can control the length of time that passwords remain valid and the minimum password size; User Rights, which defines what system functions a user can control; and Auditing, which tracks and records important system-related user events, such as logon and logoff attempts and system shutdowns.

The User Manager is a reasonably simple, easy-to-use tool for creating and managing user accounts. It enables system administrators to keep track of users without requiring the often cryptic utilities and commands that are required by most UNIX variants.

Disk Manager

Most operating systems understand only their own, native hard disk file formats and structures. DOS, for example, understands only the FAT (file allocation table) file system. Most UNIX systems understand only one or two unique file systems. Windows NT, however, understands and works with several systems, including DOS's FAT, OS/2's High Performance File System (HPFS), and NT's own NT File System (NTFS), which supports all of Windows NT's file security features.

Windows NT provides the Disk Manager as a tool for system administrators to use for local and networked hard disk management. Launching the Disk Manager displays the window shown in Figure 4.24.

Just below the menu bar, notice a bar diagram. This diagram graphically represents the partitions and available space on each disk. (The system shown here has a single hard disk. Each additional local or networked hard disk would be represented by its own bar diagram.) The diagram shows the total capacity of the disk drive and the structure of each partition.

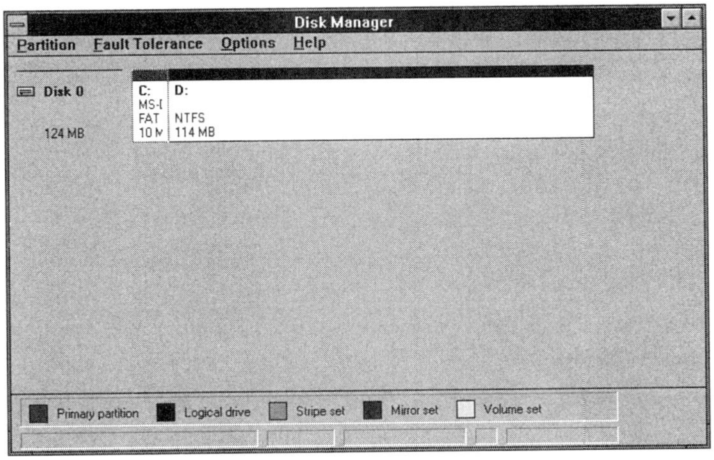

4 • *A Quick Walk Through Windows NT*

Figure 4.24. The Disk Manager window.

In this example, Disk 0's total capacity is 124M, and it is partitioned into logical C and D drives. Drive C is the Primary partition. It is 10M in size and formatted as an MS-DOS FAT volume. Drive D is a 114M logical drive. It uses the NTFS file system. To create a new partition and to modify or delete an existing partition, click the area of the bar diagram that corresponds to the disk space you want to work with. Then, choose your operation from the Partition menu.

To preserve system integrity, active (mounted) partitions such as drive C cannot be deleted. The partition containing the Windows NT system files cannot be deleted either. To delete these partitions, you must first back up all files that you want to preserve, shut down the NT system, insert a DOS system floppy disk to restart under DOS, and then reformat the hard disk.

In addition to the conventional disk drives commonly used in PCs and network servers, Windows NT also supports high reliability, high performance disk arrays used in network servers, which contain striped or mirrored drives.

Windows NT: The Next Generation

> **Striped Disk Set**
>
> A data storage system in which data is spread out across all the hard disks in an array, or set, of drives. If a single striped disk fails, you can still reconstruct your original data from the remaining drives by using NT's error correction software.

> **Mirrored Disk Set**
>
> A disk drive array in which identical data is simultaneously recorded on two drives. If one drive fails, the system can continue to operate with the data recorded on the mirror drive.

The Disk Manager Fault Tolerance menu enables the system administrator to create a striped disk set with parity or a mirrored disk drive set for data recovery. In the event of a disk failure, the Regenerate option can reconstruct the original data from the remaining drives.

The Disk Manager is a convenient, graphical means for keeping track of the multiple disk drives and file systems supported by Windows NT. With its support for striped and mirrored fault-tolerant disk drive arrays, NT is especially useful for mission-critical applications where high system reliability and guaranteed data integrity are required.

Performance Monitor

The Performance Monitor is a graphical tool useful for monitoring NT system operation. A variety of system utilization and performance measurements can be plotted individually or as a group. Figure 4.25 is an example of the Performance Monitor window plotting Privileged Mode and User Mode utilization against total processor time.

4 • *A Quick Walk Through Windows NT*

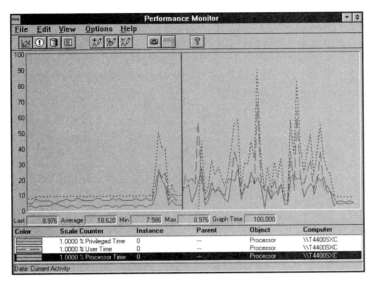

Figure 4.25. *The Performance Monitor window.*

Backup

The Backup administrative tool enables the system administrator or other authorized users to back up and restore the contents of the system's hard disks. Files can be backed up and restored by complete volumes, subdirectories, or individual files. Windows NT supports a variety of tape drives. Figure 4.26 is an example of the basic Tape Backup window. The tape drives are configured by using the Operations menu Hardware Setup selection.

Windows NT: The Next Generation

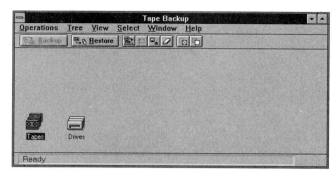

Figure 4.26. The Tape Backup window.

Event Viewer

The Event Viewer is a convenient utility for monitoring system operation logs maintained by Windows NT. These logs track unusual events, such as errors or warnings issued by system processes, attempts to violate system security with incorrect passwords, and applications that crash or otherwise abnormally terminate. Three logs can be viewed:

- System
- Security
- Application

Figure 4.27 is an example Event Viewer system log window.

Most of the system errors shown in this log come from one set of communications processes installed on the sample system. A more heavily used system has a far wider variety of errors, warnings, and other exceptions. The protected subsystem architecture of Windows NT keeps any of these errors from crashing the entire system, and a typical user never knows that an error has occurred. That's why the Event Viewer is so important for keeping track of otherwise invisible system events.

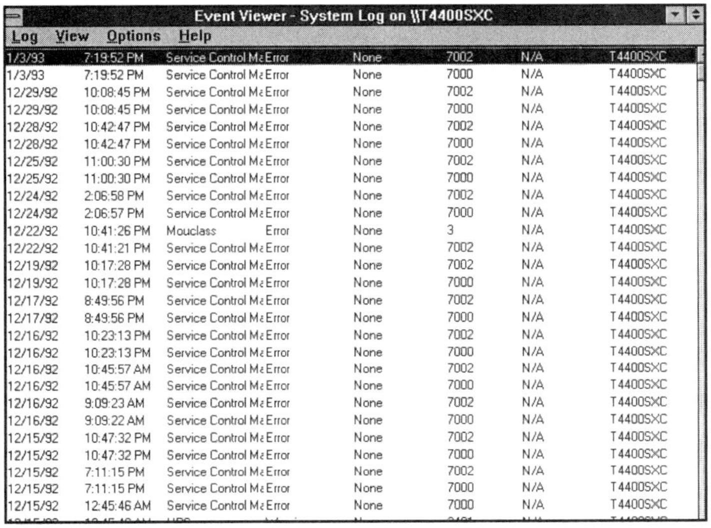

4 • A Quick Walk Through Windows NT

Figure 4.27. The Event Viewer window displaying system log.

Registry Editor

The Registry Editor enables experienced system administrators to view and edit the properties of every Windows NT *object*. As you'll see in Chapter 5, "A Developer's View of Windows NT," all operating system resources, including processes, threads, files, memory, and I/O devices are classified as objects. In fact, the Registry Editor illustrates both the object-oriented nature and the complexity of Windows NT. Every conceivable system component is represented in the Registry. Figure 4.28 is an example of this system's Registry.

Of all the tools available to the system administrator, the Registry Editor is one of the most dangerous. A seemingly trivial change to one object's properties, or deletion of an object, can kill your NT system because the Registry Editor opens up the deepest layers of NT for examination and modification. The Registry Editor bypasses the security subsystem, and if used improperly, can wreak havoc on your NT system.

Windows NT: The Next Generation

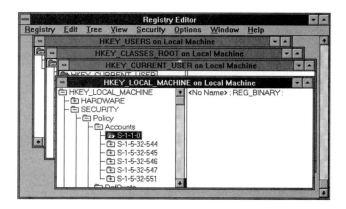

Figure 4.28. *Registry Editor window.*

The good news is that almost all the Registry Editor's functionality is available from safer, less cryptic system utilities. All key system variables can be controlled by other administrative tools, control panels, and utilities. Therefore, the Registry Editor should be used only in emergencies and only by the most knowledgeable and experienced system administrators.

File Manager

Along with the Program Manager, the File Manager is the best example of the similar look and feel between Windows and Windows NT—with two important additions. First, it includes the toolbar added to the File Manager in Windows for Workgroups. Second, it has a Security menu that provides file-level and subdirectory-level access control.

Rather than go into extensive detail about the File Manager, I'll focus on the Windows NT features that are different from the Windows features. Figure 4.29 is a typical File Manager window.

4 • *A Quick Walk Through Windows NT*

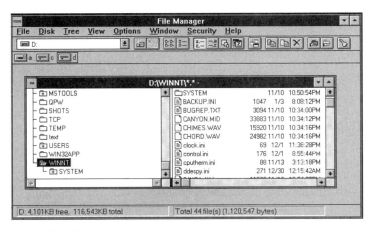

Figure 4.29. *The File Manager window.*

Notice that the upper-left side of the screen contains both a menu for drive selection and small icons representing each available drive. If this NT system were on a network, the available network drives would also be visible. The toolbar sits to the right of the drive menu. The following section describes what each toolbar button controls. It's important to know, however, that these security features are available only for Windows NT NTFS and LAN Manager volumes. If the user tries to set permissions or audit files on a DOS FAT or OS/2 HPFS volume, Windows NT displays an error message.

 Connect/Disconnect Network Drive: Selecting the first button connects a network drive to the local system. Selecting the second button disconnects a network drive. Subject to security permissions, directories and files on network drives can be opened and worked with just like directories and files on local drives.

 Name-Only/Full Information: These buttons control what file and subdirectory information is displayed. Selecting the first button displays only icons and filenames. Selecting the second button displays file size, and the date and

131

Windows NT: The Next Generation

time when a file was created in addition to the icons and filenames. Figure 4.30 shows a directory displaying only icons and filenames.

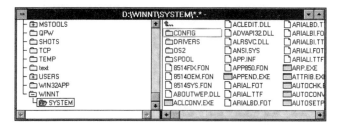

Figure 4.30. *Directory display showing only icons and filenames.*

Filename Sort/Extension Sort: The first button sorts the directory display alphabetically by filename, and the second button sorts by extension.

Filesize Sort/Creation Sort: The first button sorts the directory display by file size from largest to smallest. The second button sorts the directory display by creation date from most recently created to oldest.

New Window: Clicking this button opens a new copy of the drive window that is currently open. This feature is useful for moving or copying files from one location to another on the same volume.

Copy/Move/Delete: These three buttons duplicate the actions of the File Copy, File Move, and File Delete menu commands, respectively.

Share/Stop Sharing: The first button makes the selected local drive available for sharing by other systems on the network. The second button stops sharing the drive. Obviously, these buttons are useful only for networked NT systems.

4 • A Quick Walk Through Windows NT

 Security: This button enables you to view and change security access permissions by directory and file. For example, select a file, click the Security button, and the dialog box illustrated in Figure 4.31 displays.

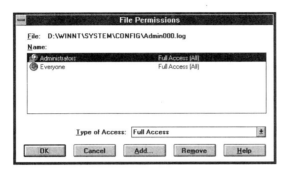

Figure 4.31. The File Permissions dialog box.

Several predefined levels of access control are provided on a group basis. By clicking the Add or Remove button, access can be granted or denied on a group-by-group basis, or even on individual user basis. If the standard access control levels are insufficient, you can define a custom combination of access controls as in Figure 4.32.

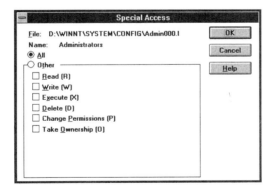

Figure 4.32. The Special Access dialog box.

Windows NT: The Next Generation

A similar mechanism is used for controlling access on a directory basis. Select a directory, click the Security button, and the Directory Permissions dialog box appears as shown in Figure 4.33.

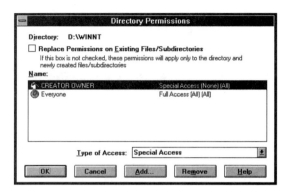

Figure 4.33. *The Directory Permissions dialog box.*

This dialog box is almost the same as File Permissions, with one important difference: if Replace Permissions on Existing Files/Subdirectories is selected, the permissions are changed on every existing file and subdirectory within the selected directory. If this option isn't selected, all the existing permission settings remain unchanged, and the revised permissions apply only to new files and subdirectories.

Two other important security features are accessed from the Security menu instead of the menu bar. The first is Auditing. This feature automatically logs any attempts to access any file or directory. Then, the log can be subsequently reviewed with the Event Viewer. This tool enables the system administrator to see who attempts to access or modify specific files or directories and serves as a way to identify potential security threats.

The second feature accessed from the Security menu instead of the menu bar is Ownership. Every file and directory has an owner, who either created or administers the file or directory. The file owner has ultimate control over a file's access permissions. Ownership can be viewed and changed with the Security menu Owner option. Unlike file and directory permissions, in which the owner can allow many users or groups access, only one group or user can be an owner. Ownership can't be assigned to another group or user by the system administrator, but the system administrator or any member of the administrator group can take ownership of a file or directory by using the Owner dialog box, illustrated in Figure 4.34.

Figure 4.34. *The Owner dialog box.*

Remember, all these security features are available only for Windows NT NTFS and LAN Manager volumes. Attempting to set up permissions or audit files on a DOS FAT or OS/2 HPFS volume will cause an error dialog box to display.

The rest of the File Manager's operation is identical to that of 16-bit Windows. I'll end my overview of the Windows NT user interface with the logoff process.

Logging Off

Unlike single-tasking operating systems such as DOS, Windows NT systems have multiple programs and processes running simultaneously. Turning off the power to shut down an NT system could cause problems by corrupting open files (although NTFS has excellent file recovery and data integrity protection features). Therefore, Windows NT provides a simple way of logging off or shutting down a system that is running Windows NT.

You can log off or shut down the system in either of two ways. You can select Logoff or Shutdown from the Program Manager's File menu, or you can press Ctrl+Alt+Del to display the Windows NT Security dialog box, which looks like Figure 4.35.

Windows NT: The Next Generation

Figure 4.35. *The Windows NT Security dialog box.*

Several access security features are provided. For example, you can lock your workstation to prevent any unauthorized person from using your system without shutting it down, or you can change your password. Selecting Logoff logs you off the system while keeping other clients logged on across the network online and all other processes running. Selecting Shutdown enables authorized users to safely terminate all running processes, close any open files, and shut down the system.

Conclusion

You've read about Windows NT from the perspective of a user/system administrator from logon to logoff. NT maintains the look and feel of 16-bit Windows, but it adds additional features for maintaining system security and managing a multitasking, multiprocessing networked environment.

Windows NT balances ease-of-use with the unavoidable complexity of a powerful operating system. In doing so, it compares favorably with most UNIX variants. NT even manages to reduce some of the nightmarish complexity of the maze of INI and PIF files in 16-bit Windows. In many cases, it is actually easier to install and maintain applications on an NT system than it is under Windows 3.1.

The 16-bit Windows user will be comfortable with the look and feel of NT. For the UNIX user, NT's concepts and capabilities will be familiar, but the ease with which its features can be used will probably be a new, happy experience. Windows NT is clearly an evolutionary, not revolutionary, improvement for users and system administrators, but it is a welcome improvement nonetheless.

5

A Developer's View of Windows NT

Windows NT: The Next Generation

This chapter discusses Windows NT from the developer's point of view. Specifically, it examines the important differences between 16-bit Windows and Windows NT that affect software development. It also focuses on some of the tools provided with the Windows NT Software Developers' Toolkit.

Software developers must be intimately familiar with the nuts and bolts of operating systems, including Windows NT. This chapter provides programmers with information about Windows NT's system architecture, the Win32 application programming interface (API), and the Windows NT Software Developers' Toolkit. This chapter, therefore, is more technical in nature than the rest of the book. If you're not a software developer, or you're not interested in learning more about the guts of Windows NT, you might want to skip to Chapter 6 ("Networking with Windows NT"), which discusses NT's networking capabilities, or Chapter 7 ("Windows NT Versus DOS and Windows"), which discusses the differences between NT and Windows for DOS.

> **NOTE**
>
> Keep in mind that discussion of features and functionality of the Windows NT environment and Software Development Kit (SDK) in this chapter is based on Microsoft's October 1992 beta release and subject to change in the final Windows NT release.

The NT System Architecture

Chapter 3, "Windows NT in Profile," examined Windows NT's architecture and discussed some of its key design features, such as user and kernel modes, protected subsystems, and the NT executive. Chapters 3 and 4 looked at user mode and the protected subsystems in considerable detail. The following section focuses on NT's kernel mode—specifically, the NT executive. Figure 5.1 illustrates the NT architecture.

5 • *A Developer's View of Windows NT*

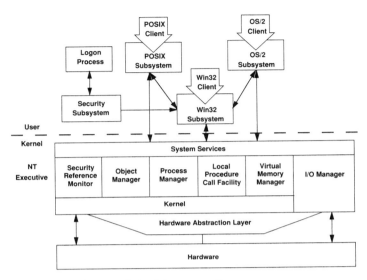

Figure 5.1. *The Windows NT Architecture diagram.*

Kernel Mode

The protected processor mode in which the NT executive runs.

NT Executive

The entire NT operating system, except the protected subsystems. The NT executive runs in kernel mode.

The NT Executive

The NT executive is the heart of Windows NT. The executive is a complete, stand-alone operating system, with the exception of a user interface, which is provided by the Win32 subsystem. Microsoft designed NT this way in order to accomplish two goals. First, Microsoft's system architects wanted to provide one uniform user interface for all operating systems and environments supported by Windows NT. Second, they wanted to be able to update and even completely replace the user interface without gutting the operating system.

By placing the user interface in user mode as a protected subsystem, the application programming interface is reasonably independent from the design of the executive. This enables the Win32 API and the executive designs to be optimized for their respective tasks. More importantly, it allows major changes in either the executive or the Win32 API to be made independently of its counterpart.

The entire NT executive is written to implement a high degree of software independence. As Figure 5.1 illustrates, the executive can best be thought of as a four-layer cake with, from highest to lowest level:

- System services
- Executive components
- Kernel
- Hardware abstraction layer (HAL)

System Services

System services are the system calls used for communication between user mode processes and the executive components. The easiest way to think of the system services is as the API for the NT executive. In operation, the protected subsystems (primarily the Win32, OS/2, and POSIX subsystems) interact with the executive by making system services calls. In other words, system services are the API for the user mode APIs.

Unlike the protected subsystems, however, the executive's system services don't create their own processes. Instead, they act on processes created by the protected subsystems. When a new application is launched by the Win32 subsystem, for example, the application process uses the Win32 API to allocate virtual memory. The Win32 API call is translated into a virtual memory manager system services call. Instead of creating yet another process, the virtual memory manager (VMM) takes temporary control of the application's running thread, allocates the needed memory, and returns control to the application. (Normally, a thread belongs to one and only one process, but as part of the memory allocation process, the thread's "ownership" temporarily transfers to the VMM, and then reverts to the original process after memory allocation is complete.) The memory allocation function is performed by the VMM in conjunction with other executive components, effectively "out of sight" of the application's thread(s).

The system services calls are designed to allow great flexibility in the design of executive components. Any executive component can be modified or replaced without requiring major changes to its system services calls. This feature allows the executive components to be upgraded without changes to the protected subsystems and their APIs, which in turn simplifies software development and allows both system performance to be improved and new features to be added without requiring applications to be rewritten.

Executive Components

The NT executive has six primary components, each of which performs a set of critical operating system functions:

- Object manager
- Security reference monitor
- Process manager
- Local procedure call facility
- Virtual memory manager
- I/O manager

Windows NT: The Next Generation

Object Manager

The object manager is responsible for creating, managing, and deleting NT executive objects. Just as the Win32 subsystem creates and manages objects of various types, including processes and data, the NT executive carries out the functions implicit in these high-level objects with its own system-level objects.

Unlike NeXT's NeXTSTEP UNIX-based operating system or Taligent, a next-generation object-oriented operating system under development by IBM and Apple, Windows NT is not a true object-oriented operating system. Although NT uses objects extensively, it uses them only where data is opened for user mode access or when data access is shared or restricted. Data structures that reside totally within one executive component are not "objectified."

Two kinds of objects exist: executive objects, which are created within the executive and accessible to the executive and protected subsystems, and kernel objects, which are available only to the executive and relate to low-level functions that can be performed only within the kernel itself. Because kernel objects are accessible to developers only through executive objects, the remainder of this discussion deals with executive objects. Windows NT defines 15 types of executive objects:

Object Type	Description
Access Token	A security ID used to uniquely identify an NT user for access control purposes
Event	A support services message that indicates a system event has occurred
Event Pair	A support services message used by the Win32 subsystem to indicate that a client thread has passed a message to a Win32 server, or that the server has returned a message to the client
File	A "handle" to a file or I/O device, such as a printer or modem

Object Type	Description
Key	The components of the system configuration registry; the Registry Editor edits these components (see Chapter 4, "A Quick Walk Through Windows NT")
Mutant	An object used to get mutually exclusive access to a system resource (one thread to one resource)
Object Directory	An object that contains a directory of defined objects (in essence, a memory-resident file system for objects)
Port	The destination of a local procedure call passed between processes
Process	An application or other program, including its virtual address space and required system resources
Profile	An object that records the proportion of time spent by a thread in various activities (used for performance optimization with the process viewer)
Section	A defined area of shared memory
Semaphore	A counter that limits the number of threads which can access a resource
Symbolic Link	A link between a common name for an object, such as a disk drive (A:) and NT's internal name for the object; sometimes referred to as an alias
Thread	The executable component(s) of a process
Timer	An object used to trigger or delay the execution of a process or thread by time

Windows NT: The Next Generation

Whenever the Win32 API directly or indirectly creates an object, the object manager does the following:

- Allocates memory

- Attaches a security descriptor to the object, which is compared with processes' access tokens to permit or prohibit access to the object

- Inserts the object's name in the appropriate location within the object directory

- Creates and returns a "handle," or pointer, to the object, often eliminating the need for the calling process to look up the actual location of the object in the object directory.

The object manager uses the security descriptor to ensure that objects are accessed only by authorized user processes, which provides the backbone of NT's access control. In addition, the object manager performs "garbage collection" functions by deleting temporary objects that have no handles attached to them. The object manager also keeps track of the amount of physical memory used by each object and ensures that individual user processes don't use too much memory, which prevents other important processes from executing due to lack of memory. In short, the object manager is essential for the efficient and secure operation of NT systems.

Security Reference Monitor

The security reference monitor works with the object manager to enforce object access control. As described in the previous section, every process includes an access token, which contains a list of the owner and authorized users of the process and their permissions. When a process is started, the security profile and permissions of the user starting the process are copied into the access token.

Access control information is also attached to every object. Each object, whether it's executable or not, has an access control list (ACL). Just as when an access token is created, the ACL initially takes on the access permissions of its creator. The owner of an object, however, can change these permissions at any time by adding entries to the ACL for every user or group authorized to access the object. Each entry specifies the permissions given to the user or group. These entries are called access control entries (ACEs).

Here's a simple example of the security reference monitor's role. Consider a database management application (a process) that manages a personnel database (a file), which contains sensitive information. When they were originally created, both the process and the file took on the same permissions as their creators. Over time, the file was given additional sets of permissions (ACEs) by its owner and system administrator, in order to enable other users and groups to access its contents. Now, when the database management process attempts to open the personnel database file, the security reference monitor compares their access control lists and grants the process access to the file only if one of the process' access control entries matches an entry in the file's ACL.

The first time a process tries to use an object, the object manager sends a message to the security reference monitor. The monitor compares the process' access token with the object's ACL. If the monitor finds an entry in the ACL that corresponds to one of the users listed in the access token, the monitor responds to the object manager with a list of the operations the user is entitled to perform. If the monitor can't match the access token to any ACL entries, however, it instructs the object monitor to deny access.

When a process has established a handle, or linkage, to an object like the personnel file previously described, no further ACL checking is required for each subsequent access. After a process terminates, however, the process' object handle table, which contains all the object linkages for the process, also disappears. The next time the process is launched, security verification must be performed again.

By separating the security monitoring functions from object management, Windows NT makes it easier to change or upgrade either the object manager or the security monitor without affecting the operations of the other. It also isolates the actual permission-checking tasks to the security monitor. A dedicated hacker would need to penetrate both the object manager and the security monitor to totally disable NT's security features.

Windows NT: The Next Generation

Process Manager

The process manager is the environment component that creates and terminates processes and threads. Like the object manager, the process manager sees processes as objects. In fact, the process manager can be thought of as simply a special instance of the object manager because it creates, manages, and terminates only one kind of object.

The procedure for creating and terminating processes is relatively straightforward. A client application (from 32-bit Windows, OS/2, or POSIX) sends a request (with an API call) to start a new process to the protected subsystem that is acting as its server (the Win32, OS/2, or POSIX subsystems, respectively). The subsystem converts the request into a uniform system services call and passes it to the NT executive, which routes the request to the process manager.

The process manager creates a process object and passes the object's handle to the object manager, which attaches an access token to the process and returns the handle to the calling protected subsystem. The subsystem then converts the handle into a form that its client application can understand.

The same basic procedure is used for creating threads. Remember that under NT, every process must have at least one thread, but the process manager doesn't automatically create a thread whenever a process object is created. The protected subsystem must request that the process manager create a thread, and it must specify which process owns the thread. The thread is given the same access permissions and execution priority as its parent process.

The subsystem takes care of automatically issuing the request to create at least one thread for every process, so the application doesn't need to create both processes and threads—launching a process is sufficient to create a thread. However, the process manager enables applications to create multithreaded processes; in this case, the application developer can explicitly create multiple threads for a single process.

The process manager also performs several protected subsystem-accessible additional functions, including the following:

- Attaching to, reading, and writing a client's address space

- Allocating and releasing a client's virtual memory
- Executing, suspending, restarting, and terminating a client's threads

The process manager enables the protected subsystems to control the creation, execution, and termination of processes and their related threads. It provides the mechanism for implementation of multithreaded applications. It also allows exquisite control over the "flow" of processes within NT, as well as adequate security safeguards that user mode applications can use to implement their own process control architectures and unique memory management schemes without violating NT's system integrity. One example of this built-in flexibility is the virtual DOS machine (VDM) with Windows on Win32. The VDM implements DOS' memory segmentation and 16-bit Windows' cooperative multitasking, within the framework of NT, which supports linear, nonsegmented memory addressing and preemptive multitasking.

Local Procedure Call Facility

Local procedure calls (LPCs) are used to pass messages between two processes running on a single NT system. NT's LPC facility is modeled on remote procedure calls (RPCs), which are a standardized means of passing messages between client and server systems over a network. LPCs are easy to understand after you understand RPCs and how they work across a network. Chapter 6 discusses NT's RPC facility in more detail as part of its discussion of networking. If you're interested in LPCs, you might want to skip to the end of Chapter 6, read about RPCs, and then return to this discussion.

In general, applications do not directly use LPCs, although they can use RPCs. LPCs are executed by the protected subsystems on behalf of their client applications. As with RPCs, there is always a client and a server in an LPC; in this case, both the client and server are processes.

Every NT server process that is open to LPC communication has at least one port object attached to it. The two kinds of ports are connection and communication. A connection port is like an in-box that accepts requests from client processes for communication. The request is sent from the client process to the server's connection port. If the server accepts the request,

Windows NT: The Next Generation

it creates two private (unnamed) communication ports, which serve as mailboxes for the client and server processes. The server returns the handle of the client's communication port to the client via the connection port.

All subsequent communications between the client and server are sent and received through the communication ports. One server communication port is always assigned to one client process exclusively. If another client requests communication, the server creates another pair of communication ports. In this way, messages from one server can't be inadvertently routed to the wrong client.

Port-to-port communications are fine for small messages, but NT supports only messages that are 256 bytes or less. If a client and server need to pass more information, the LPC facility enables the client or server to create a section object, which is a section of virtual memory available to both the client and server processes. To use a section object, the client places data it wants to send to the server in the section object, then sends a message to the server through its communication port with a handle to the section object. The server retrieves data from the section object, and when necessary, responds to the client through its communication port.

Section objects can be permanent or temporary, depending upon the requirements of the process that creates them. Permanent section objects are not deleted. Temporary section objects are automatically deleted by the object manager when the last process with a handle to the section object releases the handle.

A third form of LPC, called a Quick LPC, is used exclusively by the Win32 subsystem. With a Quick LPC, the server doesn't create a pair of communication ports in response to a request by a client. Instead, it creates a dedicated thread for handling communications between the processes, a 64K section object for passing data and messages, and an event pair object. The thread, which runs within the server process, waits for one of the two processes to place messages in memory and sets an event (flag) in the receiver's event pair. The thread then processes the message, sets the receiver's event, and waits.

Quick LPCs are the fastest way for two processes to communicate, but they add a burden to the system because every Quick LPC link requires a dedicated thread, and more threads means more system overhead involved

in managing the threads. If every client application relied on Quick LPCs, system throughput would plummet. As a result, the LPC facility limits Quick LPC use to the Win32 subsystem. Client applications and other systems are limited to the first two types of LPCs.

All three LPC approaches incorporate a mechanism, called a *callback*, which is used by one process to request more information from the other. In a system without callbacks, the client process sends a message to the server through its communication port. The server processes the message, determines that it doesn't have enough information from the client to process the request, and replies that it failed to perform the client's request. The client must then create a new message with all the needed information, send the message to the server, and wait for a response. This message loop can be repeated several times, until the server has all the data it needs to perform the client's request.

With callbacks, the client/server message loop is simplified. The client process sends a message to the server through its communication port. The server processes the message, determines that it requires additional information from the client in order to process the request, and sends a callback message to the client with the request. The client processes the request and returns the requested additional information through its communication port. The server responds with its reply to the original message. Both the client and the server can send each other callbacks—if the client doesn't understand a response or callback from the server, it can callback for more information.

Here's a hypothetical example of how callbacks work. Consider our personnel database from previous examples. The database management process sends a request to the file server to get the personnel record for John Doe. The process is looking for one unique record, but the file server locates not one, but three John Does. The file server sends a callback to the database management process asking for additional information, such as a middle initial or employee ID number, in order to narrow the search. The client process responds with more information, and the callback/response cycles continue until the file server has sufficient information to uniquely identify a single employee, after which it returns the requested information to the process.

Windows NT: The Next Generation

The LPC facility provides an effective mechanism for interprocess communications, albeit with significant system overhead. Although alternative means of interprocess communications are faster and require less processing time than LPCs, developers should at least be familiar with the LPC facility. It is likely that the LPC facility will be the precursor of a more extensive interobject communication architecture planned for Microsoft's future, an object-oriented version of Windows NT code-named "Cairo."

Virtual Memory Manager

Chapter 3 discussed NT's virtual memory capabilities and capacities. This section provides a quick overview of the NT virtual memory manager (VMM), which performs three essential functions:

- Managing each process' virtual address space
- Sharing memory between processes
- Protecting each process' virtual memory

Memory Management

The memory management function of the VMM enables each process to do the following:

- Reserve and commit to virtual memory: reserving memory simply sets aside a portion of virtual memory for a process' future use; committing memory actually allocates the reserved physical space in NT's hard disk virtual memory paging file. No operations can be performed to reserved virtual memory space until the space has been committed.
- Read and write virtual memory.
- Lock selected virtual memory pages (sections of virtual memory space) in physical memory, keeping them from being swapped to the hard disk for better performance.
- Gather information about and protect individual virtual pages.
- Flush (write) virtual pages to the hard disk for permanent storage.

5 • *A Developer's View of Windows NT*

Sharing Virtual Memory

The VMM also allows multiple processes to share one or several pages of virtual memory. As I described, the VMM uses section objects to provide two or more processes with a handle to the same area(s) of virtual memory. Section objects describe the attributes of an area of virtual memory. The memory section described by a section object is mapped into the virtual address space of each process that holds a handle to the object.

Because section objects can be very large and thus eat up lots of virtual memory for each process, the VMM allows processes to map only a portion of the section object address space to their virtual memory space. This "window" on the total section object is called a *view*, and it allows processes to work with files that are too large to fit into their own virtual memory space.

Returning to the personnel database example, the actual personnel file for a major private employer or government agency might be huge. Reserving space in a process' virtual memory space for the entire database would be extremely wasteful, especially considering that the database management process probably only needs access to a very small section of the database file at any one time. Thus, the database management process opens a window on the much larger section object and repositions the window to access different parts of the section object as needed.

Protecting Memory

The VMM enables Windows NT to protect memory from inadvertent or deliberate access by other processes. Chapter 3 discussed NT's memory protection mechanisms. The following sections examine the VMM's practical implementation of memory protection.

The VMM is responsible for mapping virtual memory address to hardware addresses. This ensures that two different processes don't access the same page of physical memory. The VMM uses whatever hardware memory management features are available in the host computer to provide page protection. All page protections not supported directly by the host computer's memory manager are implemented by the VMM in software. Individual memory pages can be defined as read/write, read-only, execute-only, and no access.

153

Windows NT: The Next Generation

The different families of processors supported by NT offer significantly different levels of support for hardware memory protection. For example, the MIPS 4000 performs read-only and read/write protection in hardware, so the VMM performs the remaining page protection functions in software.

Additionally, guard pages can be designated. If a process attempts to read from, write to, or execute anything within a guard page, a warning message is sent to the process. These pages are often used as "bookends" for a data set in memory to indicate the end of a block of data or code. If the application accesses a guard page, a message is sent to the application (this might be interpreted to mean that the dataset is running out of room in memory). The application can then request additional memory from the VMM, move the guard page protection to the end page of the expanded area, and continue.

In situations where two or more processes need to access the same memory, the VMM implements copy-on-write page protection. As long as all of the processes are reading the shared memory, all of the processes' virtual memory points to the same physical memory pages. When one of the processes wants to write to a shared page, however, the VMM copies the page to an unused page in physical memory, changes the process' virtual memory pointer to the new physical address, and allows the write operation to proceed. All the other processes continue to refer to the original, unchanged physical memory.

This mechanism insulates each process from changes made by others to shared memory. If processes want to explicitly change shared memory and have the change reflect in all the other attached processes, application developers can do so by setting the attributes of section objects. It is then up to the application developer to ensure the integrity of shared memory.

The VMM allows application developers to leave most memory management functions to Windows NT and concentrate on how their applications use virtual memory. The VMM also insulates application developers from the hardware memory management capabilities of each host computer platform because VMM provides a core set of capabilities that are performed by either hardware or software, depending upon the host memory manager.

I/O Manager

This section provides a quick overview of the architecture and features of NT's I/O system. Later in this chapter, asynchronous I/O, one of NT's most important features, is discussed.

The I/O manager is best thought of as a dispatcher, rather than a manager, of the I/O system. The I/O system communicates with the protected subsystems on one side and a variety of device drivers on the other. In NT, file systems, network drivers, and drivers for local hardware devices are all called "device drivers," and all are communicated with in the same way.

When an application issues a file or device I/O request, such as printing a file or reading data from a file on a hard disk, the application passes its request to the Win32, OS/2, or POSIX subsystems, which then passes the request to the I/O manager via system services.

The I/O manager converts the request to an I/O request packet (IRP) and identifies the correct driver to process the request. This IRP is passed to the target driver. The driver receives the packet, performs the requested operation, and either immediately returns the packet to the I/O manager or passes it to another driver for further processing. In either case, the packet eventually returns to the I/O manager, where the IRP is deleted and retrieved data and status are returned to the requesting subsystem and on to the application.

Within the NT executive, all I/O devices are seen as virtual files. Reading and writing data to and from each device is simply a matter of reading or writing the virtual file that represents the physical device or file system. These virtual files are referred to as file objects and managed by the object manager just like any other object.

When an application wishes to open a file (or connect to a device), it sends a request to the I/O manager, which passes the request to the object manager to see if a file object associated with the requested file or device already exists in the object directory. If the file object exists, the object manager passes the requesting process' access token to the security reference monitor for access control processing and then (if permitted) returns a handle to the file object to the I/O manager to make the actual connection to the file system or device.

Windows NT: The Next Generation

After the connection to a device driver is made, the drivers are responsible for controlling and queuing IRPs. In general, the two basic types of drivers are single-layered and multilayered. A printer is a good example of a device that uses a single-layered driver; a hard disk is likely to require a multilayered driver. The biggest factor in determining whether a driver needs to be single-layered or multilayered is whether a file system (either local or remote) is involved.

Printers, display controllers, and other similar devices don't have file systems. They receive and send data to and from an application or utility. If they store data, as in the case of a print buffer, they generally do so temporarily, and the storage buffer is usually not available for random access by the application. These devices need only one driver to interpret IRPs and send I/O requests directly to the hardware.

Disk drives, tape drives, and other mass storage devices usually support file systems, including directory structures. When communicating with these devices, the I/O manager sends an IRP to the appropriate file system's file object. The file system then translates the IRP's request into a device-specific message, creates a new IRP, and sends it to the targeted hard disk's driver file object. Only then is the operation actually performed on the physical device. The results of the operation are sent from the physical device to its file driver, to the file system, and back to the I/O manager.

This scheme makes it very easy to interchange and update device drivers because driver-to-process communications are executed through file objects rather than hardware-specific commands.

Experienced Windows software developers know that applications which use the Windows device driver architecture usually achieve poorer performance than that of comparable applications that bypass the device drivers and "talk" directly to the hardware. However, applications optimized for specific hardware must be modified every time the underlying hardware is changed. NT's I/O manager trades off a small amount of performance in return for hardware independence. The I/O manager allows new device drivers to be added to Windows NT on the fly, without requiring the system to be shut down and restarted. An example of this is the mechanism used by NT's networking capabilities to detect and add new network drivers. The I/O manager makes application and subsystem development easier with

5 • *A Developer's View of Windows NT*

a uniform object-oriented model of I/O operations for all file and device activities. In short, the I/O manager is designed to simplify the process of creating and maintaining both applications and device drivers.

The Kernel

The NT kernel is a core of operating system functions required by the rest of the NT executive. Because user mode applications never deal directly with the kernel, application developers generally do not have any direct access to, or control over, the NT kernel itself. The NT kernel carries out the following operations:

- Schedules and dispatches threads
- Processes interrupts and exceptions
- Performs multiprocessor synchronization
- Manages system recovery after a power failure occurs

Thread Scheduling and Dispatch

Each thread object created in response to a request from an application contains a "mini" thread object called a kernel thread object that is used by the kernel to schedule execution of the larger thread. Each thread can be ready for execution, waiting in the queue, waiting for additional resources or a specific event to occur, executing, or terminated.

The dispatcher is the portion of the kernel responsible for thread scheduling and termination. The dispatcher determines the order in which threads should by executed by examining each thread's priority, which is derived from the priority of the thread's parent process. The dispatcher has the power to suspend a currently running thread if another thread with higher priority is ready for execution. System administrators and application developers have control over the priorities of processes and their threads, and they can use these priorities to optimize the overall performance of one process or balance system performance for a variety of processes.

Interrupt and Exception Processing

Interrupts are system events that are asynchronous to the operation of the system. In other words, they can occur at any time. Interrupts are usually issued by an I/O device or the system clock/timer. Pressing a key on a PC keyboard or receiving a byte of data through a serial port, for example, automatically triggers an interrupt.

Interrupt handling requires a significant amount of processor time, so most interrupts can be turned on or off by individual applications. Exceptions usually occur when a specific operation is performed in system memory. Divide-by-zero errors and memory access violations, for example, cause NT to issue exceptions. In NT, whenever an interrupt or exception occurs, the NT kernel passes control to a *trap handler*, the memory location where instructions on how to deal with the interrupt or exception reside.

Multiprocessor Synchronization

The third major function of the NT kernel is multiprocessor synchronization. This feature ensures that only one thread can access a given system resource at a time.

In a multiprocessor-based system with shared memory, two or more processors could each be running threads that need to access the same page of memory or perform operations on the same object. Without some way of synchronizing and suspending the execution of the multiple processors, two processors could attempt to make changes in the same object at the same time, leaving the object in an unknown, but probably corrupted, state.

Both the kernel and the NT executive provide mechanisms for ensuring system integrity through synchronization. In the case of the kernel, synchronization is achieved through the use of spin locks, which are applied to critical sections of dispatcher-level instructions. When a spin lock is in place, no other processor can access the data or execute the code protected by the lock until the spin lock is released. The spin lock forces synchronization of all affected processors. The NT executive's mechanism for synchronization is the family of synchronization objects.

System Recovery

The last kernel function is system recovery in the event of a power failure. When power fails on an NT system, a high-priority interrupt is issued and the kernel executes a predetermined set of threads designed to preserve the operating system and its data integrity as much and as quickly as possible. This process starts as soon as a power failure is detected, but if an uninterruptible power supply (UPS) is connected to the NT system, the kernel can get power status from the UPS and continue operations until the UPS itself is nearing failure.

Even if the computer isn't connected to a UPS, there usually is enough power stored in the power supply's capacitors or built-in battery to at least begin an orderly shutdown. When the power level drops below a predetermined threshold, the computer's power supply issues a hardware power supply interrupt, which is intercepted and processed by NT. The operating system immediately begins shutting down the system, and it informs power status objects created by various user mode applications that power has failed.

I/O devices that could be left in an undetermined state in the event of a power failure can create a power notify object that gives the kernel the address of a power recovery routine to run in the event of power failure. After power is restored, the routine specified in the power notify object is executed by the kernel. The kernel itself also maintains a power status object that can be referred to by device drivers. If a device is about to execute a potentially dangerous activity, such as writing to a hard disk or modifying a file system directory, the device driver can refer to the power status object to determine if the power has already failed; if so, it prohibits any destructive process from occurring.

Hardware Abstraction Layer

The hardware abstraction layer (HAL) is the boundary between the NT executive and the specific host computer hardware. NT was designed

Windows NT: The Next Generation

to minimize changes in its code required by moving to different hardware platforms. Microsoft learned from the experiences of thousands of UNIX hardware and software developers who were forced to develop significantly different versions of their applications, utilities, and device drivers for every different flavor of UNIX (and there are dozens of different UNIX variants). Windows NT's first release will run on Intel-family processors, the MIPS 4000 family, and DEC's Alpha processors. Intergraph is also working on a version of NT for its Clipper family of RISC processors.

Ideally, the only change necessary for NT to support all these different architectures should be to substitute the appropriate HAL. That's still Microsoft's goal, but in reality, the kernel, the I/O manager, the VMM, and some device drivers must be modified to conform with the requirements of each processor platform, as well as to optimize NT's overall performance on that platform. In the future, Microsoft plans to further generalize these NT executive components so that the HAL is truly the only part of Windows NT that must be changed to support different processors.

Summary

The NT executive is a robust operating system platform designed for multitasking and multiprocessing, platform independence, system security and integrity, ease of application development, and ease of system updating and upgrading.

The object model implemented in the executive simplifies the development of new features, and it allows the functions of the executive to be extended in the future with new objects and classes of objects, without gutting the existing operating system.

Significant work remains to be done on Microsoft's part to make the executive fully platform-independent, but nevertheless, the NT executive is an impressive first attempt at a high-performance portable operating system for enterprise-wide applications.

The NT Development Environment

Now that I've discussed Windows NT's system architecture, this is a good point to examine the practical issues of NT software development.

First, the good news: Microsoft has worked hard to make the Windows NT software development environment look and work very much like the 16-bit Windows 3.1 environment. For experienced Windows developers, the Win32 environment holds few surprises. Now, the bad news: To take full advantage of Windows NT, developers must make big changes to their existing Windows applications and write new applications working from some fundamentally different assumptions.

If the Win32 environment is so similar to its 16-bit counterpart, why can't developers simply tweak their code to move it over to NT? In fact, they can, but without significant redesign, they can't expect their applications to run much faster or more efficiently than existing 16-bit versions do. NT's real performance advantages come from its multithreading and multiprocessing capabilities. Unless applications are written to take advantage of these capabilities, NT offers only a small advantage over 16-bit Windows (primarily from the efficiencies of NT's 32-bit linear address space). For developers willing to tackle the complexities of asynchronous I/O, multithreaded programs, and multiprocessing, Windows NT offers substantial performance advantages over 16-bit Windows.

4G Virtual Address Space

All Win32 programs, no matter how they are designed, can take advantage of Windows NT's 4G virtual address space, which reserves 2G for program space and 2G for system space. NT applications are free from the limitations of the segmented memory addressing scheme first implemented in DOS and carried on throughout 16-bit Windows. The segment:offset addressing scheme is unnecessary because NT offers a linear address space.

The address space isn't truly linear, of course, because most programs use a mix of RAM and hard disk storage, and NT pages portions of program and system space from RAM to and from the hard disk. NT's VMM, however, keeps track of both the physical and logical locations of each program's memory.

For the most part, NT developers don't need to pay attention to the machinations of the VMM. All 16-bit programs, however, must be recompiled with a compiler designed to handle 32-bit instructions and data transfers, such as the Windows NT version of Microsoft C/C++ Version 7, and they must be linked to the appropriate Win32 libraries to take advantage of NT's linear address space.

Multitasking Support: Several Paths to the Same Destination

Software developers have several ways to take advantage of NT's multitasking capabilities. The choice of which technique (or techniques) to use depends on the specific application and the degree to which the developer wants to implement a multithreaded design.

Asynchronous I/O

The simplest way for an NT application to utilize multitasking is with the use of asynchronous I/O. In a conventional I/O system such as DOS, an application requests the operating system to perform some function, such as reading a block of data from the hard disk. The operating system performs the task and returns data with status information to the application. During the time that the operating system is performing the request, the application sits "in idle" waiting for a response. This kind of processing is called synchronous I/O.

In an asynchronous I/O system such as that offered by Windows NT, an application can request the operating system to read a block of data from the hard disk, although as soon as the operating system acknowledges that it has received the request, the application program can perform other tasks

5 • A Developer's View of Windows NT

(for example, writing to the display or printing) while waiting for the data. To take advantage of this capability, the application developer must keep three things in mind:

- I/O requests must be performed specifically with asynchronous I/O system calls; otherwise, Windows NT defaults to synchronous I/O.

- No additional I/O operations can be performed to the same device while an application is waiting for the return of results from an asynchronous operation. You can't speed up operations, for example, by sending a read block command to the hard drive, immediately followed by a write block to the same drive, because NT intercepts the write command and holds it until the read operation is completed. The I/O commands end up executing synchronously, thus negating the value of asynchronous I/O.

- The application must be written to do something while asynchronous I/O is occurring. If an application expects to do nothing but idle while waiting for the I/O process to complete, nothing will be gained from asynchronous I/O. If, however, the application performs other tasks while waiting for I/O to complete, the user will perceive that the program seems "faster" than one bound by synchronous I/O.

Threads

Asynchronous I/O is a simple means for software developers to implement multithreaded applications. By definition, the act of making an I/O request starts at least one thread, running concurrently with the application program. Thus, asynchronous I/O leads to a simple way of concurrently executing at least two threads (one for the application, the other for I/O).

However, far more sophisticated means are available for implementing multithreaded operations. The concepts behind asynchronous I/O can be extended into a framework for coordinating the activities of any number of threads. Just as an application can be writing to the display while waiting for data from the hard disk, a process can look up the index number for a customer record in a database while it's simultaneously setting up a local network link to an airline reservation system.

Windows NT: The Next Generation

At some point, of course, the two threads need to connect; the customer information must be relayed to the reservation system through the network link. It's likely that one of the threads will complete its task first, in which case the application waits to continue until the second thread finishes its task.

NT uses a family of objects, called synchronization objects, to provide the means of allowing one thread to wait for the completion of another thread and enable the completed thread to signal any and all waiting threads that it is finished. Eight objects are used for synchronization signaling. Signals can be issued when any of the following events occur:

- A single thread terminates
- The last thread in a multithreaded process terminates
- An I/O operation is completed
- A specific event is set by a thread
- A semaphore counter is decremented to zero
- A timer event occurs (timer counts down to zero or a specific time arrives)
- A resource that can be used by only one thread at a time (mutually exclusive) is released

As you can see, thread synchronization can be controlled in a variety of ways, depending upon an application's requirements. In addition, a mechanism called an alert enables one thread to stop the execution of another; when used in conjunction with asynchronous procedure calls, NT can halt the execution of one thread to enable a critical operation, such as a block read request, to return its results, and allow the interrupted thread to complete its task.

Windows NT is itself implemented as a collection of multithreaded processes. At any one time, ten or more of NT's own threads can be in various states of execution, and of course, NT isn't the only operating system that supports multithreading. OS/2 and some UNIX variants also support multithreaded applications.

Object Security

Chapter 4 introduced and illustrated one facet of Windows NT's security subsystem: the elements relating to user access to NT servers and file systems. The other key facet of NT's security works to restrict access to individual objects.

Whenever a user successfully logs on an NT system, the NT security subsystem takes the user's unique identification (including personal security ID/username, group membership IDs, and system privileges) and tags that to the user's log-on process with an object called an access token. The access token is like a combination ID card and cardkey because it not only uniquely identifies the user, it also is attached to every process that the user creates and gives those processes the user's own security access.

The access token is also checked each time the user tries to access ("open a handle to") another object. The security subsystem checks the access token against an access control list, which is part of the security descriptor for every NT object. If the object's ACL has an entry for the specific user name or one of the user's groups, the security subsystem allows the user's process to access the object according to the rights assigned to the user or group. If there's no listing for the user or group(s) in the object's ACL, or if the user is listed but attempts to perform a restricted operation on the object, the security subsystem denies access to the object.

NT's object security system offers a sophisticated means of fine-grained security, well below the file and directory level, but at a relatively high price in complexity and performance. The creator of an object must set access permissions for each user or group that might use the object. On a large network with thousands of users and dozens or hundreds of groups, the object's creator has a lot of work to do. As more groups and users are added to the object, its security descriptor grows, as does the object's file size. Because the security subsystem must check more and more ACL entries before providing access to the object, performance suffers. A single file, for example, might have dozens of ACL entries, with one for each group and user authorized to access the file. Checking the ACLs on many files, each with dozens of access control entries, can take a substantial amount of time.

In reality, most object creators simply bypass the issue and set global permissions for all the objects used in a given application, selecting permission levels from a small subset of all the available groups. The resulting system isn't as secure or flexible as NT's architecture supports, but it's significantly smaller and faster than a more "robust" security implementation.

For all its safeguards and features, NT's security subsystem can't fully protect NT. An excellent example of an area in which some of these security risks occur is NT's registry editor (described in Chapter 4), which is normally available only to system administrators. With a slip of a few fingers on the keyboard, the registry editor can make mincemeat of NT system integrity (even to the point where the system may need to be completely reinstalled).

At this stage, it's clear that NT's security can be defeated, accidentally or with malicious intent, by lax administrative supervision. As with any other security system, NT's security is only as vigilant as the system administrator.

Multiprocessor Support

At this point, all the performance and security features of Windows NT are available to any software developer with a compatible compiler (obviously, Microsoft recommends its C and C++ compiler, but Borland, Symantec, and most other vendors offering 16-bit Windows-friendly compilers are expected to provide their own NT compilers) and the Win32 SDK.

To get the maximum performance out of Windows NT systems, especially for mission-critical applications, many developers and users should consider multiprocessor systems.

Multiprocessor systems extend the NT multitasking model to a new level. Instead of executing multiple threads simultaneously on a single processor (which, as previously discussed, the Intel processors really can't do—they switch so quickly between threads that it appears multiple threads are executing concurrently), multiple threads, or even multiple processes, each with multiple threads, execute on separate processors. As part of Windows NT, the Win32 API supports multiprocessing through use of the same synchronization objects previously described.

The advantage of multiprocessing is performance. If you need more performance, add more processors. Theoretically, each additional processor should provide a linear improvement in performance (two processors are two times faster than one, three are three times faster than one, and so on), but system overhead almost always limits actual performance well below the theoretical maximum. In a typical installation, adding an additional processor will provide a performance increase of 80 to 90 percent.

One of the problems of software development for multiprocessor systems is that there are no standards yet for multiprocessor architectures, unlike PC architecture, which is well defined and well understood. Hardware manufacturers have either adopted a licensed multiprocessor architecture, such as the C-Bus architecture developed by Corollary of Irvine, California, or developed their own proprietary designs.

To achieve maximum performance, software development tools must be optimized for a specific multiprocessing architecture, and this is one place where the promise and the reality of NT begins to diverge. Although NT provides a "standardized," or at least well-defined, platform for multiprocessor development, it doesn't provide any tools for support of specific hardware architectures. These tools are left to the hardware manufacturer or third-party software vendors to provide.

A variety of manufacturers currently offer Intel-based multiprocessor systems, but a new generation of systems is in development. These systems will combine NT's support for symmetric multiprocessor systems with Intel's new Pentium chip, which has special hardware features designed to facilitate multiprocessor system development.

As NT-optimized multiprocessing platforms are developed and released, software development tools supporting these platforms will become available. Until that happens, however, developers can anticipate the demands of multiprocessor systems by designing multithreaded applications. These applications can then be ported from single processor to multiprocessor systems with minimum redesign and recoding.

The Win32 Application Programming Interface

The Win32 API provides the tools necessary for software developers to communicate with and utilize all of Windows NT's capabilities. Microsoft developed the Win32 API to be as similar as possible to the existing Windows 3.x API environment. Microsoft built support for the 32-bit versions of many API system calls into the latest 16-bit version, so NT developers can achieve a good measure of backward compatibility with Windows 3.x.

For situations where developers are programming entirely new NT applications, the combination of the Win32 API, Windows NT Software Developers Kit, and a compatible compiler are all that's necessary.

Developers don't really need to worry about cross-compatibility issues unless their applications are required to also run under 16-bit Windows. For these situations, Microsoft supplies the Win32s (*s* stands for subset) API, a 32-bit API that runs under 16-bit Windows. Many, but not all, 32-bit NT applications can be run under Windows 3.x using the Win32s API. Developers can bundle the API with their applications—16-bit Windows users need not purchase any additional system software in order to run 32-bit applications.

Additionally, Microsoft is using the Win32s API to encourage existing Windows developers to migrate their applications as quickly as possible to the 32-bit NT environment. With Win32s, these developers need only develop and distribute one version of their applications, which can then run under both 16- and 32-bit Windows.

Keep in mind a few important limitations of Win32s. First, Win32s doesn't directly execute 32-bit Win32 API routines, it simply translates the Win32 routines to their Win16 equivalents for execution by 16-bit Windows and DOS. If there's no Win16 equivalent for the Win32 routine, an error is returned. In addition, many of the newly extended GDI functions of Win32 have no Win16 equivalents and thus can't be accessed through Win32s. Any 32-bit parameters to Win32 API function calls are truncated to 16 bits by the Win32s API. In short, this means that applications which take advantage of NT's special features (such as multithreading, multiprocessing, the extended GDI, and so on) aren't portable to Win16 via Win32s.

To facilitate the widest possible variety of 32-bit Windows applications running under Windows NT, Microsoft is also supplying a development utility called PORTTOOL. Some developers think that PORTTOOL is supposed to convert 16-bit Windows applications into their 32-bit equivalents. In fact, PORTTOOL makes no changes to the application source code. PORTTOOL scans 16-bit Windows application source code written in C and flags potential incompatibilities with Windows NT.

Essentially, PORTTOOL has a table of Windows 3.x and Win32 API and runtime library calls. Whenever it encounters a call in the 16-bit program that is changed or unavailable in the Windows NT environment, PORTTOOL flags the suspect call, and where possible, suggests a 32-bit alternative. Once PORTTOOL scans the source code of an application, it's up to the programmer to modify the code to conform to the Win32 API.

There are two ways for Windows programmers to develop Win32 applications: top-down and bottom-up. In the bottom-up model, the application is developed from scratch to be 32-bit compliant. If a 16-bit version of the application exists, it can be used as a model for 32-bit development. The bottom-up model is time-consuming because it duplicates a lot of the effort that went into the initial design of a 16-bit version of the same application, but it has the advantage of enabling the developer to take advantage of multithreading and other Win32-specific features that should run very efficiently under Windows NT.

The top-down model applies to existing applications. In this model, Win32 API and runtime library calls are substituted for their direct 16-bit Windows 3.x equivalents when possible. Sections of the application that were designed to maximize performance may need to be written in assembly language or tight, hand-tuned C code; these sections are initially bypassed. The user interface and many other elements of the resulting program work under Windows NT and can be used to debug and recode the rest of the application.

The top-down approach is fast and gets applications running under NT very quickly. However, the programs it creates tend to be inefficient, not because the top-down approach itself is bad, but because the 16-bit Windows environment doesn't possess many of the attributes (such as a linear address space and preemptive multitasking) that make Windows NT a superior development environment.

Windows NT: The Next Generation

Windows developers have had to add a variety of kludges and workarounds to their applications to get them to work in the obsolete DOS-based 16-bit Windows environment. The top-down approach encourages developers to port these overweight and inefficient programs to Windows NT with minimum changes rather than rewriting the applications to take full advantage of NT.

Over time, most NT developers will rewrite their applications to take advantage of the Win32 environment and eliminate the workarounds they tolerate in 16-bit Windows. Until then, NT provides sufficient compatibility with the 16-bit Windows environment so most applications can be moved with minimal rewriting into the 32-bit world.

API Functionality

The Win32 API can be thought of as a logical extension to the 16-bit Windows API that supports full 32-bit operations and the new features of Windows NT. Compared to Win32 API calls, equivalent calls in the 16-bit Windows API feature four basic categories:

- Widened
- Changed
- Dropped
- New

Widened Calls

Most 16-bit Windows API calls (more than 1,070 in the October 1992 beta release) are unchanged in Win32, although they are widened to 32 bits. The meanings of all the parameters, flags, and returned values are the same. This offers experienced Windows developers a great degree of source code compatibility between 16-bit Windows and Win32 and ensures that many 32-bit programs run unmodified on 16-bit Windows systems under the Win32s API.

Changed Calls

Changed calls are calls that survived the transition from 16-bit Windows to Win32, although they come in a modified form. Only 26 16-bit Windows API calls have been changed (most of them relate to the Window Manager). Some functions, such as MoveTo(), which formerly packed two 16-bit values into a 32-bit value, have been changed to support full 32-bit values for all parameters.

It was noted previously that there are significant differences between the 16-bit Windows and Win32 Window Managers, especially in that the 32-bit version, in order to be as platform independent as possible, makes very few assumptions about the display subsystem's underlying hardware architecture. 16-bit Windows developers should pay special attention to Window Manager calls in applications that they plan to port to Windows NT.

Dropped Calls

The 16-bit Windows API calls that have been dropped in the Win32 API fall into several broad categories:

- Device driver-specific calls, especially calls that read to or write from hardware at a low level, such as ReadComm and FlushComm

- Multimedia-related calls from Windows 3.0, such as CountVoiceNotes, SetVoiceAccent, and OpenSound, that were superseded in Windows 3.1 but not removed

- Memory management calls, such as GlobalDosAlloc, GlobalDosFree, GlobalPageLock, and GlobalPageUnlock, that are incompatible with Windows NT's new linear memory management architecture

- Miscellaneous calls

A total of 137 16-bit Windows API calls fell into this "dropped" category in the October 1992 beta release. The best rule of thumb for Windows developers to follow concerning these calls is to first bring their applications into full compliance with the Windows 3.1 API, which removes many of the Win32 incompatibilities, and use PORTTOOL to identify any remaining dropped calls.

Windows NT: The Next Generation

16-bit Windows applications that use memory management or multimedia features extensively or are heavy users of serial and parallel ports (such as communications programs and serial- or parallel port-based printer sharing or peer-to-peer networking applications) may need more extensive rewriting.

New Calls

A total of 633 new API calls have been added to the Win32 API. All of the new architectural features of Windows NT, including support for 32-bit linear addressing and memory management, true multitasking, multithreaded and multiprocessing applications, security, the client/server model, objects, asynchronous I/O, virtual files, support for multiple file systems, remote procedure calls, advanced Window Manager features, graphics primitives, and others, are covered by these new API calls. Most of the new calls are not found in the Win32s API and can't be used under 16-bit Windows.

In order to take advantage of the capabilities of Windows NT, software development is a one-way street: after a 16-bit application is ported to Windows NT, it is virtually impossible to run the application under Win32s. On the other hand, if your goal is to maintain absolute compatibility with 16-bit Windows systems, your applications will be able to take advantage of only a handful of NT's advanced features.

Microsoft has been positioning the Win32s API as a good means for running 32-bit applications under 16-bit Windows, and for some applications, that's correct. To really use the Windows NT environment to its maximum potential, however, you must use Win32-specific API calls, which limit backward compatibility.

Sooner or later, most Windows developers will "bite the bullet" and write Win32-specific applications. In this light, the Win32s API can be seen as training wheels for developers just entering the Windows NT world. The Win32s API will be used by many developers for a quick market entry with slightly modified 16-bit applications. After developers fully understand Windows NT, the training wheels will be thrown away and replaced by NT-specific applications.

Windows NT SDK Graphical Development Tools

The Windows NT SDK offers a full array of character-oriented development tools, including the Microsoft C/C++ Version 7.0 compiler, library manager, linker, help file compiler, and various debuggers. In addition to these tools, NT offers a few graphical development tools that take advantage of the NT user interface to make application development easier. As you review these tools, remember the following points:

- All of the SDK's tools were still in early beta form when this book was written. The final tools are likely to be considerably more powerful and polished.

- Third-party software developers offer a broad range of development tools for 16-bit Windows. Many of these tools are more powerful, more flexible, and easier to use than Microsoft's own tools. Some of these tools will probably be ported to run under NT.

- Many (but not all) 16-bit Windows resources, such as dialog boxes and controls, can be used with Windows NT, after they've been recompiled under NT.

Dialog Editor

Most user interaction with Windows applications is done through menus and dialog boxes. One of Windows NT's SDK tools, the Dialog Editor, makes the design and testing of dialog boxes simple. Although I'm not going to go into detail on how to use the Dialog Editor, here's a simple example of how it works: after launching the Dialog Editor, you can either edit an existing dialog box or create a new one (see Figure 5.2).

Windows NT: The Next Generation

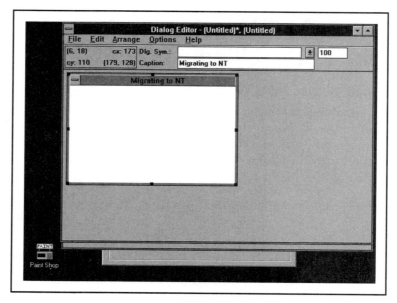

Figure 5.2. *An empty Migrating to NT dialog box.*

To customize the dialog box, use the toolbox to create a few dialog box elements. To display it, select the Options menu, then Show Toolbox (see Figure 5.3).

Figure 5.3. *The toolbox.*

At this point, create some text, position it, and add some check box buttons. To align the buttons and space them equally, click and drag a bounding box around the buttons to select them. Select Align from the

5 • *A Developer's View of Windows NT*

Arrange menu and note the graphics that visually demonstrate the different alignment options (see Figure 5.4).

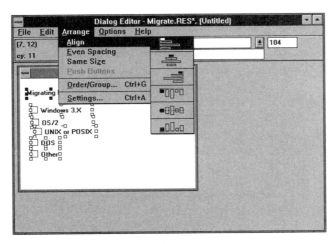

Figure 5.4. *The Arrange menu selections.*

Now align the buttons to be flush along the left side of the screen and adjust the vertical spacing of the buttons so that they are equally spaced. Select Arrange and Even Spacing and select the graphic option that represents equal vertical spacing (see Figure 5.5).

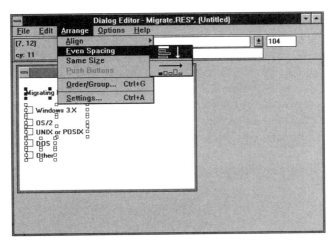

Figure 5.5. *The Even Spacing menu selection.*

Using the toolbox, you can add text fields, combo boxes, vertical and horizontal scroll bars, and more. Every element you add is identified by a user-defined symbol or name and a system-defined ID number. These identifiers are used by your application program to access and control each of the dialog box's elements. To review and modify the IDs of each element, select Order/Group from the Arrange menu (see Figure 5.6).

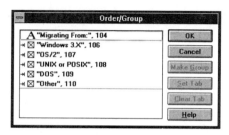

Figure 5.6. *The Order/Group dialog box.*

Using this option, you can change the order in which the user tabs between dialog box elements, and you can group elements together. After a dialog box is defined, you can connect the box to your application using the Win32 API. Dialog boxes and the fields within them can be reused by the same or different applications. The Dialog Editor speeds application development, and promotes reuse of user interface elements in multiple applications.

Process Viewer

One of the biggest problems for software developers who design multitasking and multiprocessing applications is debugging each of the application's processes. The graphical debugger, or WinDebug, is extremely useful for examining the execution of an application, although it reveals very little about that application's interactions with other user processes and the NT executive. To cover this deficiency, Microsoft includes the Process Viewer in the NT SDK. When you launch the Process Viewer, you'll see the window shown in Figure 5.7.

5 • *A Developer's View of Windows NT*

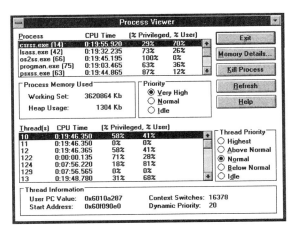

Figure 5.7. *Process Viewer window.*

Every running process and every thread within every process is tracked by the Process Viewer. Processes are dynamic, so the status of each process is constantly changing. The Process Viewer provides a snapshot of the status of every process and thread, which is updated each time the Refresh button is clicked.

To examine one process in more detail, select the NT log-on process, called winlogon.exe, process number 55, from the Process list. When a particular process is selected, the corresponding threads appear on the Thread(s) list.

In addition to examining the status of each process and thread, you can also change each thread's priority. This feature allows the developer to optimize system and application performance by fine-tuning process and thread priorities. Individual processes can also be killed using the Kill Process button. To get more information on the memory usage of any process, select the process and click on Memory Details to produce the dialog box shown in Figure 5.8.

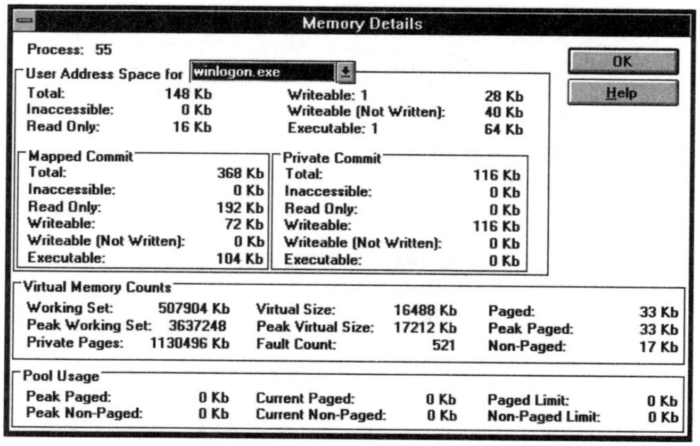

Windows NT: The Next Generation

Figure 5.8. *The Memory Details window.*

All of the specifics of memory utilization for the process, plus any and all dynamic linked libraries and other system resources attached to the process, are available for review. Developers can use this information to help determine if a process is reserving too much or too little memory, and it allows the programmer to come up with additional ways of conserving memory.

Two processes that are referring to the same data at the same time, for example, could cut down on mutual memory requirements (and implement shared memory at the same time) by sharing a section object containing the required data, or an application could reserve a large buffer for intermediate data storage, most of which is never used. The Memory Details window and Process Viewer could be used to determine the buffer's optimum size and provide useful information for using the virtual memory manager to save even more space with dynamic memory management.

Spy

Spy is a useful debugging tool that tracks and records a variety of messages passed between an application and Windows NT. Every open window can

5 • A Developer's View of Windows NT

be tracked by Spy. To select the types of messages to be tracked by Spy, open Spy and click on the Options! menu to display the dialog box shown in Figure 5.9.

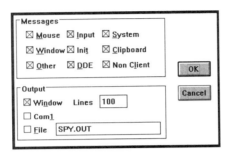

Figure 5.9. *The Spy Options! dialog box.*

If you track every possible message, you may have to work your way through a listing of hundreds of events before you find specific messages, so it's best to track just specific kind(s) of messages. To select an application or process to track, close the Options! dialog box and select the Spy window menu item to display the dialog box shown in Figure 5.10.

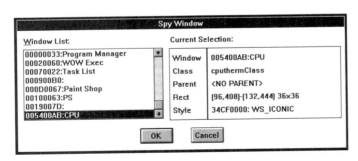

Figure 5.10. *The Spy window dialog box.*

If you select the CPU window, which refers to SDK's CPUTherm utility (a simplified version of the Performance Monitor application described in

Windows NT: The Next Generation

Chapter 4), as CPU runs, each message it generates is displayed in the Spy window (see Figure 5.11).

```
Spy - SPY!CPU
Spy  Window  Options!
005400AB WM_NCMOUSEMOVE     00000002 01B0006E
005400AB WM_NCHITTEST       00000000 01AF006E
005400AB WM_SETCURSOR       005400AB 02000002
005400AB WM_NCMOUSEMOVE     00000002 01AF006E
005400AB WM_NCHITTEST       00000000 01AD006E
005400AB WM_SETCURSOR       005400AB 02000002
005400AB WM_NCMOUSEMOVE     00000002 01AD006E
005400AB WM_NCHITTEST       00000000 01AB006E
005400AB WM_SETCURSOR       005400AB 02000002
005400AB WM_NCMOUSEMOVE     00000002 01AB006E
005400AB WM_TIMER           00000001 00000000
005400AB WM_TIMER           00000001 00000000
005400AB WM_NCHITTEST       00000000 01A9006F
005400AB WM_SETCURSOR       005400AB 02000002
005400AB WM_NCMOUSEMOVE     00000002 01A9006F
```

Figure 5.11. *CPU event messages.*

Spy's ability to track several applications simultaneously makes it very useful for debugging situations in which two or more windows must pass and respond to messages from each other, as well as those situations when a single window communicates with Windows NT.

Conclusion

Windows NT provides a very rich environment for application development. The NT executive is a powerful, flexible, and robust operating system foundation for the Win32 API and the other protected subsystems. Microsoft has gone a long way to make the Windows NT environment appear and work as close to the existing 16-bit Windows environment as possible to enable experienced Windows developers to apply their knowledge to 32-bit applications as quickly as possible.

The decision to maintain close compatibility with the Win16 environment is a two-edged sword. Just as with DOS, where Microsoft's insistence on backward compatibility limited the ability of application developers to take

5 • A Developer's View of Windows NT

full advantage of the power of new, more advanced hardware, so is NT's Win32 API limited by backward compatibility with Win16. The Windows API has developed unevenly over the years, with the addition of new functions designed to overcome the limitations of old ones. The result is a hodgepodge of overlapping functions that must nevertheless be maintained in order to guarantee compatibility between NT and all 16-bit Windows 3.X versions.

Although Windows NT is still an immature operating system and still has many of the architectural flaws and "cul-de-sacs" of 16-bit Windows in order to maintain a high degree of backward compatibility, it implements one of the most advanced OS designs in the computer industry. NT's current design paves the way to future implementations with even more powerful architectures, such as true microkernels and object-oriented operating systems.

For developers, Windows NT represents a near state-of-the-art operating system at the beginning of its commercial life—as opposed to DOS and 16-bit Windows, which are based on 15-year-old concepts and limitations that are well past their prime. Although other vendors are delivering operating systems with some features that are more advanced than NT's, only Windows NT offers the same combination of compatibility, performance, future functionality, and access to the largest installed base of computers in history.

6

Networking with Windows NT

Windows NT: The Next Generation

One of Windows NT's most important capabilities is its support for networking. NT supports both homogenous peer-to-peer and client/server networks, with NT systems serving as peers, clients, and servers. In addition, NT systems can act as servers to clients on LAN Manager and Windows for Workgroups networks, and with the appropriate software, as clients on Novell NetWare, UNIX, and other networks.

NT also supports distributed applications (applications designed to run on multiple processors across the network) by remote procedure calls. This chapter examines NT's networking features, interoperability with non-Microsoft networks and protocols, and support for distributed applications. I'll also examine the forthcoming LAN Manager for Windows NT and discuss what value it adds to NT's already extensive networking capabilities.

Networking with Windows NT: Home Run or Strike Three?

Windows NT is Microsoft's newest and strongest bid for market success in two elusive areas: industrial-strength operating systems and networking. Chapter 10, "Making the Choice: Windows NT or Not?" discusses how NT sizes up next to UNIX, which up to now has been the high-end portable (platform-independent) operating system of choice. This chapter looks at how NT addresses the needs of small to large organizations for local area networking.

Microsoft's Networking History

Windows NT is a bold thrust by Microsoft to snatch significant network operating system market share away from Novell. In order to understand the importance of NT's networking capabilities to Microsoft, it's helpful to know a little bit about Microsoft's history in the networking market and its long rivalry with Novell for market leadership.

NT represents Microsoft's third major attempt to crack the market for network operating systems. The first attempt, called MS-NET, was released in 1984 as an add-on for MS-DOS 3.1. MS-NET came out at a time when the PC industry was beginning to move away from networking systems based on proprietary hardware and software toward more open systems able to take advantage of the emerging powerful computer hardware. In 1983, a small company called Novell introduced its first version of a network operating system, soon to be called NetWare.

Neither NetWare nor MS-NET could be considered runaway successes in their first year on the market. Industry analysts forecasted that Microsoft would dominate the network operating system market for PCs as much as it did the basic operating system market with DOS. It was Novell, however, not Microsoft, that began to break away from the pack. Novell's market leadership resulted in part from a decision made by Novell early in its life.

Anyone who's attempted to install a local area network, even a very small one with a few users, knows that it's a complex process fraught with problems. From wiring the network to installing and testing the networking software, many things can go wrong. In the mid-eighties, most PCs were sold by computer dealers who understood stand-alone systems very well but were at a loss when it came to networks. A new breed of computer resellers, called value-added resellers or VARs, came to the rescue. These resellers learned everything they could about networks and took responsibility for both selling and installing networked computers.

While Microsoft sold MS-NET through the same conventional PC dealers who sold DOS and Microsoft Word, Novell focused on networking VARs. Novell qualified its VARs by making its personnel go through several networking training courses. Any computer dealer could attend the courses, but a dealer who was not certified by Novell could not sell its products. Novell became a single source for networking software and hardware, and Microsoft depended on third parties to supply critical networking hardware.

The result was that users had the perception that Novell-based networks were better (faster and easier to install and more reliable) than MS-NET systems, due to both the quality of NetWare and Novell's resellers. MS-NET dealers often couldn't answer even the most trivial questions about their

networks, while Novell resellers could not only answer the questions, they would also send someone out to the customer's site to fix problems. In this way, Novell began to build a networking empire.

In 1989, Microsoft in partnership with 3Com (a networking company founded by EtherNet pioneer Robert Metcalfe), introduced its second attempt at networking market leadership: LAN Manager. Designed around OS/2, LAN Manager was to be Microsoft's high-performance alternative to NetWare. Because OS/2 was the designated heir to DOS, LAN Manager would become the heir to the DOS-based NetWare. Industry pundits again forecasted NetWare's death, but neither they nor Microsoft anticipated OS/2's problems.

LAN Manager required OS/2 in order to run, and as discussed in earlier chapters, OS/2 1.0 was anything but a market success. LAN Manager's market penetration was tied to sales of OS/2, and as OS/2 shipments lagged far behind Microsoft's expectations, so did sales of LAN Manager. In the first year after its release, LAN Manager earned a reputation for sluggish performance and poor reliability. Shortly after its release, Novell engineers found out how to so completely crash any server running LAN Manager that not only would the network crash, but the LAN Manager software had to be completely reinstalled. Novell demonstrated these failures to key industry analysts and big networking customers. Microsoft had to spend months fixing problems and reassuring customers that LAN Manager was reliable.

Most importantly, LAN Manager was written with the assumption that most existing DOS users would quickly convert to OS/2. LAN Manager support for DOS systems was spotty at best. DOS systems could be clients to a LAN Manager server, but they couldn't act as servers themselves. NetWare, however, was written to run on top of DOS, so it didn't force users to buy, install, and support OS/2. For most PC-based networking users, LAN Manager was not a viable alternative to NetWare. Far from eliminating NetWare as a competitor, LAN Manager's shortcomings may have increased Novell's market share.

In 1992, industry analysts estimated that all of Novell's versions of NetWare combined held approximately 70 percent of the total worldwide installed base of PC networks; LAN Manager had approximately 15 percent

of the market. The size and growth of the networking market has made it a tantalizing, but ultimately frustrating, marketplace for Microsoft.

The Operating System Is the Network

Microsoft's latest strategy, expressed first in the market by Windows for Workgroups and now in Windows NT, is to incorporate networking into the operating system instead of as an add-on. Windows for Workgroups includes a powerful peer-to-peer networking capability (although still with limited support for DOS-only PCs) that seamlessly integrates into the Windows for DOS user interface and API.

Microsoft's logic? Windows for DOS is the most successful and fastest-growing graphical environment in the world. More than 12 million copies of Windows for DOS have been sold. By integrating networking into Windows and selling the resulting Windows for Workgroups product at a small premium over the price of standard Windows, most users will want to buy the networked product, and in so doing, will have no reason to buy competitive peer-to-peer products like Artisoft's LANtastic, Sitka's 10NET, or Novell's NetWare Lite. After all, the per-user cost of Windows for Workgroups is much less than the cost for Windows 3.1 plus a network operating system.

Windows for Workgroups is a good networking product for small departments and teams, but because it doesn't support dedicated servers, it's not applicable to large, enterprise-wide networks that require huge databases and centralized security and control. That's where Windows NT comes in. NT is a true server operating system, with peer-to-peer networking and security features that can stand toe-to-toe with almost any other commercial operating system. NT systems can network with each other on a peer-to-peer basis, as well as in a client/server mode. Windows for Workgroups systems can also act as clients to one or more NT servers. With NT systems as servers to groups of NT- and WFW-equipped PCs, Microsoft is well on its way to creating a viable NetWare competitor.

The rest of this chapter examines Windows NT's networking capabilities. You'll see how successful it's likely to be in stealing NetWare's thunder. This chapter also looks at LAN Manager for Windows NT, an abbreviated version

Windows NT: The Next Generation

of LAN Manager that can be thought of as a system extension to NT, rather than a network operating system in its own right. Finally, some of the decision criteria for selecting NT as a networking platform is also discussed.

The OSI Reference Model and Windows NT

Few technologies have as many buzzwords and acronyms as those that have come from networking. In order to describe Windows NT's networking capabilities, you need to know some of these terms. The following paragraphs examine some of the most important networking concepts.

Until the late seventies, communication between computers was a bit like the Tower of Babel. Every computer manufacturer promoted its own standards for communication between its computers. Generally, computers from one manufacturer could talk to other computers from the same manufacturer, but communication between computers from different vendors was difficult or impossible.

In 1978, the International Standards Organization (ISO) tried to facilitate communications between dissimilar computer hardware and software by defining a standardized communications model. This model was called the Open Systems Interconnection (OSI) reference model (see Figure 6.1), and it became the Rosetta stone of networking, the standard for defining how computers communicate.

OSI (Open Systems Interconnection) Reference Model

The International Standard Organization's software model for interaction between networked systems. The OSI model specifies seven layers of communication between systems.

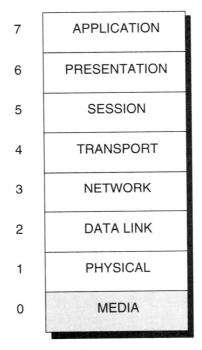

Figure 6.1. The OSI reference model.

The OSI model consists of seven layers, or protocols, numbered 1 through 7. Some form of transmission media (cables, wireless links, and so on) underlies the model and physically interconnects one computer with another; this layer is not defined by the OSI model but is commonly referred to as "layer zero." The seven layers of the model, from the lowest level up, are as follows:

Physical layer: This layer is responsible for defining the electrical and physical characteristics of how bits are transmitted on the physical media. Specifications such as connectors, voltages, minimum and maximum line lengths, data speeds, and so on are all part of the physical layer. Examples of physical layer standards include RS-232C (for serial communications), IEEE 802.3 (EtherNet), 802.5 (Token Ring), and the many CCITT standards for modem and fax communications, such as V.24, V.32, V.42, and V.17.

Windows NT: The Next Generation

Data link layer: This layer controls station-to-station communications on a single network by grouping bits into predefined frames that are transmitted from station to station. The data link layer also supports error detection and automatic data retransmission if a frame is lost or garbled in transmission. This layer also "shields" the upper layers from having to know anything about the physical layer or actual medium. OSI's High-Level Data Link Control (HDLC) and IBM's Synchronous Data Link Control (SDLC) are two examples of protocols that reside in the OSI data link layer.

Network layer: This layer is concerned with internetworking, the interconnection of computers on different networks (or, in NT parlance, domains). At the network level, groups of frames are wrapped together with the routing information necessary to determine the frames' destination and create a packet of data. The network layer controls the routing of these packets from one computer and network to another to ensure that the packet reaches its final destination. This layer also ensures that the network doesn't get bogged down under an avalanche of packets. The Internet Protocol (IP) is an example of a network layer protocol.

Transport layer: This layer manages the actual computer-to-computer communication across the network, no matter how many network links or computers stand between the originator of a message and its final destination. As far as the transport layer of the sending computer is concerned, it is always communicating directly with the transport layer of the receiving computer. The transport layer can create a virtual connection with its receiving counterpart (like a point-to-point phone call, in which there is significant work involved in creating the connection, but after it's established, lots of data can be passed across the link very efficiently), or it can establish communications on a connectionless packet-by-packet basis. The transport layer also controls data reliability by ensuring that packets are sent and received in the proper order and informing the communicating application if any data transmission errors occur. The Internet Transmission Control Protocol (TCP) and Novell's Sequenced Packet Exchange (SPX) are two examples of transport layer protocols.

Session layer: This protocol layer creates and controls the flow and progress of communications between two applications—one running on a local machine and the other running remotely. Among other things, the session layer is responsible for ensuring that file transfers between systems can be interrupted and resumed without loss of data.

Presentation layer: The presentation layer provides a means for otherwise incompatible computers and operating systems to share a common language for data interchange. A variety of standards have evolved to provide these common languages; perhaps the best known one is ASCII (American Standard Code for Information Interchange), a standard way of representing text, numbers, and control characters as one-byte binary values. The presentation layer also controls data compression and decompression (to reduce data transmission time and storage requirements) and data encryption and decryption, which are used to help ensure security and data integrity.

Application layer: The highest layer of the OSI model provides system-level services that are used by applications in communicating with their counterparts on other computers. For example, the application layer provides services that enable a local application to connect to and disconnect from other applications running on remote systems, without disrupting other applications and tasks. Windows NT's remote procedure calls, which are used for developing and executing distributed applications, rely on the services in this layer.

NT's Network Driver Interface Specification

The low-level means for getting data to and from the network resides at the physical and data link levels. Computers are physically connected to the network with a network adapter, also called a network interface card (NIC). The NIC connects the computer's internal communications bus with the

Windows NT: The Next Generation

external network. Different NICs interface computers to different types of networks, such as EtherNet or Token Ring designs.

As far as Windows NT is concerned, NICs are peripheral devices that are controlled with device drivers. In the past, different network transport protocols, such as Microsoft's NetBEUI, Novell's IPX/SPX, and Internet's TCP/IP, all required different drivers. Currently, however, Windows NT supports a device driver interface that shields devices from the differences in transport protocols. This standard is called the Network Driver Interface Specification, or NDIS. NDIS was first introduced in LAN Manager; its current version is 3.0. With NDIS, only one NIC driver is required for any Windows NT networking application. Figure 6.2 illustrates the OSI model with the NDIS interface.

Network Driver Interface Specification (NDIS)

Microsoft's standard interface for network interface card drivers, used by Windows for Workgroups, LAN Manager, and IBM LAN Server networks.

NDIS-compatible drivers identify their host NIC cards to NT's I/O subsystem. This enables NT to automatically identify any NDIS-compatible network adapters installed in the system and simplifies the process of installing new adapters and drivers. The administrator of an NT system doesn't need to know which specific adapters are installed because NT uses the NDIS-provided information to automatically identify and install all the needed software.

NT Transport Protocols and the Network and Transport Layers

Immediately above NDIS, residing in the network and transport layers, are the transport protocols. As mentioned, NT's standard transport protocol is called the NetBIOS Extended User Interface, or NetBEUI, which is already in use by LAN Manager and Windows for Workgroups. NetBEUI understands the network's physical design, or topology, and controls the parceling of structured data (such as files) into packets for transmission from one computer to another.

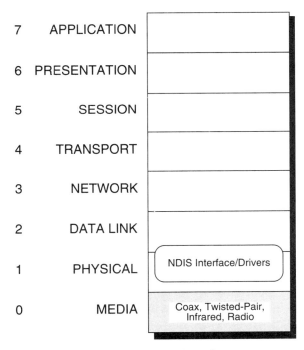

Figure 6.2. The OSI model with the NDIS interface.

Many other transport protocols are in widespread use. In fact, of installed network nodes worldwide, TCP/IP and Novell's IPX/SPX are far more popular than NetBEUI. DECnet predominates on networks based on Digital Equipment Corporation hardware, and AppleTalk is the standard transport protocol for the Apple Macintosh. If Windows NT supported only NetBEUI, Microsoft's market for NT as a network server or client would be quite limited. NT developers, therefore, came up with a way to support other transport protocols. Under NT, non-Microsoft transport protocols can be implemented either as self-contained drivers (like NetBEUI) or as streams-compatible drivers.

Windows NT: The Next Generation

Streams, originally developed by AT&T for UNIX System V and now controlled by Novell (after its acquisition of AT&T's UNIX Systems Laboratories), is a uniform transport interface to upper-layer protocols (session, presentation, and application). With streams-compatible transport protocols, software developers can write to a common transport protocol programming interface so they can safely ignore the specifics of the transport protocol itself. Any streams-compatible transport protocol written for UNIX System V or another operating system can be plugged into NT. This approach has two big advantages. First, application programs don't need to know whether they're talking to a TCP/IP, IPX/SPX, or NetBEUI network, so networked application development is easier. Second, NT users can access the broad array of transport protocols available for UNIX systems while NT-specific protocols are still under development. Figure 6.3 shows the OSI model with Windows NT network and transport layer components.

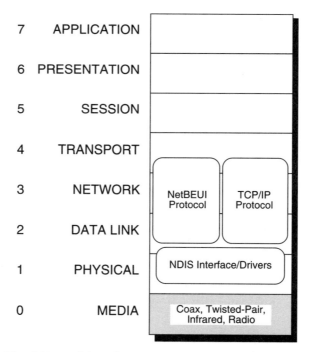

Figure 6.3. *The OSI model with NT network and transport layer components.*

Redirectors and the Session Layer

Lying above the transport protocols in the session layer are what Microsoft calls redirectors. To understand redirectors, consider the simple task of printing a file on a remote printer. In Windows NT, as with LAN Manager and MS-NET before it, a redirector intercepts your print request and redirects it across the network to the printer. If you want to read or write a file on a remote system, the same redirector intercepts your request, determines on which system the file is physically located, and redirects your request to that system.

NT redirectors look like standard I/O file system drivers, except that they work across the network. Connections to local file systems that reside on floppy or hard disks are usually quite reliable, but connections to remote file systems across a network are fragile even under the best conditions.

The network connection to the remote system can bog down or be lost as network traffic increases. In these cases, the redirector is responsible for reestablishing the connection as quickly and transparently as possible. If it's impossible to reestablish the connection, the redirector should "fail soft"— it should allow the application to retry the I/O operation without causing the entire application to crash. Because Windows NT supports several file system structures, it also supports several different redirectors, one for each of the supported file systems (DOS's FAT, OS/2's HPFS, and NT's NTFS). Additional redirectors can be installed to support new file systems in the future.

Between the redirectors and the transport protocol lies the transport driver interface (TDI). The redirector uses the TDI to create a virtual circuit, or pathway, between the local and destination systems. One virtual circuit is created between the redirector and each server to which the local system is connected, and each I/O call directed to a specific server is transferred over that server's virtual circuit.

Two additional APIs reside in the same layer. The first is the NetBIOS API, which is provided for backward compatibility with MS-DOS, Windows for DOS, and OS/2 applications, all of which use NetBIOS calls for sending streams of data across the network. The second is the Windows Sockets API, a TCP/IP-compatible means of creating a link between two systems by uniquely defining the network addresses of each system. Between the redirectors, NetBIOS, and Windows Sockets API, NT addresses all the most commonly used methods of establishing links between local and remote systems across a network. Figure 6.4 shows the OSI model with session layer redirectors, NetBIOS, and sockets.

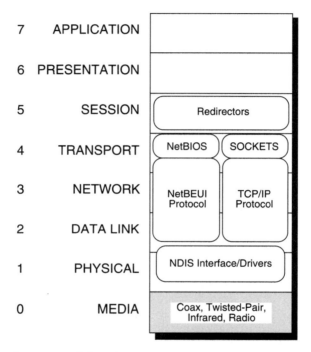

Figure 6.4. The OSI model with session layer redirectors, NetBIOS, and sockets.

Providers and the Presentation Layer

Above the session layer lies the Win32 Network API, or WNet. The WNet API allows Windows NT applications (and even system components like the File Manager or Norton Desktop for Windows NT) to connect to remote file servers and printers and utilize any kind of remote file system as if it was directly attached to the local system. The mechanism that NT uses to establish and maintain these links is called a provider. A provider establishes the local NT system as a client of a remote server. Figure 6.5 shows the OSI model with presentation layer providers.

Networking systems not supported by Microsoft (like Novell, DECnet, and others) can plug into the Windows NT networking architecture with a dynamic link library and redirector, which in effect act as the provider for their network.

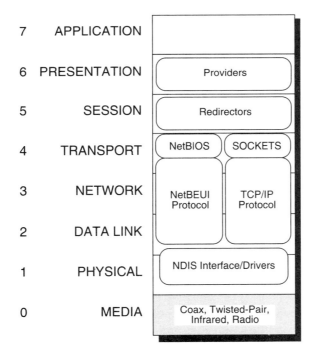

Figure 6.5. The OSI model with presentation layer providers.

The Application Layer and Windows NT

At the application layer, the highest layer of the OSI model, Windows NT provides three high-level facilities for supporting networked I/O, plus a critical system for support of distributed computing. Note the following three key facilities:

- The Win32 I/O API performs all standard file and device input/output functions (opening and closing a link to a device or file; reading and writing data to and from the file) both locally and remotely. This API allows applications to be independent of both the specific devices to be accessed (for all practical purposes, an application "talks" to a printer the same way it communicates with a disk drive) and the specific network or means of communication.

- Named pipes can be used by applications to create local or remote connections for I/O. Using named pipes, an application developer can ignore all the complexities of the network and transfer data to a local or remote application by creating, opening, and "filling" the pipe with data. The destination application opens the same pipe at its end, accepts the data, and returns data to the original application through the same pipe. Because pipes operate the same way regardless of whether the applications are local or remote, a developer can use them to create distributed applications that can either run completely on one system or be divided among two or more computers across a network.

- Mailslots are used the same way as named pipes, although they have one source and multiple destinations. An application can send data to several local and remote processes simultaneously by placing a single copy of the data into a mailslot. In turn, several processes can return data to the same application by placing data into the mailslot. Mailslots save developers the time and trouble of creating a named pipe for each process-to-process link. Mailslots are useful for passing important messages (such as "the local user just asked to exit the application—all remote processes should also begin their exit routines") to several processes simultaneously.

Figure 6.6 completes the diagram of Windows NT's networking architecture with the application layer.

6 • *Networking with Windows NT*

Remote procedure calls, or RPCs, are the final facilities provided for high-level interprocess communication.

Remote procedure call (RPC)

An API call that allows applications to be developed that consist of many processes, or procedures, which reside and execute both locally and remotely on systems interconnected by a network.

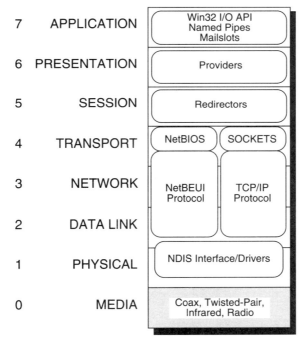

Figure 6.6. *The OSI model with all levels filled with NT components.*

Unlike the Win32 I/O API and named pipes, both of which use standard I/O calls for transferring data to and from applications, the RPC facility uses dynamic link libraries, which are linked to the application itself. These

199

Windows NT: The Next Generation

libraries can reside locally or remotely in any combination. If the application uses a library call from a remote DLL, the RPC facility goes over the network to access the remote library, performs the desired operation, and returns the results to the local application. In this way, applications, DLLs, and related data can be scattered across the network wherever they're needed. When necessary, however, they can be accessed as if they all reside locally.

NT's Key Networking Features: Peer-to-Peer Networking

Windows NT includes all the features needed for a complete peer-to-peer network. In a peer-to-peer network, all the computers on the network have equal access to system resources, such as printers and file systems. There are no servers in a peer-to-peer network; more accurately, any computer on such a network can act as a server to any other computer. Figure 6.7 is a diagram of a simple peer-to-peer network.

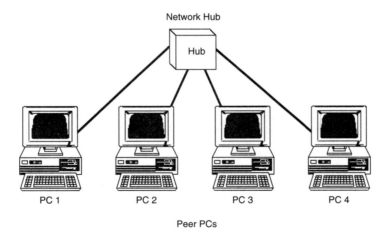

Figure 6.7. *An example peer-to-peer network.*

6 • *Networking with Windows NT*

Each computer connected to a peer-to-peer network is responsible for setting and controlling access to its own resources. For example, the user/administrator of a system could control network access to files with NT's access control security features so accounting files residing on a hard disk could be shared by other users, and a subdirectory containing personal correspondence could have restricted access. In Windows NT, the user/administrator of each computer has total control over access to files, printers, and other devices.

Peer-to-peer networks are typically small (usually no more than 20 nodes, or connected computers) and oriented toward usage in small offices or workgroups within offices in which all the members of the network need to share information, although the size of the network doesn't justify setting up a dedicated server. On such a peer-to-peer network, personnel files might reside on one system, accounting files on another, and sales forecasts on a third system. These files are shared by whoever needs them, anywhere on the network. In addition, printers can be shared by multiple users; printers can either be attached to a networked computer or directly connected to the network through a low-cost print server.

Peer-to-peer networks have several advantages. They are easy to set up and expand. As long as you install an NDIS-compatible network interface card in your computer (or if the computer comes with a pre-installed interface), Windows NT can automatically identify and configure your network adapter and driver. As you connect more stations to the network, each station identifies itself, and its system resources become available for all to use (subject to security settings, of course). Peer-to-peer networks are inexpensive. The basic networking software and utilities are built into Windows NT, so additional software isn't needed, and a dedicated server isn't required, which eliminates one of the biggest hardware costs for most networks.

Using the File Manager, any user can open and access the file systems on any other NT system attached to the same network, as long as that user has been given permission to do so by the remote system's user/administrator. (To grant permission, the user/administrator enters the remote user's user name and password into the local Security Access Manager database, which keeps track of all approved users and groups, the files and subdirectories to which they have access, and the type of access permitted.) These

Windows NT: The Next Generation

remote file systems are seen simply as additional disk drives attached to the local system. If the local system has a floppy drive as its A drive and a hard disk for the C drive, for example, the disk drive on a remote system might be referred to as the D drive, another system as the E drive, and so on. Whenever the local system wants to access the D drive, the NT redirector converts the reference to the D drive to its actual network location, makes the remote connection, and opens the requested file. This kind of network access is simple, easy, and familiar to most PC users.

Peer-to-peer networks also have several disadvantages. Perhaps the biggest disadvantage is the lack of central control. In a peer-to-peer network, each system user/administrator is responsible for managing and controlling access to files, on the administrator computer. A single user can bring the organization's operations to a grinding halt by limiting access to critical shared files, or destroy the security of the network by giving everyone access to sensitive data such as personnel performance ratings or payroll records. A single administrator could manage all the access control settings on every computer, but for practical purposes, it's impossible for an administrator to keep every system on the network under total control.

Peer-to-peer networks tend to have lower performance than client/server networks because of the lack of a dedicated server. Servers usually have high-speed, high-capacity hard disks, high-speed network interfaces, and use a 32-bit data bus (like EISA) for greater data throughput. Individual PCs usually have slower disks, slower network interfaces, and most use the 16-bit ISA bus. These systems are less expensive, but they are significantly slower than dedicated servers. Peer-to-peer networks, although reasonably efficient for small workgroups, bog down quickly as more and more stations are added because the entire network is one "zone" or domain. Tricks that are commonly used in server-oriented networks, such as breaking the network into smaller domains, each with its own dedicated server, aren't feasible with a peer-to-peer network.

If peer-to-peer networks are so limited, why bother with them? The answer is ease of installation and ease of use. Peer-to-peer networks are perfect for the following situations:

- Small workgroups (no more than 20 users)
- Temporary workgroups, such as project teams that are quickly created and disbanded
- Workgroups that need to share a lot of non-secure information between team members
- Small businesses setting up their first networks

A few things must be done to maximize the usefulness and security of peer-to-peer networks. First, because each user has so much control over their own system, it's essential that peer-to-peer network users agree on standards for file access and security. In order to facilitate the group's activities, file and directory access must be established. Even though each user controls a system, a central administrator who has full access to all systems should be appointed to manage access control, system backups, and other common network functions. The first time the user of a key system on a peer-to-peer network calls in sick or leaves the company, the availability of an administrator who has full access to the user's system will be appreciated.

In addition, rules need to be set down about such simple things as when users can shut down systems, turn off printers, or run programs that eat system resources. In a peer-to-peer network, if a user normally shuts down a system at the end of the day, other users can't access any files on that system until it's restarted. Some systems on the network may need to remain running 24 hours a day to ensure access to their files.

It's also extremely important for each user to back up files on a regular basis. As shown in Chapter 4, "A Quick Walk Through Windows NT," Windows NT includes a simple but useful file backup-and-restore utility. Unlike a server, where every file can be backed up at the same time, critical files can be scattered among several systems. To ensure system integrity in the event of a hardware or software failure, every file system containing shared files should be backed up on a regular basis.

If Windows NT peer-to-peer networking users follow these precautions and agree to appoint a central administrator to set basic rules of operation, the security and reliability of the local workgroup network will be enhanced.

Windows NT: The Next Generation

For many users, these peer-to-peer features are all they will ever need, but for others, a higher degree of network performance, reliability, security, and control are necessary. For these users, a client/server network makes the most sense.

Client/Server Networking and Windows NT

Client/server networks are fundamentally different from the peer-to-peer networks previously described, even though the physical network design can be virtually identical. Figure 6.8 is a diagram of a simple network with a single server.

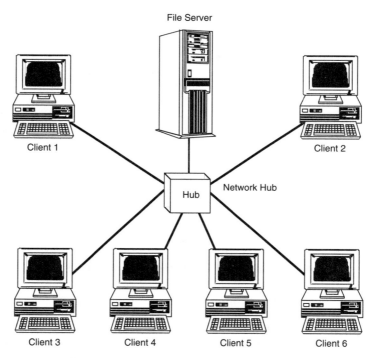

Figure 6.8. *A single-server client/server network.*

The diagram in Figure 6.8 is virtually identical to the peer-to-peer network diagram shown in Figure 6.7, although one of the peer PCs has been replaced by a file server. Client/server networks are hierarchical—one or more servers provide files for several client machines. The client machines are inherently private; the files that reside on client file systems are secure and private to that client. On the other hand, the server may contain many physical and virtual disk drives, which are shared by clients. Some server-resident files and subdirectories may be private to a specific client, while others may be shared, or common, between several clients.

Exactly the same access control features available in NT for peer-to-peer networking are also available for client/server networks. The administrator of the server, however, has much more control over network and file security with controlled access to the server. For example, a user on the network can be given or denied access to the server by the administrator. If the administrator chooses, he or she can make it impossible for a user to access private files on the server (or alternatively, make previously inaccessible files available). In short, the system administrator in a client/server network has far more control over network usage and security than a peer-to-peer network administrator.

Another advantage of a client/server system is data integrity. It's much simpler to back up files from one system than from many systems. Because a file server acts as the network's central repository for shared files, backing up the server backs up all the network's shared files at one time. The peer-to-peer problem of backing up most of the systems only to lose a critical file or subdirectory on a system that hasn't been backed up for some time is eliminated in a client/server system. Servers can be configured with redundant disk drives, disk arrays, and other technologies for preserving data integrity and reliability. (These techniques can be used for systems on peer-to-peer networks, but it's much more expensive to add these features to every system with shared files than it is to add them to one or a few servers.)

Client/server networks have a significant performance advantage over peer-to-peer networks. Figure 6.9 contains an example of a network with 20 stations.

Windows NT: The Next Generation

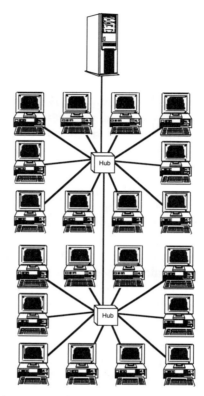

Figure 6.9. *A 20-station network with a single server.*

In Figure 6.9, all 20 stations share the same file server. As network traffic increases, the load on the server increases and network throughput declines. To compensate, the network can be reconfigured to the examples shown in Figure 6.10.

In Figure 6.10, a second server has been added, and the single network has been split into two subnetworks, or domains. Each domain contains 10 stations and one server. The number of stations per subnetwork and the message traffic has been cut in half. The load on each server has also been reduced. The result is likely to be significantly enhanced network performance and more room for expansion.

6 • *Networking with Windows NT*

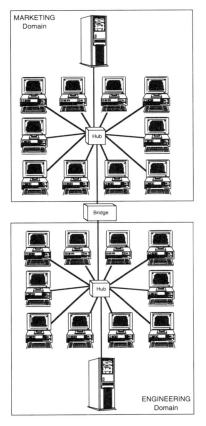

Figure 6.10. *A 20-station network reconfigured as two 10-station domains.*

> **Domain**
>
> A group or cluster of computers consisting of one or more servers and multiple clients networked together, all of which share the same security access control database.

Windows NT: The Next Generation

Windows NT doesn't directly support this kind of network, but with the addition of LAN Manager for Windows NT, this and other more complex network architectures can be supported. Windows NT allows a single domain to be defined and managed. LAN Manager allows networks with multiple domains to be defined. Each NT user is assigned to both a local machine and the domain to which the local machine is attached. This local domain is called the user's primary domain. In addition to the primary domain, users can have accounts on servers outside the local domain; they access these servers through their primary domain controller, which is a server assigned to manage security for the local domain.

Network Security: A Matter of Trust

How does Windows NT maintain security throughout the network and manage the connections between individual PCs, primary domains, and remote domains? As discussed in Chapter 3, "Windows NT in Profile," Windows NT's extensive access control security features are extremely useful for limiting access to systems, subdirectories, and files to authorized users. These security features, however, have a price. Every time an application launches a new process, opens a file, or communicates with a protected subsystem, the security subsystem intervenes to ensure that the application has permission to perform the operation. This slows down performance, compared to a wide open system like DOS that does no security checking. On the whole, however, NT's performance loss is more than compensated for by improved system security. (NT is really only usable on high-performance CPUs like the 486, Pentium, and MIPS 4000, and these systems usually have sufficient processing power to outweigh the security subsystem's processing load.)

Security in a networked environment is another matter. Consider the case of a single user who wants to run an application that resides on one server, using data from another server on the same network. First, the user logs into the local NT system (using both the log-in process and the security subsystem) and runs the application. The File Manager calls the redirector, which goes over the network to the remote server. The remote server checks the user's permissions against its security accounts manager (SAM) database before opening a link to the requested application. After the application runs,

6 • *Networking with Windows NT*

it tries to open the necessary files on a second server, and the user's security permissions are checked all over again. If the user or application needs to access any additional files or processes, more security checks are performed. On a network with many users, the servers could easily end up spending most of their time doing nothing but checking permissions and managing security.

Figure 6.11 demonstrates how Windows NT maintains tight access security on the network without drowning in security checks with a single domain.

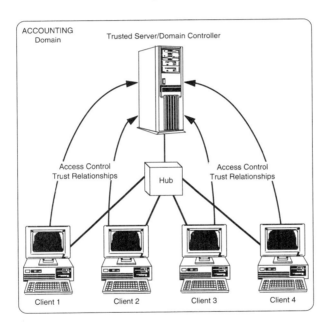

Figure 6.11. *A single domain with a trusted server.*

There are two types of access control in a domain. An NT user can log into the private system or into the domain (which contains the private system and all domain servers). If the user logs into a private system, only that system's SAM is checked before access is either granted or denied. If the user logs into the domain, however, the primary domain controller's SAM is used to determine whether to grant access. This domain SAM is shared by all the

Windows NT: The Next Generation

servers in the domain. When the user logs into the primary server, access is accepted by all the other servers. This cuts down on the processing overhead required to reauthenticate the user every time an attempt is made to access another server within the same domain.

In Windows NT's terminology, this relationship is called trust. Individual PCs (and other servers) within the domain trust the primary domain controller to provide accurate access control. Trust relationships eliminate much of the system overhead required to reauthenticate users every time they access a new server. Trust relationships also exist between domains, as shown in Figure 6.12.

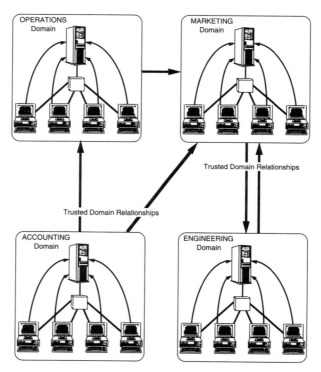

Figure 6.12. *A network with several trusted domains.*

In Figure 6.12, trusted domain relationships exist between each of the domains. Once a user has been authenticated in one domain, that user can also access any other trusted domain. The local domain's SAM is considered reliable by the remote domains, and thus the user's local privileges are extended to all other trusted domains. An engineer using a PC in Marketing could log into the Marketing domain and access the Engineering domain and even his or her personal PC. This security architecture eliminates the need to create separate accounts for every potential user on every server. As long as a user has access to a trusted domain, access to all attached trusted domains is automatically granted.

Not only does this scheme make it easy for users to virtually relocate their personal PCs to any location on the network by connecting through several domains, it also allows a central system administrator to manage all the servers and PCs included in every trusted domain. A single administrator can schedule backups, install software, maintain security databases, and perform other chores from any PC on the network, regardless of whether the network is contained in one room, one building, or spans tens or hundreds of miles.

However, trusted domains are not without their problems. If an unauthorized user manages to breach the security of any trusted domain (which could be as simple as leafing through the contents of a trash can to find an authorized user's user name and password), the intruder will automatically get the same level of access to any other trusted domains linked to the breached system. Thus, the security of several systems or an entire network could be compromised.

Fault Tolerance

Windows NT provides two types of insurance against hardware failures that can cripple a network. It offers support for fault-tolerant disk storage, and it supports redundant servers. Chapter 4 briefly discussed NT's fault tolerance features and the Disk Manager. NT supports two key disk-related fault tolerant capabilities:

Windows NT: The Next Generation

- Disk mirroring: This is a form of data protection that keeps one or more identical copies of a disk partition on one or more disk drives, preferably isolated by different disk controllers so that neither a disk crash nor a controller failure can destroy the data. If one disk crashes or a controller dies, NT can switch to the mirror partition and continue running.

- Disk striping (with parity): This technique is most commonly used with fault-tolerant arrays of disk drives called redundant array of independent drives (RAIDs). In disk striping, a disk partition is striped, or written, across several disk drives. The partition is referred to as a single volume (such as the F drive), but it in fact spans two, three, four, or more hard disks. Performance is enhanced because all the drives can simultaneously perform I/O to the striped partition. If the parity option is used, parity information is added to the recorded data so that if any drive fails, the lost data can be recovered from the remaining drives.

In addition, the NT File System is particularly robust. It can automatically identify and skip bad sectors on a hard disk on-the-fly (instead of requiring reformatting), and it automatically defragments files (takes files that are split into small segments throughout the disk and rejoins the segments into one contiguous file) in order to improve disk performance. These features require processing overhead, but NT minimizes their impact on system performance by deferring their execution until the system is idle.

These features combine with NT's automatic support for uninterruptible power supplies, or UPS. In the event of a power failure, brownout, or a dangerous overvoltage condition, an NT system that has an intelligent UPS attached to it can automatically notify users and shut down the system in an orderly fashion without losing data (without any manual intervention). It can also pass messages across the network to other servers and PCs to either shut down or reconfigure the network to work around the failed system.

NT's fault-tolerant features are extremely useful even for single-user systems, but they are invaluable in a networked environment where server downtime can cost hundreds or thousands of dollars in lost productivity and income. Under DOS, Windows for DOS, and OS/2, these features formerly required installation of LAN Manager, but they're a standard part of Windows NT.

Distributed Processing

Earlier in this chapter, remote procedure calls, or RPCs, were defined. At this point, it is useful to examine Windows NT's distributed processing capabilities and the importance of RPCs.

In a distributed processing system, applications can access both programs and data that reside on remote computers as if they actually were located on the local system. An insurance claims processing application could retrieve customer information from a local server, but if the customer records aren't available locally, the application could automatically send a message to a remote system to retrieve the records (from wherever they are located on the network) without the user knowing anything about the actual record location. The remote server could even send messages to other servers to ask them to search for the records until one of the servers locates and retrieves the desired information.

This form of processing distributes tasks across the network to the servers that are best suited for the given task. It also places the processing power at the data location, which cuts down on network traffic. It's much faster and easier to send a request for data to a remote file server and let the file server search its local database and retrieve the requested records, than it is to search the file server's entire database from a remote location. Only the search request and the returned results of the search are actually passed across the network—a total of a few hundred or thousand bytes, instead of millions of bytes of raw data. To make this kind of processing work, applications must be written to work with remote processes, as if they were an integral part of the application. Windows NT provides this facility through remote procedure calls.

When an application is created by a developer, many critical functions (such as database management and serial communications) are provided by prewritten libraries of system functions, called dynamic link libraries or DLLs, which are the building blocks of NT's APIs. To access these functions, the application issues a local procedure call, or LPC, which refers to one of the routines in a DLL. For example, an application could call a routine in a DLL provided by Microsoft to search for, read, and write records in a FoxPro database. By substituting a DLL from Borland, the same application could search a Paradox database.

Windows NT: The Next Generation

This procedure works fine if the application and the DLLs all reside on the same computer, but what if they do not? What if the database and its associated DLLs reside on a server across the network? In this case, instead of using LPCs, the application uses RPCs. As far as the application is concerned, the actual library routine used is the same, whether the DLL is local or remote.

In this case, however, the local DLL is a "dummy" that performs no function other than identifying the location of the real library across the network. Whenever a function call is made to the dummy library, NT's RPC facility routes the application's request to the server where the real library resides. The remote library procedure performs the requested function and returns the result to the local application. If any network glitches occur during the procedure, NT's requester/redirector mechanisms attempt to reestablish the network connection. This can usually be done "silently" without interrupting the application.

To take advantage of this distributed processing capability, applications need only link up with the local "dummy" DLLs at runtime. Once linked, the only other key requirements are that the local and remote systems can talk to each other (they both support a common transport protocol like NetBEUI, IPX/SPX, or TCP/IP, and the remote procedure calls on both systems are compatible). Microsoft's RPCs are written to conform with the specifications of the Open Software Foundation's distributed computing environment (DCE) standard. This means that Windows NT applications can connect to procedures on servers running not only NT, but the OSF/1 operating system and a variety of other UNIX variants as well.

NT's remote procedure calls ease the development of distributed applications. NT's architecture allows software developers to use the same basic libraries of procedures that work on a single computer and expand applications to work across networks. Because the RPCs can work with other transport protocols and operating systems, distributed applications can run on the platforms best suited for them, without forcing every user and system on the network to adopt Windows NT.

Caveats and Conclusions

Windows NT's networking capabilities are very appealing. Peer-to-peer networking, client/server networking, interoperability with a variety of network operating systems and protocols, network-wide security, fault tolerance, and distributed processing are valuable resources.

Although all of these capabilities are expected to be built into NT's first release, not all of them may work with your installed networks. For example, Novell and Microsoft are currently feuding over the inclusion of Microsoft's transport protocols and redirector in both Windows NT and Windows for Workgroups. Novell claims that Microsoft's rights to its software are limited to Windows for DOS 3.X only, not NT or Microsoft's networking products. Novell has developed and publicly demonstrated its own redirector and provider for NT, which will be marketed directly by Novell, instead of being licensed to Microsoft. In this way, Novell can (at least temporarily) control the interoperability of NT systems on NetWare networks and limit NT's role to that of a client.

When Windows NT ships, it will be able to interconnect with LAN Manager, Windows for Workgroups, and IBM LAN Server networks, as well as UNIX and other TCP/IP networks. Connection to these networks will be quite straightforward, and in the case of NetBEUI-based networks, NT systems will be able to act as clients or servers.

However, if you use another networking architecture, especially Novell NetWare, your connectivity with NT systems may be quite limited, especially in NT's first release. It's unlikely that NetWare users will be able to attach NT systems to their networks as servers, although it is likely that either Microsoft or Novell will offer the capability to use NT systems as clients to NetWare servers. DECnet users, on the other hand, are probably in luck because Microsoft and DEC have been working closely to port Windows NT to DEC's new Alpha processor series. DEC will most likely offer broad connectivity with NT clients, servers, and networks.

Windows NT: The Next Generation

Another issue for NT users to consider is the real value of LAN Manager in the NT environment. Most of the network-oriented features that LAN Manager added to OS/2, including peer-to-peer networking, security, client/server processing, and fault tolerance, are standard features of Windows NT. In fact, the only key feature of LAN Manager that has been left out of NT is the ability to establish multiple network domains and trust relationships among the domains.

So why would Microsoft or its customers bother with LAN Manager at all? Why not simply build LAN Manager's functionality directly into NT? It's really more of a marketing dilemma for Microsoft than it is a technical issue. Some networking users may be willing to pay a substantial price for LAN Manager's multiple domain support, while other users might decide that it's not worth the price. However, if Microsoft is aggressive, the combination of Windows NT and LAN Manager can be priced so low that the per-node cost of a LAN Manager network (supporting Windows for Workgroups clients and Windows NT clients and servers) is less expensive than Novell's NetWare 4.0.

For customers installing new networks, an aggressively priced LAN Manager/NT network may be hard to resist, especially if Microsoft delivers on its promises for extensive interoperability with other networks. Existing NetWare users may be more inclined to wait out the Novell/Microsoft feud before making a big investment in NT to see if Novell will allow NT systems to act as NetWare servers or only as clients.

If you're already a LAN Manager user, if you're installing a network for the first time, or if you want to interconnect with TCP/IP networks, it makes sense to carefully consider the combination of LAN Manager, Windows NT, and Windows for Workgroups. Microsoft is packaging a lot of networking (and distributed processing) value in its core operating environments. For many users, it's all the networking power they need.

7

Windows NT Versus DOS and Windows

Windows NT: The Next Generation

Making investment and development decisions in a world of new operating systems and hardware architectures can be risky and even dangerous under some circumstances. Not knowing what will be available in hardware and software combined with not having enough information available to formulate future needs could make for a short career.

New products, and particularly new operating systems, force computer users and developers to stop and think about their needs. With these new products, they carefully consider the job they do, their goals, requirements, and performance. Can we do this in a better way? Are we meeting everyone's expectations? What will we need in the future?

This chapter discusses the Windows NT decision from the perspective of the manager who has made commitments to the DOS and Windows platforms and from the viewpoint of the user who is thinking about changing from DOS-based Windows to Windows NT. You'll read about the expanded choices that Windows NT introduces—in networking, security, multiprocessing, and other areas. I will consider each of these new features in light of existing operating system environments, which for most users means DOS and Windows.

I will also present the additional requirements that these new choices bring. These new features create added responsibilities, and you can measure those against the increased benefits.

Why Look at Windows NT?

This is a fundamental question. Before you consider an option, you must understand why you are even looking elsewhere. You will often find the answers you need. The reason you are looking at Windows NT shapes the reasons you would implement it.

Take the time to consider all the applications running within your organization. Which applications would you consider mission-critical? Where is the data that could most benefit from a more robust and secure operating system? Which users know they have the need but have no ability to express it? Can you find the answer for them?

7 • Windows NT Versus DOS and Windows

You must also consider your role in your organization and what type of impact your decision would have on existing users. If you are a manager of programmers, your view of Windows NT's features differs from the view of a manager of data entry clerks. A manager of network administrators would view the Windows NT decision in light of the need for compatible, reliable operation and with topologies and domains in mind.

Whatever your first impression of Windows NT may be, you must also review other elements that it brings to the table. If you require its multiprocessor capabilities, also investigate its transaction tracking features. If you're interested in its networking capabilities, be sure to review its capacity as a dedicated server. Each of these new features is related because they are fundamental to the way NT operates. NT, like any operating system, has a bundle of capabilities and limitations. Before making a commitment to NT, understand all the different ways in which its features will affect your applications and operations.

NT and the Windows Family

Microsoft has created a family of operating systems and environments. From the MS-DOS product created over 10 years ago to today's Windows NT with LAN Manager extensions, Microsoft has worked to create platforms for each type of user. Because these products come from a single vendor, an organization has an easier time intermingling them. The different layers of Windows products (shown in Figure 7.1) create a work environment in which sharing information becomes easier by using common tools.

Windows NT is Microsoft's flagship operating system in terms of product features such as speed, security, networking, and application flexibility. It performs more operations and offers more to more people than any of Microsoft's previous products.

Notice in the illustration that Windows NT has its roots in all these products except DOS. Windows NT does not run on top of DOS like Windows 3.1 does, but is an operating system unto itself. Windows 3.1 for DOS and Windows for Workgroups are not operating systems but rather are operating

Windows NT: The Next Generation

environments. DOS and Windows NT are the only two operating systems pictured here; everything else is a graphical environment that runs on top of either DOS or NT.

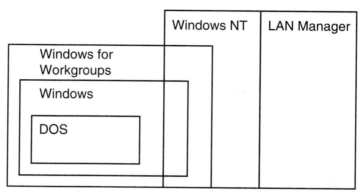

Figure 7.1. *Microsoft Windows family portrait.*

I've covered each of these operating environments and operating systems one at a time, taking into consideration not only the features of each, but also how they relate to overall computing requirements. You'll find that no single product can meet everyone's needs, but each can play a role in an organization's computing strategy.

MS-DOS

MS-DOS, Microsoft's workhorse operating system, lies at the simplest level. It is at once the most confining and the most reliable of options. DOS is confining for programmers because it places fixed limits on the size and capabilities of applications. On the other hand, it's a reliable choice for decision makers because of its huge installed base, wide selection of application software, and enormous market acceptance.

With more than 10 years of support, DOS is a standard now and will be for many years to come, no matter the quality of future operating systems. DOS has sold more than 100 million copies, with more than 10,000 applications available. Few managers or users want to throw out this amount of

resource and knowledge. Therefore, any viable operating system alternative must be able to run most available DOS software.

Ease of Use

Few people would describe DOS as easy to learn. In fact, whole industries have developed around training users on the fundamentals of DOS. Companies have created books, videotapes, and training software to help users conquer their fear of the `C:\>` prompt.

Starting with MS-DOS 4.0, Microsoft included a shell program so the user could avoid the prompt by launching programs, performing directory navigation, and executing other operations with the shell. Each version of DOS after 4.x has improved this shell. In general, however, DOS users continue to prefer the command-line interface to the DOS shells of either Microsoft or third parties.

Accessing DOS from Windows NT

Windows NT contains the standard Windows graphical user interface, reducing the retraining needs for users who are running DOS-based Windows. But for diehard command-line users, the Windows interface is useless overhead at best. These users have mastered the DOS command set and can accomplish more in less time than they ever could by pulling down menus and clicking choices. For these DOS users, both Windows NT and regular Windows 3.1 have facilities for running DOS applications. On DOS-based Windows, the *DOS box* is essentially a session where you can run a DOS program or operate at the DOS prompt.

When Microsoft first released Windows 3.0, many users adopted it not for its graphical user interface but for its capability to multitask DOS applications. These users opened up several DOS windows, ran a different application in each one, and used the mouse to jump from program to program. Under NT, the DOS box is much more sophisticated. It not only emulates the entire DOS software and hardware environment, but it also launches DOS/Windows applications and character-based OS/2 applications and executes NT commands. It extends and expands the capabilities of DOS while maintaining backward compatibility with most DOS applications.

Windows NT: The Next Generation

How Windows NT Does DOS

You can run most DOS applications on Windows NT. The exceptions are applications that require direct access to hardware. For instance, disk caching programs will not run under Windows NT, nor will some communications programs that directly write to and read from the serial ports for improved performance.

Windows NT implements DOS differently than ordinary Windows does. NT creates what is called a *virtual DOS machine* (VDM) for running DOS applications. The VDM captures all the DOS application's attempts to write to the screen, open and close files, or access memory. The VDM then translates these to Windows NT calls, and the NT kernel executes them. Consequently, Windows NT security is maintained, and no DOS application can bring down the whole system.

One way to tell if you will have trouble converting from DOS to Windows NT is to look in your DOS CONFIG.SYS file. If device drivers are present that applications must have in place to do their task, these applications might not be compatible with NT. With NT's OS Loader dual-boot feature, however, you can always boot the machine into DOS mode and still run any standard DOS application.

Contact your vendor to find out if a special Windows NT version of the software is available. DOS programs that require DOS device drivers will not run under Windows NT because you cannot use DOS device drivers with the VDM. This is because DOS device drivers expect to have full access to the hardware—a situation that Windows NT prohibits. When evaluating a move to NT, this point is critical. If you have several DOS applications with special drivers, expect significant compatibility problems that require new NT-specific drivers, special patches, or new versions of the software.

Even with this potential incompatibility issue, DOS users can run most applications under NT without modification. Microsoft estimates that more than 90 percent of existing DOS applications will run within the Windows NT VDM. The good news is that Windows NT will trap any programs that don't run correctly and prevent them from damaging the core operating system or any other running applications.

Viruses

This protection from errant DOS applications is also advantageous because it eliminates some virus concerns. Windows NT's capture of the offensive calls prevents viruses from being able to format users' hard drives or destroy the FAT tables of DOS partitions. I'm not saying NT prevents all viruses, but because Windows NT works so hard to prevent DOS applications from destroying the overall system, it stops most viruses that attempt to wreak havoc. Over time, however, programmers will likely develop viruses specifically for NT, which will in turn lead to a new generation of antiviral software.

Necessary Hardware

The minimum hardware platform for running nearly all popular DOS applications today is a system with 1M of memory, a 40M hard drive, a graphics monitor and adapter, and a 286 processor or better. If you intend to have DOS users connecting to networks, of which Windows NT would be a server, you should consider PCs with at least a 386-class processor. Microsoft's Workgroup Connection software for creating network access requires 386 equipment to take full advantage of its features.

Two Important DOS Limitations

DOS does not provide any type of file system integrity process. It offers the CHKDSK program to evaluate the state of a file volume, but it has no proactive method for ensuring integrity of transaction processing. A number of third-party tools make up for DOS's deficiencies with volume repair, but again, these tools are not built into the operating system and therefore might not be as compatible as one that ships with the operating system.

Another key deficiency of DOS is security. By itself, DOS has no access control security features whatsoever. When one user is away from the equipment, another user could simply start up the system to obtain full access to all programs and data.

Networking Within DOS

With Version 3.30, DOS gained rudimentary extensions for networking. The Share program was added so the operating system could recognize that some files may be busy while attempting a write, and the operating system gained the capability to recognize many more drives. However, these improvements didn't turn DOS into a network operating system. Rather, they enabled clients on a network to use DOS systems. DOS users could access remote drives on servers based upon other operating systems.

DOS users could also access Windows NT servers using the various protocols available for NT, including TCP/IP, IPX/SPX, and NetBEUI. With NT as a server, the DOS user will mount network drives as an extension of the local drives; for example, if the local PC has a C and D drive, network drives will be mounted as E, F, G, and so on. LAN Manager's Net Use command or Novell NetWare's MAP command apply here.

Microsoft has also created a DOS client services software package called *Workgroup Connection*. With this new software product, DOS users can share disk drives and printers with other users on the same network. The Workgroup Connection software consists of a terminate-and-stay-resident (TSR) program called NET.EXE. This software stays resident on the workstation and creates the client/server environment in the background.

Only 386-based computers can take advantage of the best feature of the Workgroup Connection—the capability to use a machine as a server. By connecting 8088 and 286 machines to various networks as clients, however, organizations can salvage their investment in otherwise obsolete computers and can therefore offer tremendous cost savings. In addition, a DOS version of MS Mail ships with the Workgroup Connection, whereby DOS users can utilize the same electronic mail format that ships with Windows for Workgroups and Windows NT.

The point of this discussion is that DOS systems still have tremendous value as clients on both Windows for Workgroups- and Windows NT-based networks. Thus, the adoption of Windows NT doesn't necessarily mean that every PC incapable of running NT is headed for the scrap heap.

The Future of DOS

Even with the advent of powerful 32-bit operating systems, DOS is still a viable option for most PC applications. In Version 6.0, MS-DOS will gain features—such as disk compression and tape backup services—that have normally been available only through third-party tools. While these planned enhancements don't change the fundamental structure of DOS—its file system and memory management—they will make life easier, and less expensive, for its users.

Rumors in the trade press have circulated concerning Microsoft's plans for future versions of DOS beyond Version 6. These future versions may be based on an integrated 32-bit Windows operating system, without the Windows GUI, or they may be closer to NT's VDM implementation in that they emulate DOS in a window under a more robust 32-bit operating system. Regardless of the implementation, though, DOS and DOS applications will be supported for many years to come.

Evaluation Points

If you are considering a jump from DOS with no Windows installed to Windows NT, consider the following:

- If you have no current graphical application requirements, your cost to upgrade existing DOS systems to run NT will probably be very high. You should plan on continuing to use DOS unless features such as true multitasking are essential.

- If you are currently using Windows applications (or plan to do so in the near future), determine the costs for necessary hardware and software upgrades before committing to NT. You may find that 16-bit Windows is more than adequate for your needs, and that you don't need to rush into NT.

- Give Windows NT time to mature and allow time for software developers to move to this new 32-bit application platform.

Windows NT: The Next Generation

The Windows Revolution

Windows has introduced users to the idea of using a multitasking environment for getting work done. Windows enables users to switch from one application to another with relative ease. It also enables users to transfer data easily from among those applications through a single source, the clipboard, as well as by a process called *dynamic data exchange (DDE)*. DDE is a service in which applications can set up a communications channel between themselves and pass data back and forth.

Microsoft has sold more than 10 million copies of Windows and reshaped the way people view their hardware needs. For DOS-based applications, an 8088-based computer could be adequate and a 386-based machine could be incredibly fast. Windows-based applications, on the other hand, can feel sluggish on a 386-based computer that doesn't have either enough memory or a fast enough disk drive. This can affect the hardware budgets for the companies that include Windows in their corporate strategies.

The key point here is that moving to Windows—whether Windows 3.1 or Windows NT—can (and most likely will) cause a budget impact beyond software acquisition and upgrading costs alone. Windows has saved money in many organizations by reducing demand for user training. Its consistent interface means that users feel right at home while moving from one application to the next. This level of comfort makes people loyal to Windows.

Graphics

The graphical user interface in the Windows version is just that—a combination of text and graphics images. The graphics engine behind Windows, the part that draws everything onto the screen, has never been considered state-of-the-art. It doesn't contain API calls to perform advanced curves and shadings, and its display performance is mediocre at best without the addition of hardware graphic accelerators. Still, it's powerful and flexible enough so that users can perform specialized tasks such as video editing, page layout, and 3-D graphic manipulation. Windows NT offers a somewhat more advanced version of 16-bit Windows' graphics display capabilities, but for most users, the differences are subtle.

7 • *Windows NT Versus DOS and Windows*

Though a Windows-based system might not be the platform of choice for sophisticated graphics applications, a manager must consider the company's overall plan for integrating data among users. Therefore, information created using a DOS- or Windows-based system in some cases may be integrated into a report or publication more easily than if the data or files came from a mixture of different platforms.

Device Drivers

Hardware and software must communicate with each other. Spreadsheet programs must know how to draw numbers on-screen and print numbers to the printer. Word processors must be able to save their files to disks. Printers must be able to relate information about their status back to the software.

DOS by itself has never been known for supporting a wide range of hardware. DOS allowed for *device drivers*—small programs that help software talk to hardware—but offered only the most limited support. The job of utilizing the hardware's special features has always been left up to the application software.

In the early days of personal computing (1981 through 1986) few standards existed. If you purchased a brand-new hardware item, such as a video card or modem, you could only hope that the software you used would support it. If you depended on a charting program that drew graphics on-screen, you needed a video driver for your hardware that completed the interface between your graphics board and that software. If none were available, you were out of luck. Finding drivers for software became quite a chore. Each new hardware item needed a driver written to connect it in a software sense with all the application software available for DOS.

The appearance of Windows introduced the personal computer community to the idea of device driver support built into the operating environment. Consequently, the programmer creating an application would write the application so that it used the driver for Windows, and the user would use the driver for Windows that was appropriate for their hardware. Hardware vendors needed to create a driver for only one software package: Windows.

Windows NT: The Next Generation

Windows was designed to serve as a standardized layer between the software application and the hardware upon which it ran. This concept is called *device independence*, and it performs three functions:

- It enables programmers to return to the task of creating innovative software rather than writing device drivers.

- Hardware vendors can expect that their products will work with all existing software.

- Users can take full advantage of all their hardware and software's features.

Because Windows 3.1 for DOS is not an operating system, non-Windows programs cannot use its device drivers, and Windows NT can't use them either. Thus, hardware vendors must create new drivers to take advantage of Windows NT. While this might add to the expense of implementing Windows NT in a corporate environment, the new operating system's expected popularity will mean that appropriate hardware drivers will eventually be readily obtainable.

As with DOS, you must consider the time needed by your hardware vendors, application suppliers, and in-house software developers to complete NT-specific drivers. Be sure you determine that your most important peripherals and applications will have compatible drivers before you switch over to NT.

Networking Windows

DOS-based Windows provides some network functionality through the implementation of WinNet APIs. Windows contains interfaces that enable a programmer to code at a level higher than the specific network operating system. For example, a programmer could make a function call to connect to a network drive. The programmer makes the same call regardless of the network operating system installed, so the application works on NetWare, LAN Manager, and so on. NT applications work the same way. The application developer writes a generic routine to read or write data from a hard disk, and an NT network redirector converts the application's request into a format for identifying a specific disk drive across the network.

7 • *Windows NT Versus DOS and Windows*

In addition, the tools that ship with Windows are built with network users in mind. The Windows File Manager can connect to remote drives if it senses that a network has been installed. The Control Panel has options for network access that have been provided in conjunction with major network vendors. With these options, users can change their network parameters in much the same way they change other Windows configuration items.

Necessary Hardware

An absolute minimum platform for running most Windows-based applications is a 286 processor with 4M of system memory, a 40M hard drive, and an EGA monitor. The operative word here is minimum. In almost every case, the limitations of such a platform would frustrate a user.

To take full advantage of Windows, a 386 is a minimum. At least 8M of memory, a large hard drive, and a VGA monitor are also recommended. A good graphics accelerator also helps make Windows seem a bit snappier, and like most PC hardware, graphics accelerators are becoming less expensive every day.

Limitations

A fundamental difference between DOS-based Windows and Windows NT is that Windows is an operating environment, and Windows NT is an operating system. This may seem like a subtle distinction, but it is actually rather significant.

An *operating environment* creates an interface between applications and the operating system. When DOS-based Windows needs memory or disk access, it must request these from DOS. How DOS handles that request is based on its history as a single-tasking operating system. Windows creates an environment where many things can happen at once, but DOS was designed to perform only one task at a time. This imposes significant overhead on Windows as it tries to queue tasks in a way that DOS can efficiently process them.

Windows NT: The Next Generation

Windows NT, on the other hand, is an *operating system* and as such doesn't run on top of DOS or anything else. NT completely controls all hardware devices and grants access to these devices as it sees fit. Therefore, Windows NT doesn't have the same limitations that DOS does. The first time this may become apparent to experienced DOS users, often called power users, is when they realize that all hardware devices are active at the same time (as opposed to under DOS, when only one can be operating at a time). For example, a user with two hard drives running on two hard drive controllers, such as an IDE and a SCSI, can have I/O processes accessing both hard drives at the same time under Windows NT. This offers a tremendous performance advantage, particularly if Windows NT is acting as a server.

Integrated Drive Electronics (IDE)

A hard disk drive and controller electronics combined in a single device.

Small Computer System Interface (SCSI)

An interface for up to eight devices daisy-chained together on a single bus. (A bus is an internal pathway along which signals are sent from one part of the computer to another.) The SCSI host adapter, which controls the SCSI bus and must be installed in the host computer, always counts as one of the eight devices.

The Future of DOS-Based Windows

DOS-based Windows will undoubtedly be around for quite some time. Already, *Chicago* (also called Win32c)—Microsoft's code name for a combination Windows 4 and MS-DOS 7—is being touted as the next generation of Windows running on DOS. Some press reports indicate that this will be a full

32-bit implementation of Windows on top of a multithreaded version of DOS. Details are not clear, but the humble Windows user can be sure the product is alive and has a future.

As a key point to remember, if you are obtaining acceptable performance with your existing Windows applications, Windows NT offers you few advantages except a platform for future, higher-performance applications. Don't fall into the trap of automatically assuming that Windows NT will be the default upgrade for DOS-based Windows, because it isn't—for the following reasons:

- Many DOS/Windows device drivers will be incompatible with NT and will need to be updated or rewritten.

- All 16-bit Windows programs run in the same address space. Therefore, as long as all your applications remain 16-bit, you won't gain any multitasking advantages under Windows NT. The programs will need to be rewritten to take advantage of the NT platform.

Windows and Win32s

For 16-bit Windows users who would like to take advantage of the 32-bit 386 environment, Microsoft has developed an API called Win32s. This set of DLLs enables developers to write—and users to run—32-bit applications on top of 16-bit Windows. Win32s is a subset of the full Win32 API set that composes Windows NT. The items missing from Win32s include the new high performance graphic subsystem, security, multithreading, and other features not supported under 16-bit Windows. As an advantage, a developer can write a 32-bit program that will run on DOS-based Windows and Windows NT with no changes. The Win32s API gives applications some advantages, especially when accessing memory.

Keep in mind, however, that these 32-bit applications will, in effect, execute as 16-bit applications because that's how DOS-based Windows operates. When you need services from DOS or the other Windows services, they are 16-bit requests. A 32-bit Win32s call is *thunked*—translated to 16 bits. This *thunking layer* takes a toll in the form of degraded performance.

Windows NT: The Next Generation

Remember that if developers or vendors start touting their applications as 32-bit compatible, investigate to determine how the applications actually perform under DOS-based Windows. Performance can vary greatly from that of native 16-bit versions, depending upon whether the application is processor-intensive or I/O-intensive.

Win32s was scheduled for a release concurrent with the initial commercial release of Windows NT, and software developers first received beta versions of the API in fall 1992. Developers can ship the libraries with their applications, so you shouldn't need to purchase any additional software beyond these new 32-bit applications to run them on your existing Windows-based systems.

Limitations

Software using Win32s won't run on DOS-based Windows machines that cannot run Windows in enhanced mode; this includes all 286-based machines. The minimum hardware platform is a 386-based system with 4M of system memory, an 80M hard drive, and a VGA monitor.

Windows for Workgroups

One of the best features of the Windows product line is its extensibility created through the use of dynamic link library (DLL) files. Windows for Workgroups (WFW) exemplifies that feature. Microsoft took the original Windows 3.1 and added the necessary extensions to create a peer-to-peer networking environment. WFW permits the sharing of resources among a collection of computers joined by transport protocols that are grafted onto Windows itself.

WFW is a significant product for those considering Windows NT because it contains some of the same tools and features as NT. Although WFW doesn't possess the same level of security and robustness that NT offers, it may be a good intermediate choice for users or organizations that are growing out of single-user Windows.

Why, then, would a company consider purchasing WFW instead of Windows NT? The first reason is cost. WFW for two users, including network cards, cable, and the WFW software, sells for about the same price as the expected price for a single client copy of Windows NT. Additionally, WFW can run on older, 286-based computers—though in a very limited fashion.

You don't have to make an either-or choice between WFW and Windows NT, however. You can run both platforms in a single networked environment. In many cases, Windows NT acts as a high-performance server (running, for example, a large centralized database), whereas WFW workstations use peer-to-peer services for printing and other general-use applications.

Network Tools

Marketed as a workgroup's first network, WFW brings several applications with it to help beginning network users get started:

- Schedule+ is an application that provides workgroup features for scheduling resources, such as people and meeting rooms. It's simple, but fully functional.

- MS Mail provides users with a full-fledged electronic mail platform that can send and receive mail to DOS-based systems running the Workgroup Connection software for DOS, as well as Windows NT systems.

- Chat is a program that enables two Windows users to have a real-time conversation across the network using the keyboard.

Each of the new workgroup applications is intended to spur users into thinking of new ways to communicate and share information. Versions of these applications are also scheduled for inclusion in Windows NT.

Schedule+

Having scheduling software available on a network is helpful in planning group meetings; this is Schedule+'s greatest strength. Intended as a personal

Windows NT: The Next Generation

scheduler to help people track their appointments and reminders, Schedule+ also enables users to delegate other users as assistants for help in managing their time. Because it is a networked project, others can see as much or as little of your schedule as you want them to see. Figure 7.2 is an example Schedule+ window.

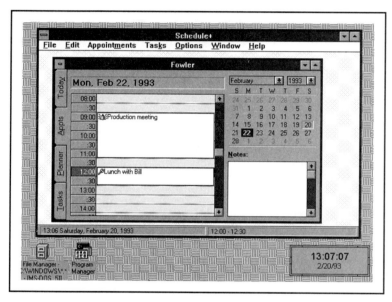

Figure 7.2. *Schedule+ window.*

Schedule+ does not replace more advanced third-party appointment products any more than a bare-bones graphics application such as Windows Paintbrush replaces Corel Systems' CorelDRAW! WFW (and Windows NT) ship with Schedule+ to show that these types of applications have a place in workgroups.

MS Mail

Microsoft's electronic mail system, MS Mail, is more than just a token program that ships with WFW and Windows NT. MS Mail is a fully functional cross-platform electronic mail system, with versions for all flavors of Windows, as well as DOS, OS/2, and Macintosh System 7. MS Mail centers around

7 • *Windows NT Versus DOS and Windows*

the Workgroup Postoffice, a server location that each workstation can attach to and use—as the name suggests—as the central post office. The Workgroup Postoffice can be located on a WFW machine acting as a server, on any Windows NT machine, or even on a Novell NetWare server. Figure 7.3 illustrates an MS Mail window.

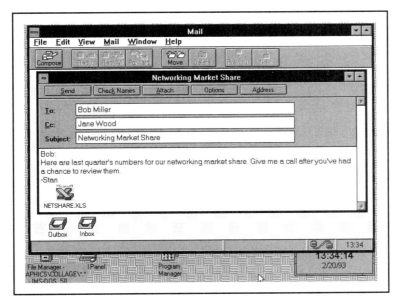

Figure 7.3. *MS Mail for Windows.*

The WFW and Windows NT MS Mail programs share the same interface. Therefore, users can move more easily from one platform to the other. Because the interface for creating messages is Windows-based, it is possible to take advantage of object linking and embedding (OLE). Thus, users wanting to create a link to a spreadsheet or graph within the E-mail message can do so. Receivers can also make changes to the embedded object. Because OLE support is specific to Windows, OLE services are not available for DOS users of MS Mail.

MS Mail has an intuitive in/out box feature, along with a useful folder system built into the product. New mail received is placed in the in-box. The user can read the new mail, then either delete or store it in folders within the in-box. Users can create new folders under any name they choose and

Windows NT: The Next Generation

decide if the folder is private or public—that is, available to be shared on the network.

For instance, a user may want to create a folder called "June 1993 Budget," and share it with other members of the workgroup. When the user wants to create mail discussing the June 1993 budget, he first composes the message, then drags it into the out-box folder by that name. The mail will go to everyone who is on the receiving list of the message, and everyone who receives the mail will find it in their in-box folder by that name. This helps keep mail organized by subject, enabling users to look for the most pertinent mail first.

Chat

Some users will say Chat is the new WFW application that's the most fun, whereas others will complain that it's nothing but a drain on productivity. When running, Chat sits at the bottom of the screen as an icon that resembles a telephone. When another user tries to reach you, the telephone rings, and you answer it by double-clicking the icon. Figure 7.4 shows a Chat window.

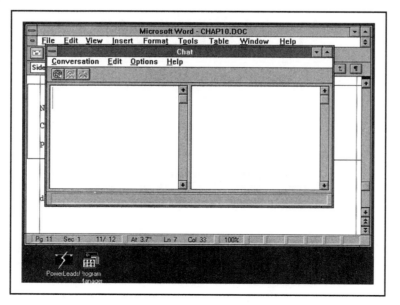

Figure 7.4. *Chat.*

7 • Windows NT Versus DOS and Windows

When you answer the phone, you have completed a two-way keyboard link between yourself and another user on the network. You can then type messages back and forth. The top of the window shows the messages you have typed, and the bottom shows those received from the remote user. You can change font styles and colors for each of the windows so you can more easily distinguish messages from the two users.

Network Clipboard

Users familiar with Windows know that it provides a *clipboard*, which accommodates quick data transfer from one application to another. Users can copy a block of text, a graph, a file, or other information to the clipboard, then paste it into other locations, once or many times. Figure 7.5 shows an example Clipboard screen.

Figure 7.5. *Windows Clipboard.*

WFW and Windows NT expand on that idea by creating a network clipboard, so other people in the workgroup can view the contents of the

Windows NT: The Next Generation

clipboard, and paste from it into their own applications. Clipboard items can be saved into files, creating a library of data from which anyone on the network can paste.

WFW Limitations

Running WFW in Windows standard mode prevents the computer from functioning as a server on the network. The user can still run in client mode, attaching to remote drives, accessing mail, and using other workgroup applications, but other users won't be able to share the resources (disk drives and printers) of that system.

Because Windows can run only in standard mode on a 286-based computer, these systems can't act as servers on a Windows for Workgroups-based network. This could be a critical limitation for sites with many existing 286-class PCs. One way around this is to dedicate one or more 386 computers to work as servers, while the clients use the 286 machines. Consequently, files can be shared on the servers, but printers located at users' machines cannot be shared. You must attach any printers to be shared to a server under Windows for Workgroups.

WFW Advantages

Windows for Workgroups introduces DOS-based Windows users to networking in a pleasant and easy-to-understand manner. It also serves as an easy upgrade path to Windows NT. WFW's workgroup applications are simple, both in features and in ease of use. They won't form the backbone of an organization-wide network, but they will introduce concepts that users may not have seen before.

Windows for Workgroups is also a good choice if you want to hook one or a small cluster of PCs into a main corporate LAN. WFW makes better use of conventional memory for installing network drivers than DOS does. In the single-user Windows world, you load device drivers or TSRs before you start Windows. With WFW, these drivers load with the operating system, thus avoiding TSR or DOS device driver memory conflicts.

7 • *Windows NT Versus DOS and Windows*

Windows NT

Windows NT sits at the summit of Microsoft's operating system strategy. Windows NT has more features and benefits, and it creates more responsibility for the user than any other product I've discussed so far.

Windows NT contains all the features of Windows 3.1 for DOS and Windows for Workgroups, including support for the same applications, the same connection options, and the same user interface (see Table 7.1). Windows NT also is a full 32-bit operating system. Programs created to take full advantage of Windows NT will most likely outperform similar programs designed for DOS-based Windows or WFW. This of course assumes that the programmer wrote the application with NT in mind and optimized it to take full advantage of the operating system's features.

Table 7.1. A comparison of Windows NT and the rest of the Windows family.

Feature	16-Bit Windows 3.1	Windows 3.1 with Win32s	Windows for Workgroups	Windows NT
Virtual Memory	yes	yes	yes	yes
Multitasking	cooperative	cooperative	cooperative	preemptive
Multithreading	no	no	no	yes
Symmetric Multiprocessing	no	no	no	yes
Portable	no	no	no	yes
Access Security	no	no	no	yes
Runs 16-bit Real Mode Windows Applications	yes	yes	yes	no
Runs 16-bit Standard Mode Windows Applications	yes	yes	yes	most

continues

239

Windows NT: The Next Generation

Table 7.1. continued

Feature	16-Bit Windows 3.1	Windows 3.1 with Win32s	Windows for Workgroups	Windows NT
Runs 16-bit 386-Enhanced Mode Windows Applications	yes	yes	yes	yes
Runs 32-bit Windows Applications	no	yes	no	yes
Runs OS/2 Applications	no	no	no	1.X Character Mode Only
POSIX Support	no	no	no	yes
Supports DOS FAT	yes	yes	yes	yes
Supports OS/2 HPFS	no	no	no	yes
Supports NTFS	no	no	no	yes
Built-In Networking	no	no	yes	yes
Built-In E-Mail	no	no	yes	yes
386 or Higher CPU Required	no	yes	yes (In Server Mode)	yes

In the following sections, I'll discuss the key advantages and disadvantages of Windows NT.

Security

Windows 3.1 for DOS offers no security features beyond those available through DOS or any other network operating system that runs in conjunction with Windows. Because DOS has very little capability to control how resources such as memory, files, and hardware devices are used, Windows 3.1 for DOS has few security or system integrity safeguards.

In contrast, when users sit down to Windows NT, they must log into the operating system. Because security is such a strong focus in Windows NT, users must identify themselves to the operating system and authenticate their identification with a password to gain access to the system. Additionally, unlike third-party access control features for DOS-based Windows that tend to be all or nothing controls, NT can control user access to the system on a file-by-file and program-by-program basis.

Windows NT offers U.S. Government C2 Class security. Three components maintain this level of security:

- The security subsystem
- A user mode subsystem for managing initial system access control
- Two NT executive subsystems, the Object Manager and Security Reference Monitor

New to Windows NT, these subsystems track the creation and usage of all resources available to the operating system. They provide facilities for allowing system administrators to set the privileges that each user has to access these resources, and they provide a common mechanism for using resources.

Under Windows NT, resources can include more than just the simple items described earlier. A programmer creating an application specifically for Windows NT could designate a record from a database as a resource (or object) for management by the operating system. Therefore, the operating system controls who can view, change, or delete that record. The system administrator can grant privilege to that object, and access can be controlled and logged.

Windows NT: The Next Generation

When an application requires access to an object, it sends a message to the operating system, requesting the item. The operating system then forwards that message to the object manager to see if the application—based upon the user who logged in—has sufficient privileges to that object. If so, the object manager returns a message granting access, and the operating system forwards the resource to the application. If the resource is unavailable, the object manager notifies the operating system, and the application decides whether to wait for the resource to become available or continue without the resource. All this activity takes a significant amount of processing time, but the benefits offered by a secure operating environment usually outweigh the performance penalty exacted by this procedure.

DOS does not contain such a facility for resource management, and therefore clashes that occur when two programs want the same resource at the same time are not uncommon. This usually results in a hung system or (under Windows 3.1) a general protection fault. Then the user must decide how to handle the conflict, but in many cases, the user is forced to reboot the system, often resulting in a complete loss of work in progress.

Windows NT Protected Subsystems

Imagine you had several pairs of glasses, and each one presented you with a different view of the same thing. This is similar to the concept of the Windows NT protected subsystems. The Win32 subsystem is the most prominent of these subsystems. Others include the OS/2, POSIX, and VDM subsystems. These Windows NT extensions provide the elements that programs written for their native environments need in order to run.

While running a DOS program, the VDM subsystem gathers the DOS system resource requirements and presents them to Windows NT for processing. Likewise, the OS/2 subsystem catches all the needs of OS/2 programs running under Windows NT before passing them on to the operating system. Because the protected subsystem is the program's first contact with Windows NT, the program thinks it is running in its native operating system.

Protected subsystems run as programs under Windows NT, rather than as a part of the operating system itself, so they can be modified and updated without requiring traumatic changes to the entire operating system. When

later versions, of OS/2 or POSIX arrive, their subsystems can be updated to reflect necessary changes and improvements. This also means that when new operating environments become available, Windows NT's extensible nature offers the possibility of compatibility through new protected subsystems.

For the decision maker, having these protected subsystems on a client machine means that the user can run applications from a variety of sources and can trade information among them. Managers are not forced to change all their data processing systems at once, but users can still work with existing systems while taking advantage of the latest technology.

Hardware

Windows NT running as a client system will eventually work on a 486 system with 8M of RAM and a 200M hard drive, but early versions of NT will more likely require 12M to 16M of RAM for acceptable performance.

Windows NT is a portable operating system, meaning that it can run on more than one processor architecture. In addition to Intel 80x86-based computers, NT users have the option of computers based upon the MIPS 4000 and DEC Alpha RISC processors. For example, DEC is preparing to introduce an Alpha PC that combines the Alpha CPU with a 32-bit EISA bus and local-bus video. In beta test benchmarks, this system significantly outperformed a comparable 486-based PC also running Windows NT.

Symmetric Multiprocessing

The feature of Windows NT filling the role of unsung hero is its capability to perform *symmetric multiprocessing*—it can work on computers with more than one CPU, dividing the processing tasks among the processors. Symmetric multiprocessing is a complicated task for an operating system, but if the operating system architect and application developers have implemented it well, it happens completely behind the scenes for users. To activate the multiprocessing, the user doesn't need to make adjustments, modify files, or set levels.

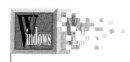

Windows NT: The Next Generation

Few people understand the benefits this offers because so few computers have the hardware for this to happen. Mainframe and minicomputers have been doing this for years because their operating systems can take advantage of the feature. If computer manufacturers widely adopt multiprocessor architectures, this feature could save millions in upgrade costs over the years. When users want more speed from their system, they could simply add another CPU. The user will not need to throw out the old system to produce a dramatic speed increase.

The soon-to-be-released Pentium (586) chip includes features that make the task of developing multiprocessor systems easier for computer designers. The Pentium also implements a new feature called *CPU redundancy*, so that if one CPU fails, the others are notified and directed to pick up the slack without causing a system failure.

NT File System

The NT File System (NTFS) can replace the DOS FAT file system under Windows NT if the user chooses. NTFS offers greater speed and caching as well as supporting longer filenames (up to 254 characters). The NTFS is implemented—as are all drive I/O systems—as a subsystem under Windows NT. The user can designate one drive as HPFS (High Performance File System—OS/2's standard file format), another as NTFS, and still another as DOS FAT. In fact, multiple file systems can reside in different partitions on the same hard disk. Windows NT contains an Installable File System (IFS) architecture, which means others can create file systems that interface directly to Windows NT.

As an important consideration, applications developed with one file system in mind may produce unpredictable results when run with another file system under NT. For example, NT has no problem working with the DOS FAT file system, except that NT can't implement its security and data integrity features under FAT. When a DOS application attempts to access NTFS files, however, conflicts may occur. DOS filenames are limited to eight characters plus a three-character suffix, whereas NTFS filenames can run up to 254 characters. DOS applications truncate NTFS filenames, and filename conflicts (in which the first eleven characters of two or more filenames are not unique) are a constant possibility.

Conclusion

This chapter reviewed the basic capabilities of DOS, 16-bit Windows, Windows for Workgroups, and Windows NT and compared NT with each of the alternatives. As you've seen, NT provides both connectivity to and an upgrade path for these sister Microsoft operating systems and environments.

For many users, the existing Windows environment, running on top of DOS, provides all the power and features they need. For them, the cost of upgrading to Windows NT probably outweighs the benefits. For those users and organizations that have simply outgrown the capabilities of DOS or for organizations planning to make a major commitment to networking, however, Windows NT offers a solid application and file server platform.

The next two chapters compare OS/2 and UNIX, respectively, with Windows NT. If you're interested in these operating systems, I encourage you to read these chapters. To round out your understanding of all the issues involved with selecting a computing platform, I strongly suggest that you read Chapter 10, "Making the Choice: Windows NT or Not?" for a practical guide to choosing among NT and the many other available operating systems and Chapter 11, "The Future of Windows NT," for some insights into future operating system developments.

8

Windows NT Versus OS/2

Windows NT: The Next Generation

The OS/2 operating system and Windows NT have a common heritage: they are both derived from the IBM-Microsoft joint development agreement for OS/2. As described in Chapter 1, "The Road to Windows NT," in 1991 IBM and Microsoft decided to go their separate ways with respect to 32-bit operating systems. IBM continued work on OS/2, and Microsoft's OS/2 3.0 project became the foundation of Windows NT. Because of their common ancestry, OS/2 2.1 and Windows NT have much in common. Not surprisingly, however, they also differ in function and features.

This chapter compares the capabilities of OS/2 with those of Windows NT. Each of the major elements in both operating systems is examined, and the OS/2 2.1 implementation with the Windows NT equivalent is compared or contrasted. (Unless otherwise specified, all references in this chapter to OS/2 pertain to the most recent version: OS/2 2.1.)

Neither Windows NT nor OS/2 can possibly be all things to all people. At times, one of them may more properly fit your particular environment than the other. This chapter should give you the information and knowledge to enable you to understand, on a feature-by-feature basis, why one system may be more appropriate than the other.

OS/2 Explained

OS/2 has a graphical user interface, similar to that of Windows and the Apple Macintosh, known as the Workplace Shell. OS/2 operates only on Intel (or compatible) 386, 486, or Pentium-based computers and provides a 32-bit protected-mode processing environment on which OS/2 16-bit, OS/2 32-bit, DOS, and Windows 3.1 applications can run together.

OS/2's Workplace Shell provides the user interface for the operating system. However, it is more than just a windowing interface for users. The Workplace Shell is an API that allows reusable and interconnected components—or objects—that enable programmers to integrate their applications with the Workplace Shell. This means that a well-written OS/2 application can appear like another component of the operating system and take advantage of all the drag-and-drop possibilities and a consistent user interface

design. The Workplace Shell is currently available only for the OS/2 operating system, and applications closely linked to the Workplace Shell's architecture may not be portable to other environments, such as Windows NT, without significant redesign.

OS/2 is now well-accepted in the marketplace, especially by the large corporate computer users who have historically formed the backbone of IBM's market (although its success in the small office, workgroup, and individual user market segments is not as great).

OS/2 2.1 is the sixth version of the operating system, first delivered as OS/2 1.0 in 1987. Over the years, OS/2 has shed its reputation for sluggish performance and gained many new features and capabilities. IBM positions OS/2 as an integrating platform on which you can run DOS, Windows 3.1, and OS/2 applications. It is also a solid environment for networked, enterprise-wide, mission-critical operations.

Windows NT is similar to OS/2 in many respects. Technically, it has most of the features included with OS/2, and it also contains some additional features not offered in OS/2.

OS/2 2.1 Features

OS/2 is a full-featured, 32-bit operating system. Many of its features are available in Windows NT, although they may be implemented in a slightly different way; other features are unique to the OS/2 operating system. This chapter discusses the features offered in OS/2 2.1. The 2.1 version includes many improvements over the 2.0 version, including enhanced support for Windows 3.1 applications, video display adapters, printers, and other hardware devices like PCMCIA cards, as well as better system performance and reliability. Although memory requirements remain largely unchanged, you need more hard disk space to accommodate the new features, principally the Windows 3.1 support.

Windows NT: The Next Generation

> **PCMCIA**
>
> Personal Computer Memory Card Industry Association, an international nonprofit group that establishes hardware, software and interface standards for credit card-sized memory and I/O peripheral cards for portable computers.

Multitasking

OS/2, like Windows NT, is a true multitasking operating system. This means that a user can perform a number of tasks simultaneously, even tasks involving the hardware of the computer. DOS-based Windows appears to make this happen, but actually it only shifts its attention from one task to another very rapidly, under the control of each application, not the control of the operating system. OS/2 and Windows NT implement multitasking by setting up separate virtual processors and registers for each task.

Windows NT and OS/2 implement multitasking using a very similar process. However, handling input messages (for example, from the keyboard and mouse) is different. As discussed in Chapter 7, "Windows NT Versus DOS and Windows," both Windows NT and OS/2 work by passing messages between the applications and the operating system. These messages enter a queue for processing, and all messages are processed in the order in which they arrive in the queue.

OS/2 sets up only one message queue for all input messages for all applications. Messages are removed from this queue and passed on to individual queues, one for each application, only when each application is ready to receive more input.

However, any message stuck in the first input queue (because it can't be processed) prevents any other application from receiving input. This can appear to cause the entire system to halt because none of your keyboard or mouse activity appears to be received by the system. In fact, this is not the

case; all application threads that are not waiting for any input message continue to execute. This is important for mission-critical communications and network environments. It also explains why most well-designed OS/2 applications have multiple threads—one to process input events and others to do the actual work.

Windows NT, however, creates a separate message queue for input to each application. Windows NT checks the queues for each application, executes what it can in the time allotted to that application, and moves to the next. If a message is stuck, Windows NT moves on to the next application. This design means that if one application fails to respond to an input message, it does not affect any other application in any way—you can still type text, use the mouse buttons, and have each application (except the hung application) respond.

Windows NT's design is generally considered to offer a better environment for running most user interaction-intensive applications, and it is likely that a future version of the OS/2 operating system may also adopt a similar technique. Because applications are implemented with multiple threads and processes, the failure of another application does not affect them. This makes both NT and OS/2 well-suited for network servers and mission-critical applications.

More Memory

Both OS/2 and Windows NT overcome the limits of DOS by implementing huge memory addressing for each application. Both systems have an architectural limit of 4G of memory addressability. Windows NT reserves 2G for its own use and allows up to 2G for applications. OS/2 2.1 currently limits each application to 512M.

On OS/2, DOS and Windows applications request memory through one of the three standard memory management schemes used by DOS-based applications: XMS, EMS, or DPMI. Limitations in the XMS and EMS architecture prevent OS/2 from supplying more than 16M and 32M, respectively, for each DOS session. For DPMI, however, OS/2 can provide anything up to the full 512M for each session. Note that neither OS/2 2.1 or Windows NT support the VCPI standards because it would compromise the protection built into both systems for DOS applications.

XMS

Extended Memory Specification, a memory management scheme that allows DOS programs running on personal computers based on Intel 286 or greater processors to use extended memory.

EMS

Expanded Memory Specification, a memory management technique originally developed by Lotus, Intel, and Microsoft that allows DOS to work with up to 32M of additional memory. Unlike XMS, which requires an Intel 286 or greater processor, EMS runs on any Intel processor from the 8088/86 on up.

DPMI

DOS Protected Mode Interface, a DOS extender specification that enables DOS-extended (XMS-compatible) programs to cooperatively run under 16-bit Windows without crashing the system.

> **VCPI**
>
> Virtual Control Program Interface, a DOS extender specification for Intel 386 or greater processors that enables DOS-extended programs to run together in a cooperative multitasking environment with DOS real mode programs.

All these memory numbers seem large, but they are, in fact, theoretical. In practice, the amount of memory that OS/2 and Windows NT can actually supply to your applications depends on the sum of the amount of physical memory you have in your computer and the amount of free space on your hard disk drive.

In both operating systems, virtual memory can make each application believe it has more memory than it really does. The memory an application uses is created in physical memory first, then in disk space. The operating system swaps disk space memory in and out of physical memory as needed. This means that as long as disk space is plentiful, no application will run out of memory, despite the size of the physical memory installed.

Virtual memory is both a blessing and a curse. It makes a trade-off of disk space for memory, but the price paid is time. If you are running applications that need a great deal of memory, you should consider the costs of additional memory for your computer versus the amount of time spent waiting for disk swapping to occur. Do not underestimate the performance improvements possible by installing only a couple of extra megabytes of memory if you find that the operating system is extensively swapping data and programs to and from hard disk.

Application Compatibility: DOS, Windows, and OS/2

IBM currently has an agreement with Microsoft to review and use programming code from Windows for use in OS/2. Similarly, Microsoft may review and use the programming code from OS/2.

Windows NT: The Next Generation

These rights enabled IBM to incorporate support for Windows applications in OS/2 (first, for Windows 3.0 in OS/2 2.0, and now for Windows 3.1 applications in OS/2 2.1). However, it's important to keep in mind that all of IBM's rights to future Microsoft code expire in September 1993. After that time, IBM will need to maintain compatibility with future versions of DOS and 16-bit Windows without the advantage of being able to examine Microsoft's source code.

Even with access to much of Microsoft's source code, it took IBM more than a year to add Windows 3.1 support to OS/2. If Microsoft picks up the pace of development of future 16- and 32-bit Windows environments, it's likely that IBM will fall behind even further. One of IBM's strategies for OS/2 is to position it as an integrating platform for a variety of application types. OS/2 2.1 provides a high level of compatibility for Windows 3.1 applications, including enhanced mode, and DOS applications. It is even possible to run a specific version of DOS in OS/2 if you want, for example, DR DOS 6.0.

Whether OS/2 continues to offer compatibility for applications designed for possible future operating environments remains to be seen. IBM includes support for Windows 3.1 and DOS applications in OS/2 2.1 because there are thousands of applications for these environments that its customers would like to use.

If a large number of applications appear for a future version of DOS or Windows and there is demand from its customers, it is fair to anticipate that IBM will try to accommodate these needs, although, as discussed, IBM's ability to maintain full compatibility with future Microsoft operating systems and environments is an open question. It's also possible that IBM might strip out support for 16-bit Windows—and possibly even DOS—from a future "lite" version of OS/2.

With OS/2 it's possible to run DOS, Windows, and OS/2 applications on the same desktop, all executing together on the same system. IBM's term for OS/2's ability to run Windows applications on the same desktop as other applications is *seamless windows*. In OS/2 2.0 you can do this only if you use a regular VGA video adapter. OS/2 2.1, however, now supports this feature on almost any video adapter supported by the OS/2 operating system. This includes many Super VGA adapters, as well as IBM's own range of adapters (see Figure 8.1).

8 • *Windows NT Versus OS/2*

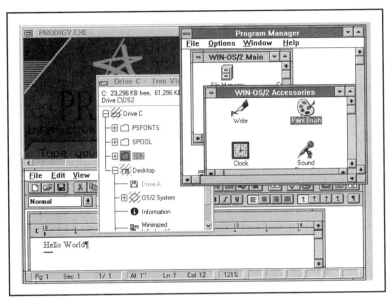

Figure 8.1. *Windows, OS/2, and DOS applications on the same screen.*

IBM has not announced support for the Win32s extensions for Windows 3.1, Windows for Workgroups, or Windows NT. Some of the Windows for Workgroups utilities, however, do work on OS/2 2.1. Applications written specifically to take advantage of any of these products may not work on OS/2. Although very few applications that require the Win32s API, Windows for Workgroups, or Windows NT currently exist, the probability is that many applications will be developed for all three during the next few years. OS/2's inability to run these applications could ultimately limit the functionality of its Windows support capabilities.

Both OS/2 and Windows NT provide enhanced file systems not normally available to DOS applications: OS/2's high performance file system (HPFS) and the NT file system (NTFS). DOS applications running on real DOS or Windows 3.1 cannot access data files held on a hard disk formatted with one of the enhanced file systems. When running on OS/2 or Windows NT, however, they use the services of the underlying operating system for all file

Windows NT: The Next Generation

access. This permits access to data on these file systems, with significantly improved performance and data integrity. There are two problem areas here for DOS applications that are common to both OS/2 and Windows NT: long filenames and extended attributes (EA).

Windows NT can run OS/2 1.3 character-based applications. A few text editors and word processing applications can run in this environment, but this level of OS/2 compatibility in Windows NT is not terribly useful. Most OS/2 applications written in the last few years use the Presentation Manager (PM) to provide a graphical user interface.

On the other hand, few horizontal OS/2 applications—word processors, spreadsheets, databases, and so on—do not have equivalent versions that run either on DOS-based Windows now or Windows NT in the near future. In contrast, Windows currently supports thousands of horizontal applications that are not available in native OS/2 versions. OS/2's greatest appeal is to incorporate in-house application developers for vertical applications. Very few users or organizations have committed to OS/2 because of its available library of horizontal applications.

Adobe Type Manager Font Support

In a graphical environment, it's important to make the computer's display accurately represent what a printed page or document will look like; this capability is called WYSIWYG (what you see is what you get). The accurate display of text is particularly difficult because of the endless variations in type fonts, sizes, and styles. OS/2 and Windows NT offer similar mechanisms for ensuring that text on the screen looks like printed text—OS/2 uses Adobe's Adobe Type Manager, or ATM; Windows NT uses TrueType.

ATM was first created as an add-on for the Apple Macintosh to enable it to display the same type fonts printed by Apple's LaserWriter laser printer. Later, ATM was moved to Windows 3.0; it is currently supported under 16-bit Windows and Windows for Workgroups. Compared to the bitmapped screen fonts supported by the Macintosh itself, ATM's PostScript fonts were smoother and could be enlarged or reduced to virtually any size without distortion. ATM allows one set of PostScript fonts to be used by both printers and displays. Under OS/2, you can install new fonts for use by Presentation Manager applications, Windows applications, and printers.

IBM adopted an ATM and PostScript standard for OS/2, and Microsoft and Apple jointly developed a different font-rendering program called TrueType. TrueType uses a technology similar to ATM, although its fonts are not compatible with PostScript. TrueType is built into all Windows products including Windows 3.1 and Windows NT. Since the release of Windows 3.1, TrueType has become the predominant font-rendering technology for Windows systems, primarily for two reasons:

- TrueType is included in Windows at no extra cost (ATM is sold separately).

- Microsoft and other companies sold libraries of TrueType fonts at a fraction of the cost of comparable PostScript typefaces. For the cost of one family (four styles—normal, bold, italic, and bold italic) of Postscript typefaces, TrueType users could purchase a library containing 40 to 60 fonts.

OS/2 2.1 includes TrueType only for Windows applications. Third-party utilities, such as Ares Software's FontMonger, can convert typefaces from TrueType to PostScript, or vice versa, so your investment in a font library of either format can be preserved if you decide to switch to a different font rendering program.

High Performance File System (HPFS)

OS/2 includes an optional HPFS that you can install and use, or you can choose to continue to use the FAT system originally introduced with DOS. In fact, for most OS/2 users, FAT is an ideal choice. In OS/2 2.0 the FAT system was considerably enhanced (incorporating some of the features found in HPFS) to improve its performance over DOS.

Windows NT: The Next Generation

OS/2 2.1 can work with either or both file systems. If your hard disk is less than 120 megabytes in size, or if you have limited memory (less than 8 megabytes), stick with the FAT system. The improved performance of HPFS begins to become significant only for larger hard disks—the environment for which it was designed.

HPFS does not simply extend FAT, it replaces it. It allows for larger filenames, larger files, and has multithreaded input and output—it can read and write files while the user is busy getting other things done by caching data in memory and later writing it to the physical disk drive. Termed *lazy write caching*, this feature is also incorporated into the OS/2 implementation of FAT.

The primary motivation for creating HPFS was to improve performance when accessing data on very large hard disks. HPFS accomplishes this well and also introduces other enhancements: long filenames and extended attributes (EA). Long filenames extend the familiar eight-character (with a three-character extension) format of DOS (FAT) filenames. HPFS allows up to 254 characters, as many periods as a user deems necessary, and other characters not allowed by the FAT system. For example, you can include spaces and mixed-case characters in HPFS.

Remember, however, that you can run DOS and Windows 3.1 applications on OS/2. Because most of these applications are unable to work with filenames longer than the eight characters, using long names prevents you from accessing data in that file from a DOS or Windows application. This, of course, is also true for these types of applications running on Windows NT.

The most advanced feature of HPFS is extended attributes (EA). The attributes of a file can be used to describe the file in ways that the actual file content may not be able to do (for example, whether the file is write protected).

The extended attribute mechanism permits you to attach a pointer to a collection of information about the file that can include most anything. A programmer of a word processor, for example, who wants to record the name of the author of a file, might store that name in the file's extended attributes. The Workplace Shell on OS/2 2.1 allows you to enter information into the most common extended attribute fields using the File section of an object's system settings notebook (see Figure 8.2).

8 • *Windows NT Versus OS/2*

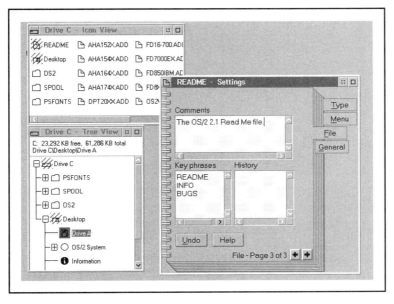

Figure 8.2. *The File section of an object's system settings notebook.*

OS/2 uses extended attributes in a number of ways. The most significant is that the Workplace Shell attaches object information to a file's EAs—for example the icon to use when the object is visible on your desktop. Other applications are free to make whatever use of EAs they choose.

Both OS/2 and Windows NT support FAT and HPFS file systems. In addition, NT supports its own file system, called NTFS, that offers significantly more capability than HPFS. First and foremost, NTFS includes extensive access control security features. Access to every file and subdirectory in an NTFS volume can be restricted by user groups or individual users. NTFS offers sophisticated error recovery capabilities and support for fault-tolerant features, such as disk mirroring and striping with parity, in the event of hardware, software, or power failures. (A modified version of HPFS, available with IBM's LAN Server software for OS/2, also supports fault-tolerant features.) Chapter 3, "Windows NT in Profile," and Chapter 4, "A Quick Walk Through Windows NT," provide more information about NTFS.

Windows NT: The Next Generation

Application Protection

OS/2 implements a protected-mode environment for all running applications, whether they are DOS-, Windows-, or OS/2-based. Windows NT offers similar protection for native NT applications and for the NT-protected subsystems (see Chapter 3). If an application tries to grab memory outside of its allotted area, OS/2 senses the fault and issues a message known as the Hard Error Popup. You have the option of displaying debug register information (as shown in Figure 8.3) or simply terminating the offending application.

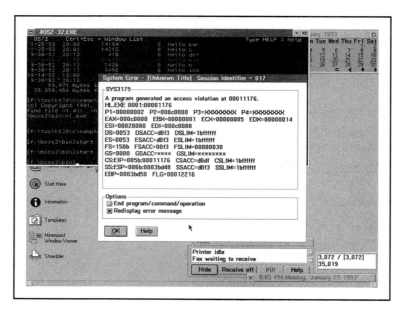

Figure 8.3. Register contents after a fatal protection violation in an application program.

OS/2 runs nearly every DOS application. The technique it uses employs a feature of 386 or higher Intel processors known as virtual 86 mode. In OS/2 and NT, this is usually called a virtual DOS machine (VDM). The virtual 86 mode allows OS/2 to use the built-in features of the Intel processors for hardware protection between running applications. If one DOS application does

something it shouldn't—which, on Windows 3.1 or real DOS, may cause a system fault—OS/2 detects the error and prevents the fault from causing any side effects on the operating system or with any other application that may be executing at the same time. In this regard, Windows NT employs exactly the same technique as OS/2. Windows NT, however, is also designed to run on non-Intel processors. In this environment, all DOS application support must be provided by software emulation via the virtual DOS machine, or VDM, described in Chapter 3. Regardless of the hardware platform, NT's VDM will not be as efficient at running DOS programs as an Intel-based PC running DOS as its native operating system would be, by virtue of the fact that the VDM emulates the Intel hardware architecture in software. This technique, however, does enable 16-bit Windows applications to run on otherwise incompatible hardware.

When accessing hardware devices—for example, the disk drive or input/output ports—both OS/2 and Windows NT exert control by requiring a virtual device driver (VDD) to oversee the operation. VDDs ensure that no more than one DOS application is accessing a single hardware device at the same time. They also ensure that a DOS or Windows application that accesses a hardware device does not leave it in a state that is unusable by some other application.

Should a DOS or Windows application access a hardware device illegally, or attempt to use the hardware in a way that would corrupt the system, both OS/2 and Windows NT can detect this situation, and you can then terminate the offending application. It is not possible for the application to cause any damage to any other part of your operating environment, be it OS/2 or Windows NT.

OS/2 supports Windows applications in the same protected environment that it offers for each DOS application. You can execute each Windows application in a separate virtual DOS machine or run all your Windows applications in the same VDM.

Running all your Windows applications in the same VDM improves performance because each application can share the same Windows system code. However, it exposes you to all the inherent problems of Windows 3.1 on DOS. Should one of your Windows applications cause a fatal error, it may cause all your other Windows applications to fault as well. The difference in

Windows NT: The Next Generation

OS/2 and Windows NT, however, is that this fault does not affect any of your other types of applications (you won't have to reboot your computer to clear the problem).

Windows NT runs DOS applications in virtual DOS machines, with one VDM per DOS-based program. Each VDM is a separate subsystem, so any one DOS application crash won't affect other DOS applications. On the other hand, 16-bit Windows applications share a single emulator, called Windows on Win32, or WOW. 16-bit Windows applications running under WOW are subject to the same limitations and problems as applications running under native DOS-based Windows; an application crash could also crash other 16-bit Windows applications and possibly even WOW itself. However, a WOW crash won't take the entire Windows NT system with it.

REXX

OS/2's REXX is a modern programming language designed to solve an old problem. Originally created to replace an awkward and difficult batch language used for decades on IBM mainframes, REXX's design goals were to make it friendly, easy to learn and use, yet extremely powerful. Relatively new when compared to other languages, REXX is only now beginning to receive international standardization attention.

Although it was created by IBM for use on large mainframes, REXX was designed to be machine-independent. Versions of the language are now available on a wide range of computer systems, including UNIX systems, Amiga multimedia computers, DOS and Windows and, of course, OS/2. Even Macintosh has a shareware REXX-clone language version available.

REXX is more than just a batch language. It is used within OS/2 as a command and macro language. You can create and modify Workplace Shell objects from a REXX command, for example, and use REXX to create macros for the OS/2 Enhanced Editor (included with OS/2 2.1). Some see REXX as one of OS/2's major assets. It is not a language meant for building interactive graphical programs, although some companies have built tools for this purpose. You can use REXX to create small programs that work with existing software for automated tasks.

A financial analyst, for example, might create a REXX batch program to start a communications program each evening to download the latest stock quotes. The REXX program could transfer the information into a spreadsheet and print graphs. The small program could be instructed to run automatically every evening so that the graphs are completed when the analyst arrives in the morning.

Windows NT does not contain a direct equivalent to REXX, although it does include a macro recorder that can record keystrokes and mouse movements and replay by pressing a function key or command key combination. NT also has a command language that can be used in a command-line interface mode, even from within DOS. This command language can be used to develop simple applications. With the vast popularity of 16-bit Windows, it's only a matter of time until some of the third-party batch/macro languages available for it are ported to NT.

The Workplace Shell and the System Object Model

The Workplace Shell is more than just a replacement for the Windows Program Manager. It is the user interface employed to control all aspects of the OS/2 operating system through a desktop, object-oriented metaphor (see Figure 8.4).

In Figure 8.4 the icons represent application programs, devices (like printers), data files, and folders. Folders are special objects that can contain any number (and type) of other objects, and you can use them to arrange the contents of the desktop into a logical order. Each desktop object also carries with it characteristics that are alterable, often by the same dialogs. The settings on your printer, for example, can be changed from the same printer icon used to print reports.

Contrast the Workplace Shell desktop with the desktop provided by Windows NT (see Figure 8.5). The Windows NT desktop is very similar to the one provided with Windows 3.1, and it comprises separate application programs for the Program Manager, File Manager, Print Manager, and so on. Each of these applications can hold icons that represent the type of data that they

 *Windows NT: The Next Generation*

are designed to work with. For example, it is not possible for an icon representing a data file to appear in a Program Manager group window. You cannot move an icon from the Program Manager to another location on the desktop.

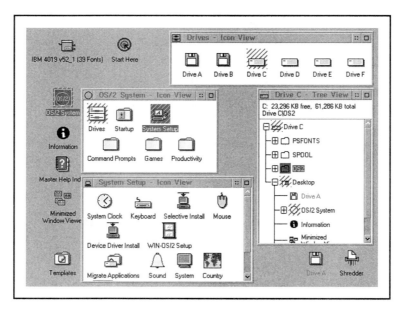

Figure 8.4. *A typical Workplace Shell desktop on OS/2 2.1.*

As discussed in Chapter 2, "Microsoft's Blueprint for the Nineties," Microsoft and third-party software developers are aware of the limitations of NT's Program and File Managers. Microsoft has publicly acknowledged its intention to merge the Program and File Manager into a single, unified desktop in a future version of NT. Symantec has publicly committed to shipping Norton Desktop for Windows NT, which will provide a similar unified desktop. In short, the Workplace Shell's advantages are likely to be short lived.

8 • *Windows NT Versus OS/2*

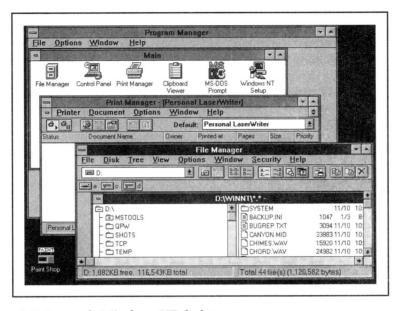

Figure 8.5. *A sample Windows NT desktop.*

The Workplace Shell is implemented in the C language but uses a feature of OS/2 known as the System Object Model (SOM). Created out of a standard from the Object Management Group, an industry consortium, this model allows for the creation, management, and communication of objects. SOM objects can represent any programming construct that the application developer chooses. In the OS/2 Workplace Shell, the objects are used to represent things like text files, printers, or spreadsheets. SOM allows for a common, programming language-independent method for controlling these objects.

Workplace Shell Advantages

By creating tools that can be shared by all of your applications, files, and icons, the Workplace Shell provides you with a consistent and familiar interface. If you want to change the characteristics of an object, you perform

Windows NT: The Next Generation

much the same action, and see much the same dialogs, from one object type to another.

The Workplace Shell may be one of OS/2's biggest advantages over Windows NT, especially with its underlying object-oriented nature, although its lead over NT is likely to be temporary. The Shell is the only application that ships with OS/2 2.1 that takes full advantage of SOM, and IBM showcases it as the future of applications development.

The Workplace Shell in OS/2 2.1 includes a number of programming interfaces that application developers can use to integrate their programs more closely with the OS/2 user interface. Even end users can customize and program the Workplace Shell with the REXX interfaces provided in the operating system.

OS/2 Connectivity

OS/2's ability to connect to other systems (mainframes, minicomputers, or microcomputers) is one of its strong points. Products from both IBM and third-party suppliers enable you to connect computers running OS/2 to a variety of IBM and third-party systems.

OS/2 applications that support IBM's own Systems Network Architecture (SNA), as well as other protocols like NetBIOS, TCP/IP, LU 6.2, APPC, and others are available. You also have a wide choice of connection hardware, including Token Ring, EtherNet, coaxial, twisted-pair, and fiber optic cable connections.

Networking

OS/2 is an established platform for local area network (LAN) servers. Both Microsoft's LAN Manager and IBM's LAN Server network operating systems are based on OS/2, although once NT is released, LAN Manager will migrate to Microsoft's new flagship operating system. OS/2 systems can act as both

clients and servers on Novell NetWare systems; NetWare runs as a "parallel" API alongside the OS/2 API. IBM's commitment to NetWare support, and Novell's direct participation, are critical due to NetWare's overwhelming PC LAN market share.

OS/2 is used today as a client on NetWare, LAN Manager, LAN Server, Banyan VINES, or UNIX (TCP/IP) servers. Redirectors to connect to each of these networks are available for OS/2 2.1. IBM and other suppliers provide excellent SNA protocol drivers for connection to 3270 equipment, both mainframe and mini.

Windows NT can also serve as a client on all these networks. It supports NetBEUI and TCP/IP transport protocols, and Novell supplies IPX/SPX protocols and network redirectors for NT client applications. Unlike OS/2, however, NT includes both client/server and peer-to-peer networking support. NT systems can also be "servers" to Windows for Workgroups networks, and as mentioned, NT can form the backbone of LAN Manager.

Novell NetWare

Currently, Novell NetWare is the most popular network operating system on the market. OS/2 is well-supported in the NetWare environment. You can easily add OS/2 clients to existing NetWare networks, and NetWare has support for HPFS filenames, through name services, as well as tight integration with the Workplace Shell. OS/2 supports both Novell's ODI network device interface and the NDIS interface jointly supported by IBM and Microsoft.

Novell has declared its intention to market client networking software for Windows NT. Novell will supply IPX/SPX transport protocol software and NetWare redirectors so that NT systems can connect to NetWare servers. Novell, however, has no intention of supporting NT as a NetWare server. Novell's goal is to sell its UnixWare operating system as an alternative to NT for application servers. In order for NT to become a NetWare-compatible server, either Microsoft or a third party will have to develop compatible server software that doesn't infringe on any of Novell's patents or copyrights.

LAN Server

IBM's LAN Server 3.0 works on top of OS/2, inheriting its features and adding support for an extended version of HPFS, coprocessor support for disk access, fault tolerance, disk mirroring, and other features.

LAN Server provides a file system called HPFS-386, making file access significantly faster by allowing it to run at a higher processor priority, one that is equal to the OS/2 kernel. Performance is further increased by adding an optional second processor. This allows some of the disk access and processing to be off-loaded to this second processor, freeing the main CPU for other tasks. This is known as loose coupling of processors, and it should not be confused with NT's more sophisticated support of symmetric multiprocessing.

Disk mirroring and fault tolerance create a system that becomes more stable in the event of trouble. Having these features allows users to implement mission-critical applications.

LAN Manager

Microsoft's LAN Manager Version 2.1 is a network server that sits on top of an enhanced version of OS/2 1.3. Although you can connect OS/2 2.0 and 2.1 clients to the network, the server is unlikely to be updated for use with OS/2 2.0 or 2.1. Existing LAN Manager users will have to eventually move to Windows NT in order to use the latest versions of the network operating system.

Because LAN Manager supports some of the major protocols for network access, including NetBEUI, IPX, and TCP/IP, it is possible to intermix LAN Manager servers, IBM LAN Server servers, and even Novell servers. You can expect to be able to connect DOS, Windows 3.1, and OS/2 2.1 clients to the LAN Manager server, even though the server itself will run on Windows NT.

What Windows NT Has That OS/2 2.1 Doesn't

The preceding sections of this chapter highlighted many of the features that the OS/2 operating system offers. In many cases these features were compared and contrasted with equivalent features in Windows NT. In some areas, OS/2 2.1 and Windows NT are roughly equal in capability. Windows NT, however, has many additional features that are not offered by the current version of the OS/2 operating system. With these features, Windows NT offers a challenge not only to OS/2, but also to existing UNIX platforms.

Portability

End users and network administrators hunger for speed. In fact, performance is the leading driver for hardware implementation, far ahead of new features. For years there have been RISC-based processors and entire systems that perform faster than any Intel-based computer, but it has always been impossible for DOS users to take advantage of those machines—examples include the new DEC Alpha series and computers based on MIPS processors, such as Silicon Graphics' systems.

Moving an operating system from one style of computer to another is a feature called portability. For an operating system to be moved, that feature must be built in. The current versions of OS/2 are not portable, but IBM has demonstrated an operating system based on the Mach microkernel technology that can execute OS/2 programs. The Mach technology provides portability for IBM's future operating systems.

Portability for operating systems is of great interest to system software developers because it enables them to move their products at a reasonable cost into a marketplace where they may not have competed before. Windows NT has a hardware abstraction layer (HAL) that isolates function calls to hardware. When vendors of non-Intel hardware platforms want to port Windows NT to their systems, they need only provide a new HAL for that computer.

Windows NT: The Next Generation

Portable operating systems enable application developers to move their software from one computer hardware architecture to another with a minimum of modifications. In many cases, the software must only be recompiled on the target computer in order to run; in other cases, some software rewriting may be necessary. This enables UNIX applications, for example, to move from an Intel-based computer, a Sun SPARC-based system, a MIPS system, or a Digital VAX Ultrix system, and it protects both the software developers' and end users' investments. Windows NT applications will have similar portability, albeit between fewer platforms. OS/2, because it's limited to Intel-compatible systems, depends on third-party development tools for cross-platform compatibility.

Symmetric Multiprocessing

Symmetric multiprocessing (SMP) is a feature of an operating system that permits it to make use of two or more similar microprocessors in the same computer. This can significantly improve the performance of applications—providing the application program is designed, with multiple threads, to make use of it. Windows NT and some UNIX systems include SMP capability, and IBM plans to include SMP in its future microkernel OS.

With SMP, it is possible for hardware vendors to produce equipment that closely links a number of CPUs inside one computer. The operating system handles the job of balancing different tasks among these CPUs. Try to imagine the speed at which a machine with eight 486 chips could perform a processing-intensive task like a large spreadsheet recalculation or the rendering of a complex graphics image. There is some performance degradation due to the job of processor scheduling, but having eight CPUs means that applications designed with parallel processing in mind can run nearly eight times faster.

Extensibility

Increasingly, users are demanding operating systems that are capable of running all of their applications. This is because of the heavy investment

8 • *Windows NT Versus OS/2*

needed to implement and create strategy around any single operating system. Both OS/2 and Windows NT run 16-bit Windows and DOS applications. With Windows NT, Microsoft can add support for other types of applications by creating a new environment subsystem. This can be used to add the capability to run programs from other operating systems. As discussed in Chapter 7, environment subsystems can be added to Windows NT without restarting the operating system because they run in much the same way that applications do.

Should Microsoft release an environment subsystem for OS/2 applications, users would only need to install the product while running Windows NT to begin running it immediately. Currently, Windows NT includes support for only 16-bit, full-screen text applications. Given Microsoft's stated intention to offer only one GUI for Windows NT (the Win32 API), it's unlikely that an officially-sanctioned 32-bit Presentation Manager API will be offered. However, the door is open for third-party software developers to provide graphical OS/2 functionality under Windows NT.

Extensibility, like portability, is a way for end users and application developers to protect their current investments in software. It's a "hedge" against the future. With an extensible operating system such as Windows NT, end users will have the opportunity to adopt popular applications from a variety of current and future operating systems without abandoning NT as a whole.

Security

Windows NT's native security and system reliability features far exceed those of OS/2. System, file, and directory access control at the user and user group levels is built into NT; a limited subset of these same features is tacked on to OS/2 by utilities and the IBM LAN Server. Under NT, the security model is extended to virtually every operating system object. Individual processes, threads, memory, I/O devices, and other system resources are all kept under access control. OS/2 has no such mechanism.

Windows NT: The Next Generation

Windows NT also offers an extensive security logging facility that tracks attempted access violations throughout the system, as well as regular events such as user logons and system shutdowns. OS/2's logging facilities are minimal at best, and they are managed only through LAN Server. NT's security features enable it to offer C2-level security as specified by the U.S. government.

Fully 32-Bit Operating System

Parts of the current OS/2 operating system are carried over from earlier, 16-bit versions, making OS/2 2.1 a 32-bit-capable operating system, but not a fully 32-bit-implemented operating system.

This will change over time, and in fact, it is already changing. For example, in OS/2 2.0 the graphics subsystem and display drivers were all 16-bit. In OS/2 2.1 this has changed to 32-bit. Significantly, however, this was done transparently to applications, whether they were 16-bit or 32-bit programs.

Windows NT is entirely 32-bit throughout for its components that support 32-bit Windows applications. Like OS/2 2.1, it continues to contain some 16-bit components to support existing DOS and Windows 3.1 applications—when running on an Intel processor.

NTFS

The NT file system (NTFS) includes all of the features of the HPFS, although it offers greater security, greater data reliability and recoverability, and support for fault-tolerant features. It also supports larger file volumes and longer filenames. NTFS, if it lives up to its initial specifications, will provide a better foundation for mission-critical applications than HPFS.

Conclusion

This chapter examined some of the features of OS/2 2.1 and compared them to the equivalent features in Windows NT. This chapter also discussed some of the additional features available in Windows NT that are not currently offered in any version of the OS/2 operating system.

The following items contain a few final thoughts about the two operating systems that might help you make an informed choice:

- If you're already using OS/2, and you're satisfied with its performance and security and don't foresee the need for multiprocessing support or other advanced features in the next 18 to 24 months, your best bet is to stick with OS/2. By the time your needs outgrow OS/2's capabilities, IBM's microkernel operating system will most likely provide a compatible upgrade path.

- If you're a Windows user who has outgrown your current system and you're trying to decide whether to move to OS/2 or Windows NT, keep September 1993 in mind. IBM's ability to continue to provide you with a fully compatible upgrade path will be sorely tested in the years ahead. IBM claims that OS/2 is actually more compatible with DOS and 16-bit Windows than NT is, but that claim is less and less likely to be valid as time goes on.

- If you have an existing NetWare network, both OS/2 and Windows NT can act as clients. However, OS/2 systems can act as NetWare servers right now; it may take a year or more for NT to gain the capability to act as a NetWare server.

- If you're currently using LAN Manager, you need to start making transition plans. As LAN Manager moves to NT, you'll either have to adopt NT as well, switch to IBM's LAN Server to stay with OS/2, or jettison them both in favor of NetWare or TCP/IP networks, both of which work with a wide variety of clients and servers.

Windows NT: The Next Generation

- If yours is a "true Blue" organization, only OS/2 will come with IBM's full service and support. The value of being able to get all your technical service and support from one source is still considerable. Although Microsoft is developing its own support organization, IBM has a decades-long head start and the resources necessary to provide service whenever and wherever it's needed.

Summary of Features

Table 8.1 lists some of the major features highlighted in this chapter.

Table 8.1. A feature comparison of OS/2 2.1 and Windows NT.

Feature	OS/2 2.1	Windows NT
Portability	No	Yes
Symmetric Multiprocessing	No	Yes
Virtual Memory	Yes	Yes
Object-Oriented User Interface	Yes	No
Internationalization	Codepage	Unicode
C2 Level Security	No	Yes
DOS FAT File System	Yes	Yes
Enhanced FAT File System	Yes	No
High Performance File System (HPFS)	Yes	Yes
NT File System (NTFS)	No	Yes
Runs DOS applications	Yes	Yes
Runs 16-bit Windows applications	Yes	Yes

Feature	OS/2 2.1	Windows NT
Runs OS/2 16-bit applications	Yes	Text only
Runs OS/2 32-bit applications	Yes	No
Runs 32-bit Windows applications	No	Yes
Application Protection	Yes	Yes
Multitasking	Yes	Yes

Your decision on which operating system (or systems) to adopt may well be broader than the choice between OS/2 and Windows NT. Chapter 10, "Making the Choice: Windows NT or Not?" and Chapter 11, "The Future of Windows NT," compare NT with DOS-based Windows, OS/2, and UNIX on seven important criteria and discuss both the present and future of each operating system. Before you make any choice, please read these chapters for a deeper understanding of your options.

9

Windows NT Versus UNIX

Windows NT: The Next Generation

This chapter investigates how Windows NT stacks up against UNIX. To say that there's only one UNIX is really incorrect. Unlike DOS, Windows, and OS/2, which are controlled by Microsoft and IBM respectively, UNIX has one "parent" (the UNIX System Laboratories) but many different "flavors" and versions. I'll discuss how this variety of UNIX flavors came to be, look at the architecture of the official UNIX—UNIX System Laboratories' System V—and then compare it with Windows NT.

Next, I'll examine the most important PC-based UNIX variants:

- NeXTSTEP, from NeXT Computer
- SCO UNIX, from the Santa Cruz Operation
- Solaris, from SunSoft
- UnixWare, from Univel/Novell

This chapter concludes with some final guidelines on how Windows NT stacks up against its UNIX competitors.

UNIX: Coming of Age on the Desktop

At first glance, a head-to-head comparison between Windows NT and UNIX seems akin to a duel with an unarmed man. Isn't UNIX that cryptic operating system that requires you to have a Ph.D. in computer science in order to understand it? Doesn't it require tons of memory and tens of megabytes of hard disk space? Haven't companies been trying to sell UNIX for PCs for years with virtually no success? Didn't Microsoft offer its own version of UNIX, only to eventually abandon it to the Santa Cruz Operation (SCO)? Isn't it thoroughly character-oriented, beyond the engineers and scientists who would use it? Aren't there dozens of different, incompatible versions of UNIX in use?

All these questions were relevant to UNIX at one time. Yes, it was once virtually impossible for mere mortals to understand UNIX. Yes, it was a system resource hog. Yes, few companies have succeeded in selling UNIX for

9 • Windows NT Versus UNIX

PCs. Yes, Microsoft developed its own flavor of UNIX called XENIX, which it eventually turned over to SCO in return for a sizable share of the company. Yes, UNIX was character-oriented and offered little in the way of graphics support. Yes, UNIX's biggest marketplace is still the engineering and scientific community, and yes, dozens of versions of UNIX exist.

In the last few years, however, UNIX has changed radically. The differences between the old and new UNIX are at least as significant as the differences between DOS and Windows. Like Windows, new UNIX is built on the foundation of the original operating system, but unlike DOS, UNIX offers a far more robust and powerful foundation.

UNIX today supports powerful graphic user interfaces and APIs that are, in many cases, better application development platforms than DOS-based Windows. Although there continue to be many versions of UNIX, most versions were unified at the system level a few years ago and are thus quite compatible.

Many of the features, and much of the architecture of Windows NT, have been derived from UNIX. UNIX experts who have always turned up their noses at DOS and Windows may now find NT and UNIX to be more alike than different.

Microsoft's networking nemesis, Novell, currently controls the core UNIX architecture through its acquisition of AT&T's UNIX Systems Laboratories. NT will soon find itself competing on the desktop PC with world-class UNIX variants from Novell (UnixWare), SCO (SCO UNIX), SunSoft (Solaris), and NeXT (NeXTSTEP). It's becoming clear that the ultimate battle for control of client/server computing on the desktop is likely to be between NT and UNIX.

This chapter provides a brief introduction to the UNIX design and compares it to that of Windows NT. It also examines the four most likely UNIX competitors for NT on Intel-based PCs: UnixWare, SCO UNIX, Solaris, and NeXTSTEP. This chapter also provides some additional recommendations for determining where and when you should use either NT or UNIX.

Windows NT: The Next Generation

A Quick Introduction to UNIX

As I first discussed in Chapter 1, UNIX's origins date back to 1969 at Bell Labs, when it was designed as a simple multitasking and multiuser operating system for Digital Equipment's PDP-7 and, a year later, for the PDP-11. UNIX's popularity grew over the years, as AT&T (the parent of Bell Labs) licensed UNIX to colleges and universities for little more than the cost of the magnetic tape and paper needed to distribute the operating system.

Unlike Microsoft and other companies that kept tight control over the source code of their operating systems, AT&T licensed both compiled versions of UNIX and source code that schools could modify and compile for their own computers. The result was that academic support for UNIX exploded in the late seventies and early eighties. Hundreds of thousands of future programmers, scientists, engineers, physicists, and mathematicians were first exposed to computers with UNIX.

At the same time, it seems that every university's computer science department tweaked the UNIX source code a bit to meet its own specific requirements. Some of these UNIX variants, such as a version created at the University of California, Berkeley—called BSD (Berkeley Software Distribution) UNIX—were themselves widely distributed and became the "seeds" for even more UNIX flavors, such as Sun Microsystems' SunOS (now Solaris) and Carnegie-Mellon University's Mach (a radically redesigned flavor of UNIX based on BSD Version 4.3).

AT&T also licensed UNIX to computer manufacturers and software developers such as Digital Equipment Corporation, Hewlett-Packard, Sun Microsystems, IBM, Microsoft, the Santa Cruz Operation (SCO), Interactive Systems, and others. Each of these companies made their own changes to UNIX and released their own versions.

The result was a chaotic mix of semicompatible operating systems, all based at some level on UNIX, but most were significantly different from each other. The most popular UNIX base variants are

- UNIX System Laboratories (USL) System V. USL, which took over UNIX licensing from AT&T and is now wholly owned by Novell, has three widely-used versions of System V: Version 3.2, which is the first

9 • *Windows NT Versus UNIX*

version that unified System V and Microsoft/SCO Xenix; Version 4.0, which added compatibility with BSD UNIX and SunOS and in so doing unified all the most popular flavors of UNIX in a single product; and Version 4.2, the most recent version, which adds a standard GUI, and improves security and reliability, among many other new features.

- University of California, Berkeley BSD. BSD's advantages over AT&T UNIX included integral networking support and bigger filenames (up to 255 characters). The most popular versions of BSD are Versions 4.2 and 4.3.

- Carnegie-Mellon University Mach. Although some UNIX purists don't consider Mach to be a true UNIX variant because it employs a microkernel operating system design that's simpler and much more compact than System V, Mach's architecture owes a great deal to BSD 4.3 and is compatible with BSD UNIX at the API level. Mach's importance as a base variant is because it was adopted as the model for a number of advanced operating systems, including the Open Software Foundation's OSF/1, NeXTSTEP, and IBM's forthcoming microkernel operating system designed to subsume both OS/2 and AIX.

Any list of UNIX variants is inevitably incomplete because of AT&T's many source code licenses, but the following is a list of some of the other most popular variants not already discussed:

- UnixWare from Univel (Novell)
- OSF/1 from the Open Software Foundation
- AIX from IBM
- A/UX from Apple
- ULTRIX from Digital Equipment
- Solaris and Interactive UNIX from Sun Microsystems
- HP/UX from Hewlett-Packard

- NeXTSTEP from NeXT Computer
- XENIX, UNIX, and Open Desktop from the Santa Cruz Operation
- Coherent, from Mark Williams

As you read the discussion in the following section, keep in mind that it refers to the "generic" UNIX System V. As you've seen, some versions of UNIX have significantly different architectures. NeXTSTEP, for example, which is based on Mach, uses a microkernel-based, object-oriented architecture. Functionally, however, it is UNIX. Later on in this chapter, you will see how NeXTSTEP differs from generic UNIX. Figure 9.1 shows a simplified block diagram of the UNIX system architecture.

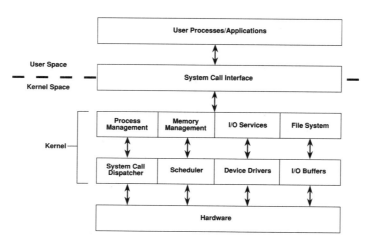

Figure 9.1. *UNIX system architecture.*

The most important thing to remember about UNIX is that it's a multitasking, multiuser operating system. All variants of UNIX, whether they run on a huge application server or a one-person RISC workstation, are based on the same foundation—one computer and many users. Most of UNIX's key capabilities come from this foundation:

- Sophisticated process management
- Multiprocessing
- The file metaphor
- Device drivers
- Interprocess communications
- 32-bit linear memory addressing and virtual memory management
- Spaces and modes
- System call interface (SCI)
- Shells, X Window, and APIs
- Security
- Networking

Sophisticated Process Management

UNIX's Process Scheduler controls the execution of each process, or program. The Process Scheduler determines which process to execute and when by means of priority, the amount of time elapsed since the process received a slice of processor time, and the security permissions of the owner of the process.

The Process Scheduler also enables processes to create, or spawn, subprocesses that are necessary for the parent process' operation. It synchronizes the activities of these processes and subprocesses to ensure that tasks are completed in the correct sequence. It also ensures that no process is left idle for an extended period of time while it waits for another process to complete. Windows NT performs much the same functions with the Process Manager and Object Manager components of the NT executive.

Windows NT: The Next Generation

Multiprocessing

Currently, most UNIX variants support some form of either asymmetric or symmetric multiprocessing. (See Chapter 3, "Windows NT in Profile," for a discussion of multiprocessing techniques.) UNIX System V Release 4 and the variants based on it include support for remote procedure calls, or RPCs, which enable a process running on one UNIX system to spawn and communicate with processes running on remote systems, just as if all the processes were executing locally. (Chapter 6, "Networking with Windows NT," discusses RPCs in more detail.)

Some specialized flavors of UNIX, especially those used for computation-intensive engineering and scientific applications, support parallel processing. This allows an application to spread processes or threads across several CPUs and execute them all in parallel with tight synchronization.

The File Metaphor

One of the most important concepts underlying UNIX is that virtually everything appears to the operating system as a file. All UNIX files are either random-access or sequential. Random-access files exist in RAM and on high-speed memory devices like hard disks. Data in these files can be read and written by directly addressing a block (usually 1 kilobyte) of storage. Sequential files are written to and read from with a stream of data. It's impossible to directly access a single byte or block of data from a sequential file.

Conventional mass storage devices like magnetic tape drives are inherently sequential, but within UNIX, input/output (I/O) devices—such as terminals, displays, keyboards, printers, modems, and others—also appear to be sequential files. Even processes are sequential files. NT uses virtually the identical design in its I/O manager and expands upon it. Within NT, files, I/O devices, processes, memory, and other elements are objects, which are connected to and communicated with much like UNIX's files. The file metaphor not only makes application development easier by filtering out the distinctions between devices, it also allows data to be rerouted from one destination to another with one command. This routing is done through UNIX's Interprocess Communication capability.

A UNIX file system manages data stored within it and arbitrates access to the devices attached to the file system. Like NT, UNIX's directories are hierarchical, with a root directory and several subdirectories below it. A single directory structure can provide access to mass storage and I/O devices. For example, UNIX's utilities are commonly found in the /bin subdirectory, and its I/O device drivers (and the connections to I/O devices) reside in the /dev subdirectory. In this way, the entire hardware and data storage architecture of a UNIX system is accessible from within the UNIX directory structure. Again, NT mirrors UNIX's structure: the I/O manager is responsible for maintaining and communicating with NT's supported file systems, device drivers, and network drivers. To higher levels of the NT executive and user mode processes, the device drivers and network drivers also look like file systems.

Device Drivers

As discussed, UNIX device drivers look like files to applications, and they are managed like sequential file devices. In the past, device drivers were "hard-configured" into the UNIX kernel: the specific device drivers to be supported by a UNIX system were installed as part of the initial software system installation.

If drivers needed to be updated or added, the UNIX system had to be shut down and selectively reinstalled with the new drivers. This was a very time-consuming process that could cause additional problems if an inexperienced system administrator accidentally changed other parts of the system configuration during the driver's installation.

As with much of UNIX, this situation has changed dramatically in the last few years. Current versions of UNIX allow new drivers to be added to a UNIX system without reinstalling or rebuilding the operating system. This capability also exists in Windows NT, and it is extremely useful for adding or changing peripherals (for example, installing a new display controller or attaching a mouse or digitizer). Windows NT also uses the capability to add and configure new drivers "on the fly" to intelligently recognize and install network interface cards and other devices.

Windows NT: The Next Generation

Interprocess Communications

Just as Windows NT provides a mechanism for objects, including processes, to communicate by passing messages to each other or sharing memory, UNIX does the same thing explicitly between processes.

Two subprocesses spawned from the same parent process, for example, can pass data between themselves with a pipe, a special sequential link between two processes. For example, UNIX systems use the ls command to display the current hard disk directory or subdirectory. UNIX's default is to route the directory listing to the user's display. However, if you want to print the directory, all you need to do is type ls ¦ pr, where ¦ is the symbol for a pipe, and pr is the printer process to which the physical printer is attached. NT offers a similar facility with its support of named pipes for interprocess communications. UNIX processes can also communicate through the following items:

- Shared memory, which uses a mechanism that is similar to NT's, for requesting, specifying, and managing regions of shared memory.

- Message queues, which are managed like shared memory except that the queues are generally used to pass short messages or commands between processes instead of large data structures.

- Semaphores, which are used like NT's synchronization objects, to synchronize the execution of multiple processes.

- Signals, which are used to communicate changes in status of a process, including termination, continuation of a suspended process, and various errors.

- Sleep and wake-up calls, which are issued by processes to suspend their execution pending the completion of a specific task by another process (sleep), or to signal a sleeping process to continue execution (wake-up). The NT kernel's dispatcher offers equivalents to sleep and wake-up calls. A thread in the waiting state could be thought of as sleeping, while a thread in standby state has been given a "wake-up call."

32-Bit Linear Memory Addressing and Virtual Memory Management

Like NT, all UNIX flavors implement a flat, linear memory addressing scheme instead of the clumsy segmented addressing implemented in DOS and 16-bit Windows. The actual amounts of physical and virtual memory supported by UNIX differ by hardware platform and UNIX variant, but typically, a UNIX system can support 64M or more of physical memory (RAM) and 2G or more of virtual memory. (NT supports up to 4G of virtual memory per process, of which 2G is available to the process and the remaining 2G is reserved for NT's own use.) The memory management system implements process memory protection so one process cannot inadvertently or deliberately view or modify the memory of another.

Spaces and Modes

As Figure 9.1 illustrates, UNIX is split into user space and kernel space, corresponding to user mode and kernel mode in Windows NT. Application processes run in user space; operating system functions run in kernel space.

User space processes are not allowed to interfere with each other's memory or resources, except through the interprocess communication capabilities previously discussed. Kernel space processes, on the other hand, can interact with other kernel and user space process resources as needed.

One big difference between UNIX and Windows NT is that in UNIX, a process can start in user mode, switch to kernel mode to perform operating system-level functions, and then switch back to user mode. In NT, user mode processes are dispatched and executed by the kernel, but they never run in kernel mode. If an application wants to have the operating system perform a specific task, it issues a system call to its associated user mode protected subsystem, which in turn issues a system services call, which then spawns one or more kernel mode processes or threads. NT's approach is, at least theoretically, more secure. Since UNIX user mode processes can penetrate kernel mode, rogue applications could perform system operations in kernel

mode that are otherwise prohibited in user mode, while NT user mode processes can never get into kernel mode, and thus cannot directly perform kernel mode functions.

System Call Interface

UNIX's equivalent to NT system services calls are system calls. Each UNIX variant has its own set of system calls. The System Call Interface (SCI) allows user space processes to access memory and devices, spawn subprocesses, and perform other system level functions. The SCI forms the boundary between user and kernel space, and user space processes are converted to kernel mode processes through the SCI.

Shells, X Window, and APIs

One UNIX user interface tenet is "each to his own taste." Historically, UNIX systems have used a command-line interface, like DOS' COMMAND.COM, for running programs and executing system commands. Over the years, UNIX developers created their own preferred libraries of utilities and programs for processing commands. These programs are called shells, and they run on top of the UNIX SCI. Shells are actually simple programming languages, somewhat like the batch commands of DOS, that can be used to execute even reasonably sophisticated tasks without requiring use of a programming language like C.

In the last few years, UNIX's text-oriented shells have been augmented by graphical user interfaces built on top of a library of primitive graphic display commands called X Window. X Window is commonly, and mistakenly, thought of as a graphical user interface (GUI). Actually, X Window can be thought of as a library of graphic routines used by a GUI to perform its functions.

UNIX GUIs are layered on top of X Window. Many different GUIs and variations on GUIs have been developed over the years, but currently, the two most popular versions are OSF/Motif and OPEN LOOK, both of which are APIs available to developers.

Motif was developed by the Open Software Foundation, and it has been adopted by most UNIX system vendors as their standard GUI. OPEN LOOK was designed by Sun Microsystems and was initially promoted as an industry standard, although Sun remains the primary proponent of OPEN LOOK. It's important to note that both Motif and OPEN LOOK are available for most popular UNIX systems—users have GUI choice and retain full compatibility with the UNIX kernel. However, only a small percentage of all UNIX applications are available in versions for more than one GUI. Thus, UNIX users' choices of applications are limited by their choice of GUI (or they must switch GUIs to run a wider assortment of applications).

One of Microsoft's most important goals for NT was to offer a single GUI for all applications and protected subsystems. Thus, NT users and developers don't need to choose a GUI, nor must they learn and support multiple GUIs. While some UNIX users might decry NT's lack of GUI choices, in practical terms NT's single GUI is less confusing, easier to learn, and easier to support than UNIX's multiple GUIs.

Security

From its origins as a multiuser operating system, UNIX has required extensive access control features. UNIX's access control is very similar to that of Windows NT, though generally without as many levels of file and directory access permissions. Most UNIX implementations comply with the U.S. government's specifications for C1 security, or Discretionary Security. Some UNIX vendors, like SunSoft, offer add-ons for their versions of UNIX that bring them up to the same higher-level C2 Controlled System Access level that NT offers.

Some deliberate (and accidental) holes in the system security of many UNIX variants were created for ease of use, and these holes must be closed to create a C2-level system. One such deliberate hole is the su command.

In many UNIX systems, any user can gain access to administrator-level privileges by executing the su, or superuser, command after logging in. All the user has to do is enter an authorized superuser password to gain the

Windows NT: The Next Generation

powers of a system administrator. A UNIX administrator has virtually unlimited control over the system. For example, he or she can access any file or device on the system, no matter what its nominal access control permissions. The superuser can read the "passwd" file, which contains the user name, privileges, and encrypted passwords of every system user. Any user's profile file, which contains information about the user's preferred shell, home directory, accessible subdirectories, and other information can be modified by the superuser. Among other features, UNIX C2-level add-ons restrict or eliminate the ability of system users to request superuser powers.

The most recent versions of UNIX include advanced file security and integrity features. UNIX System V Release 4.2, for example, includes Veritas, a journaling file system that maintains redundant file information and supports disk mirroring and striping with parity. During file read/write activity, Veritas can recover from power failures that corrupt the file systems of earlier versions of UNIX. In general, Veritas' capabilities are superior to those of OS/2's unenhanced HPFS, and on par with those of NT's NTFS, which also has advanced data integrity protection and data recovery support features. In addition, NTFS supports automatic disk data defragmentation for better performance, a feature unaddressed by Veritas.

Networking

UNIX systems offer robust networking capabilities, primarily based on the TCP/IP transport protocol. Different flavors of UNIX may use slightly different protocols at each level of the OSI model (see Chapter 6), but the overall architecture is quite similar to Windows NT. The exception is that most UNIX implementations provide little to no support for DOS-based protocols (NDIS, NetBEUI, NetBIOS). The STREAMS interface for alternative transport protocols used in NT originated in UNIX, as did remote procedure calls.

In the OSI model, everything above the session layer (presentation and application layers) resides in user space; everything below the session layer (transport, network, data link, and physical layers) resides in kernel space. The session layer is a set of system calls added to the System Call Interface in order to support networking.

At the application layer, UNIX systems support several distributed network file server systems that enable users to access remote file systems as if they were connected locally. NT supports much the same capabilities, but full accessibility of remote file systems is limited to systems running NT and the NT file system; UNIX distributed file systems can access a variety of UNIX and non-UNIX file systems. The two most popular distributed file systems are Sun's Network File System, or NFS, and USL's remote file system, or RFS.

Both NFS and RFS support file sharing across the network. The biggest difference between the two is that NFS is implemented as a virtual file system that is "superimposed" on top of the remote server's native file system, while RFS requires all clients and servers to use the same UNIX file system. NFS's virtual file system architecture enables it to support a variety of server file systems, and thus, many different operating systems. NFS already supports the DOS FAT file system, OS/2's HPFS, the UNIX and BSD file systems (as well as a number of other UNIX variant file systems), Digital's VMS, and others. It's likely that NFS will support NT's NTFS in the near future, via software from Microsoft, SunSoft, or a third-party vendor.

While NFS can run with a variety of operating systems and file systems, RFS is limited to UNIX systems only. However, RFS has two advantages: First, it uses standard UNIX file system calls, so it allows RFS systems to perform the same file sharing operations on local or remote computers. (NFS uses special calls for remote file sharing, so some file operations that can be performed locally can't be done remotely.) Second, RFS allows I/O operations such as file printing to be performed remotely, and it allows remote peripherals to be shared across the network. NFS, on the other hand, supports only file sharing, not peripheral sharing.

Actually, most UNIX systems implement a mix of distributed file systems to meet the needs of different applications and environments. RFS is most commonly used in homogeneous UNIX networks where transparent file and device sharing are required. NFS is usually used in heterogeneous networks where, for example, UNIX, NetWare, and LAN Manager servers and network segments might be mixed.

Windows NT's network file system capabilities are a mixture of NFS's and RFS's features. On NetBEUI networks, NT can share the files and peripherals of remote NT-based systems, and it can access different file systems, so

Windows NT: The Next Generation

long as those file systems are supported by the local NT system. On IPX/SPX (NetWare) networks, NT systems are limited to sharing the files and peripherals of NetWare servers, while on TCP/IP networks, NT systems can share files and peripherals with other NT systems. A capability like NFS is required to share the files of remote non-NT systems.

UNIX and Windows NT: Differences

UNIX has many additional features, but the features already discussed should give you a basic understanding of UNIX's architecture and capabilities. After reading this chapter in the context of the first half of the book, it should be clear that UNIX and Windows NT are far more alike than different. Their architectural details are different, but their functionality (especially from a user's perspective) is quite similar.

If UNIX and Windows NT are so similar, how can you choose between them? The following sections contain brief lists of some of the pros and cons of the two operating systems.

UNIX Advantages

- UNIX runs on many more platforms than Windows NT, from PCs to mainframe computers. UNIX variants are marketed and supported by virtually all of the world's major computer companies. Initially, NT will run only on Intel-architecture PCs and computers based on the MIPS 4000 and DEC Alpha processors.

- UNIX has been in use for almost 25 years, and it is extremely well-tested and reliable.

- UNIX is a multiuser operating system that is designed around the "one computer, many users" model, and it allows systems to be shared via inexpensive terminals. NT, on the other hand, is a single-user operating system based on the "one computer, one user" PC model. Multiple users can share an NT server, but they must be networked and cannot connect with dumb terminals.

- Two generations of computer engineers and scientists learned about programming and system development through academic experience with UNIX, and there is an enormous pool of trained UNIX users, programmers, and system administrators.

- UNIX has support for advanced features such as parallel processing and shared distributed file systems that don't require foreknowledge about the physical location of a file anywhere on the network. NT's parallel processing support is more limited (synchronized multithreading, but no vectorizing compilers like those used to support true parallel processing supercomputers with many processors). Its own shared distributed file system is planned for introduction as part of Microsoft's Cairo next-generation operating system.

- UNIX users have access to thousands of applications and system utilities that take advantage of the full power of their UNIX systems, including multitasking, multiprocessing, and multiuser features; Microsoft is just beginning to generate third-party support for NT applications that take similar advantage of NT's full suite of features.

- UNIX's X Window client/server graphics system enables multiuser graphic windowing applications to be supported across the network on low-cost X terminals or PCs running X server software.

UNIX Disadvantages

- There are many UNIX variants, and even though good programming practices often minimize the amount of software rewriting necessary to move an application from one version of UNIX to another, the time, effort, and expense of such efforts can be substantial.

Windows NT: The Next Generation

- There is no standard UNIX GUI. Users must choose from OSF/Motif, OPEN LOOK, Workspace Manager, and a variety of different GUIs from smaller vendors. Microsoft, however, made the development of a single GUI for Windows NT a high priority. Proliferating GUIs can lead to user confusion and increased training and productivity costs.

- UNIX is big. The complete UNIX System V Release 4.2 package requires 93 disks or access to a quarter-inch tape drive. Depending on the installed features, 60M to 98M of hard disk space is needed. The minimum amount of RAM required for acceptable single-user performance is 8M. (It's impossible to fairly compare this to NT until Microsoft releases and ships its client and server versions.)

- UNIX is old, and it carries a lot of baggage. Over the years, more and more functions have been added to UNIX. These functions add to UNIX's appeal, but they also make it harder to install, maintain, and master. (Newer UNIX variants, such as NeXTSTEP, implement a microkernel architecture that strips everything but absolutely essential functions out of the kernel and places everything else in subsystems in user space.)

NT Advantages

- NT is a new operating system with a new architecture. Although NT isn't fully object-oriented, and it doesn't have a microkernel OS, it is considerably more advanced than most UNIX implementations.

- NT was written from the ground up with a single GUI in mind, unlike UNIX, which sported a command-line interface for years and only added a GUI (actually, several different GUIs and APIs) in the last few years.

- Because Microsoft will not license the source code for NT to anyone (except under extraordinary circumstances), its APIs are totally under Microsoft's control and will not be subject to the same kind of incompatible improvements made in UNIX by its many licensees over the years.

- NT's GUI and programming interfaces will be very familiar to Windows users, which represent a much larger population than the number of active UNIX users.

- NT has the potential for more transparent networking connections than UNIX, although Novell's UnixWare may well be superior to NT in this area.

- NT can run DOS, 16-bit Windows, NT, character-mode OS/2, and POSIX applications; some UNIX variants can run DOS or Windows applications with a software emulator, as well as POSIX applications.

NT Disadvantages

- NT is new and untested. Its networking features were particularly troublesome in beta testing. It's highly unlikely that NT's first commercial release will have UNIX's stability and reliability.

- Very few applications will exploit NT's capabilities to the extent that UNIX applications now take advantage of their operating system's strength. It may be two years before users start to see a significant population of applications that take full advantage of NT's strengths.

- Right now, NT is big (requiring 8M of RAM for adequate performance and 60M to 100M of hard disk space) and slow. However, it's reasonable to withhold judgment until Microsoft makes its first customer shipments.

- Some UNIX systems exceed NT's functionality with support for parallel processing architectures, transaction processing, advanced fault tolerance, and other features suitable to enterprise-wide mission-critical applications.

- NT's short-term network connectivity capabilities are questionable, especially while Novell and Microsoft feud over the rights to NetWare client and server software.

Windows NT: The Next Generation

The PC UNIX Contenders

The choice of which operating system to use for what application depends not only on the generic differences between UNIX and Windows NT, but also on the differences between different UNIX implementations. The following sections focus on four UNIX variants that are, or are likely to be, the most popular choices for PC users migrating to client/server computing systems:

- NeXTSTEP from NeXT Computer
- SCO UNIX from the Santa Cruz Operation
- Solaris from the SunSoft division of Sun Microsystems
- UnixWare from Univel/Novell

NeXTSTEP: Object-Oriented UNIX

Sometimes, important software products come from unusual sources. Such a product is NeXTSTEP, an object-oriented version of UNIX from NeXT Computer.

When the NeXT workstation shipped to customers in September 1989, the big news was the computer hardware, not the software. However, a combination of high price, poor performance, and design quirks, such as supporting monochrome displays only when other competitors were moving to color, and using a slow erasable optical disk instead of the combination of a fast hard disk and floppy drive for mass storage, put a damper on sales. The company introduced a new family of computers in 1991. While these systems supported color displays and offered significantly better price/performance than the original NeXT workstation, NeXT's hardware sales still didn't meet company expectations.

While NeXT was struggling to put together the right combinations of hardware features, pricing, and target markets, its operating system and development tools won high praise. Users were impressed with the user interface, which borrowed elements from many different GUIs to create an environment that was both pleasingly familiar and yet arguably unique. But it was the development tools that really caused the excitement. Software developers who had been "evangelized" by NeXT to support their programs on the NeXT platform found that the Interface Builder, a graphical object editor for developing applications, combined with a rich, extensible library of reusable objects, could cut the time needed to create commercial-quality applications from several person-years to several person-months.

Innovative applications like Lotus' Improv spreadsheet made it clear that there was hard evidence of the quality of NeXT's development environment. Developers for other platforms, including Windows, Macintosh, and other flavors of UNIX, began clamoring for the same tools or the same kinds of tools.

Unfortunately, as they soon learned, NeXTSTEP was an island. While millions of PCs and Macintoshes, and hundreds of thousands of RISC workstations were being sold, NeXT sold only 50,000 workstations from the end of 1989 to the first quarter of 1993. NeXTSTEP and the Application Builder weren't portable to other platforms, and software developers were unwilling to make big commitments to an unpopular hardware design.

In the first quarter of 1992, NeXT announced that it would port NeXTSTEP and its development tools to the Intel 486, thus broadening the market potential and appeal of NeXTSTEP beyond NeXT's proprietary hardware. Development delays and the departure of key personnel, however, forced NeXT to postpone the release of NeXTSTEP for the 486 (shown in Figure 9.2) for more than a year.

Figure 9.2. *NeXTSTEP 486.*

Windows NT: The Next Generation

Although it was rumored for months, the final stroke came on February 9, 1993, when NeXT announced that it was abandoning its hardware business to concentrate on NeXTSTEP for the 486 and other platforms. NeXT's hardware designs were sold to its largest investor, Canon, and its manufacturing plant was put up for sale. Half of the company's employees (250 out of 500) were laid off. The "neat" operating system of the original NeXT computer has become the company's sole business, and NeXT has begun the process of transforming itself from a hardware to a software company.

Basic Architecture

NeXTSTEP is based on Mach, the object-oriented operating system developed by Carnegie-Mellon University. Mach, in turn, is based on the University of California, Berkeley's BSD 4.3 UNIX variant.

NeXTSTEP is a multitasking operating system that can also be used for multiuser applications, although it is optimized for networked client/server environments in which the "one machine, one user" model applies.

Like NT, NeXTSTEP relies on a series of protected subsystems for its API. Unlike NT, however, even core functions like the Object Manager's and Security Reference Monitor's NeXTSTEP equivalents are object-oriented subsystems outside the kernel. This enables NeXTSTEP to have a very small, compact, efficient microkernel, and promotes its ability to add and change system functionality without major changes to the kernel as a whole by swapping in new objects.

Graphics and GUIs

The NeXTSTEP graphical environment differs significantly from other UNIX variants. Instead of X Window graphic primitives, NeXTSTEP uses Adobe's Display Postscript Level 2 for rendering 2-D text and graphics, and Pixar's RenderMan Version 3.2 for rendering 3-D images.

The advantage of this approach is that PostScript and RenderMan are device-independent, so exactly the same graphic primitives are used to display or print. X Window, on the other hand, is display-oriented and isn't appropriate for print applications, so significant conversions are required to get X Window images on paper with full resolution. The downside of this approach is that NeXTSTEP isn't compatible with the X terminals and X server software that are becoming popular in UNIX environments.

The Workspace Manager is NeXTSTEP's GUI. It includes a rich library of text and graphic elements, including hierarchical pull-down menus, scroll bars, scrolling text and image fields, 3-D buttons, and more. The user can customize the "desktop" with the colors, backgrounds, fonts, language, and other elements, then save the customizations in the profile file.

No matter what NeXTSTEP system the user logs onto on the network, the preferred desktop will be available. The Workspace Manager is not compatible with OSF/Motif or OPEN LOOK, although NeXTSTEP users shouldn't have a hard time moving from one GUI to another.

Networking

Like other UNIX systems, NeXTSTEP supports the TCP/IP protocol. NeXTSTEP systems can serve as either clients or servers, although the NeXTSTEP networking architecture is primarily focused on the client side (Sun's Network File System [NFS] Version 4.0 is included so any NFS server can be used as a NeXTSTEP server). This client-side bias stems from the hardware design of NeXT's computers, which were generally designed as single-user workstations. As NeXTSTEP develops, it's likely that NeXT will add more server-oriented capabilities.

NeXTSTEP can also act as a client on Novell NetWare and Macintosh AppleTalk networks. In addition to its native file system, NeXTSTEP can also mount CD-ROM, DOS, and Macintosh file systems. These features provide excellent connectivity with other desktop computers and networks, and are especially useful in situations in which one or a handful of NeXTSTEP systems must share data with an existing base of PCs and Macs.

Development Tools

NeXT supplies a rich set of development tools for NeXTSTEP, including the following items:

- Interface Builder is a graphical object editor for building applications. The Interface Builder enables developers to design and test user interfaces without programming. A library of predefined GUI objects is available; objects are selected, connected, and resized with the mouse. Relationships between objects are created simply by drawing lines between objects. In this way, an application's GUI can be built without programming.

  Another advantage of the Interface Builder approach is that it uses the same objects used by the Workspace Manager to create the NeXTSTEP GUI, so Interface Builder applications are inherently consistent with the Workspace Manager.

- Database Kit is a toolkit for developing object-oriented interfaces to industry-standard databases, such as Oracle and SYBASE. Instead of using the database vendors' querying languages or interface toolkits, NeXTSTEP developers using the Database Kit can develop applications that use exactly the same user and programmatic interfaces to connect to many different, and otherwise incompatible, databases.

- Distributed objects enable interprocess communications and remote procedure calls at the object level, which enable object-oriented applications to communicate on a single computer or across a network.

- NeXTlinks is a mechanism, similar to 16-bit Windows' and Windows NT's object linking and embedding (OLE), that allows a single instance of a dataset (such as a graph, spreadsheet, word processing document, image, or database table) to be automatically updated for all users when any user makes a change. This feature is very useful for groupware or collaborative computing.

- 3D Graphics Kit is a 3-D imaging model based on Pixar's RenderMan standard that allows 3-D support to be added to any dimension. Like Display PostScript, the 3D Graphics Kit enables any 3-D object to be displayed or printed at the maximum resolution supported by the output device.

- Object libraries: in addition to the Database and 3-D objects kits listed above, NeXT supplies an application kit, which is the object library used with the Interface Builder; the sound kit, which supports sound I/O and processing; and the NetInfo kit, which provides access to the NetInfo database used for network administration.

- Languages and other development tools: NeXT supplies object-oriented Objective C and C++ compilers, debuggers, object management tools, editors, and development utilities. NeXT's primary language is Objective C, and both its development tools and internal architecture revolve around Objective C objects. Unlike C++, relatively few programmers and system developers have extensive Objective C experience.

SCO UNIX

As discussed in Chapter 1, "The Road to Windows NT," Microsoft dabbled with UNIX in the early eighties by creating its own AT&T-licensed version called Xenix. Microsoft quickly realized that Xenix wasn't like its core PC software products. Xenix required enormous developer support resources, which weren't required in an end-user, consumer-oriented software business like DOS. Xenix also had to be ported to different computers and different processor architectures: a 68000 for Tandy, an 8086 for someone else (remember that Xenix actually predated DOS). Xenix required a level of support and customization that didn't make sense.

To provide marketing, support, and customization services, Microsoft turned to a small company in Santa Cruz, California, called the Santa Cruz Operation (SCO). SCO was founded by the father-and-son team of Larry and Doug Michaels to enter the new market for desktop UNIX solutions. The business arrangement was simple. Microsoft licensed its Xenix source code to SCO and referred potential customers to the company. SCO published and sold copies of Xenix for a variety of different platforms (and processors) and paid a royalty to Microsoft for each copy.

Windows NT: The Next Generation

Over time, Microsoft grew less and less interested in fixing Xenix bugs and coming up with new versions, so the task of updating the operating system also fell to SCO. Microsoft retained a significant financial interest in the company (approximately 20 percent), but effectively turned its UNIX business over to SCO, which expanded its business charter to include application software. The company became a distributor for customized versions of a number of horizontal applications, including Xenix clones of Lotus' 1-2-3 spreadsheet and FoxPro, a clone of Ashton-Tate's dBASE database management system. SCO quickly built up a dominant market share in the nascent PC UNIX business, in part because they were the first single-source supplier of operating systems, applications, and development tools.

In the late eighties, AT&T began an intensive campaign to regain control of the ever-fragmenting definition of what was UNIX. The many different UNIX variants kept any one version of UNIX from developing a sufficiently installed base to spark an explosion in the availability of shrink-wrapped applications like the one that propelled DOS to absolute domination on the desktop.

AT&T enlisted SCO's help, as the leader in desktop UNIX, to start bringing order to the chaos. AT&T and SCO agreed to merge the functionality of UNIX System V and Xenix. Starting with Release 3.2, UNIX System V and Xenix would be source-code compatible, meaning that, in theory at least, Xenix applications could be compiled and run under System V with little or no modifications. SCO agreed to sell its own version of UNIX (SCO UNIX).

Even after the merger of Xenix and UNIX, Xenix continued to sell briskly because many developers and users postponed the switch to UNIX until all the bugs in the new release could be resolved. SCO sweetened the pot for its customers by introducing Open Desktop, the first widely supported GUI environment for PC UNIX, along with a developer's kit and an assortment of compatible applications. Open Desktop didn't actually ship until almost a year after its introduction, but once it did, Xenix sales nose-dived when many customers moved to the graphic interface.

Currently, SCO UNIX is the leading PC UNIX variant, with approximately 70 percent of the market. SCO is still selling UNIX System V Release 3.2

(although the current release level is 4.2). SCO claims that it has added compatibility features that make its version of UNIX virtually equivalent to System V Release 4, but its API is not fully compatible with Release 4.

System Architecture

SCO UNIX is based on UNIX System V Release 3.2, and it is highly compatible with other Release 3.2 implementations. SCO UNIX is multitasking and multiuser; in fact, its appeal (and that of Xenix) over the years has stemmed from its multiuser capabilities. SCO UNIX is a plain-vanilla implementation of UNIX, and its architecture is well-described in the first part of this chapter.

Graphics and GUIs

SCO UNIX supports the X Window library of graphic primitives, and it can run X-based applications either locally or on remote X Terminal servers. Open Desktop is SCO's GUI, which is based on X. Both OSF/Motif and OPEN LOOK have been implemented under SCO UNIX, so developers and users have their choice of available GUIs.

Networking

SCO UNIX can be either a client or server on a TCP/IP network, and the operating system comes with a complete suite of networking applications and utilities. In addition, SCO UNIX can be configured as a NetWare client.

Development Tools

A suite of development tools, including language compilers, debuggers, editors, and utilities, is available for SCO UNIX. Because SCO UNIX is based on standard UNIX System V, a wide variety of third-party development tools are also available.

SunSoft Solaris

Sun Microsystems is the world's leading vendor of RISC-based UNIX workstations and servers. Over the years, Sun has developed a reputation for world-class operating systems based on standard hardware platforms.

In 1987, Sun broke away from the Motorola 68000 family of processors and introduced its own CPU, a RISC-architecture design called SPARC. Since then, Sun has made a number of attempts to establish the SPARC architecture as an industry standard (including a somewhat halfhearted attempt to stimulate competitors to develop Sun workstation clones based on the SPARC processor), but the company has had little success to date. Sun has never stopped trying to position SPARC-based systems as the natural successors to the PC, however.

In early 1991, a massive rethinking of Sun's products and strategies led to a breakup of the company into a number of business units. One such unit was SunSoft, which was formed by pulling Sun's operating system and application developers into a new software development group. In September 1991, SunSoft announced its intention to develop an Intel version of its SPARC operating system called Solaris 2.0. That same month, the company purchased INTERACTIVE Systems Corporation, publisher of an enhanced version of UNIX System V Release 3.2, from Eastman Kodak Company. This acquisition, plus the preannouncement of Solaris 2.0, placed SunSoft in direct competition with SCO.

The strategic reason for Sun to enter the Intel market is clear. The size of the installed base of Intel-based PCs dwarfs the SPARC installed base. In order to be a serious contender for adoption by PC users moving up to more complex client/server networks, SunSoft had to provide a compatible upgrade path. By first migrating customers to Solaris on PCs, it makes it much easier to further migrate these customers to Solaris-based SPARC systems when their server needs can no longer be fulfilled by PCs.

9 • Windows NT Versus UNIX

The strategic goal is clear, but the execution still needs some work. By September 1992, Sun was distributing only early release (beta-level) copies of Solaris 2.0 for PCs. Figure 9.3 is a screenshot from Solaris 2.0. Two months later, the company preannounced Solaris 2.1, and stated that the new release would be available for PCs early in 1993. Much of the product description for Solaris 2.1 for the PC isn't available yet. The following capsule description, therefore, is based on Solaris 2.0, with information about Version 2.1 when it was available.

Figure 9.3. *SunSoft's Solaris 2.0.*

System Architecture

Solaris is based on UNIX System V Release 4, which incorporates source-code compatibility with Berkeley BSD, UNIX System V Release 3.2, Sun's SunOS, and SCO Xenix into one product. System V Release 4 was the "grand unifier"

Windows NT: The Next Generation

of the UNIX world because it merged all the most popular UNIX variants into a single product. In theory, at least, this enables a high degree of compatibility among UNIX applications and platforms.

In addition to the basic capabilities of System V, which includes supports for multitasking and multiuser applications, Solaris also supports multithreading and symmetric multiprocessing, as well as extensions for real-time processing (where time-critical processes can be executed precisely when they are needed).

Solaris also implements a distributed object-oriented architecture at the application development level. The Solaris implementation, called Project DOE (for distributed objects everywhere), supports interobject communication both locally and across a network.

Solaris includes a family of graphical utilities designed to simplify the normally complex system administration tasks, both locally and across the network. The following network-savvy utilities are included:

- Online Backup, an automated mass storage backup and restore utility
- User Manager, which adds new accounts and builds user directories anywhere on the network
- Database Manager, which manages the central system administration database (not unlike NT's Registry Editor)
- Print Manager, which controls and connects print servers
- Host Manager, which connects client systems to the network as stand-alone systems, diskless clients, or dataless clients
- Software Manager, which allows administrators to access, install, and configure applications locally and across the network

Finally, Solaris SHIELD brings Solaris' security up to the full C2 level, and ASET allows system administrators to audit security on any PC or server on the network.

Graphics and GUIs

Sun has always been a leader in bringing graphic capabilities to UNIX, and SunSoft continues this tradition in Solaris. Above the System Call Interface level, Solaris offers the OpenWindows application development platform. OpenWindows encompasses both X Window and Networked Window Server (NeWS, a Sun-proprietary graphics primitive library) functionality. In effect, OpenWindows is the Solaris API for graphics application development.

Above OpenWindows, Solaris offers the OPEN LOOK GUI. As mentioned earlier, OPEN LOOK was originally designed by Sun and still finds its greatest popularity on SPARC platforms, but other UNIX vendors also offer OPEN LOOK, generally as a substitute for their "default" GUIs.

Also included is DeskSet, a suite of 15 workgroup and personal productivity applications. DeskSet's applications can be thought of as a UNIX equivalent to the standard mini-applications, or applets, included in Windows for Workgroups. Additionally, Solaris' equivalent to Windows' OLE functionality is called ToolTalk. Solaris supports XGL, a library of graphics primitives for 2-D and 3-D graphics applications, which consists of an API, a hardware device driver interface, and a runtime environment.

Networking

Network support is one of the strongest features of Solaris. SunSoft calls its network support capabilities ONC+, for Open Network Computing. It supports TCP/IP, Novell NetWare IPX, and other protocols.

Both the standardized remote procedure call interface and Sun's proprietary mechanism for standardizing network data representation, called External Data Representation or XDR, are available. The Network File System (NFS) is supported, as is the Network Information Service Enterprise Naming Service (NIS+). NIS+ is a secure repository of information about all the users, printers, and servers on the network, which enables network management to be done from any system on the network. It also enables new systems just attaching to the network to instantly come up to speed about the network's current configuration.

Windows NT: The Next Generation

A variety of additional networking features are available, including an automatic mounting facility that mounts remote file systems as needed for access, without manual user intervention. JumpStart enables a single system to install and configure the software on every system across the network simultaneously, without user interaction. This same facility enables software upgrades to be installed selectively or on every networked system.

Application Development Tools

Both SunSoft and a host of third-party developers provide programming languages, debuggers, editors, object libraries, device driver libraries, and other development tools. Because Solaris is the most popular UNIX workstation operating system, many compatible development tools will be available. (However, the library of UNIX development tools pales by comparison with the existing range of Windows tools, and Windows tools are usually also more widely available and less expensive than their UNIX counterparts. It will, of course, take quite some time for a broad range of NT-specific tools to reach the market.)

Univel UnixWare

Univel's UnixWare is both the newest (because it only began to ship in late 1992) and oldest (because it's a direct descendent of AT&T UNIX and a complete implementation of the latest version of UNIX, System V Release 4.2) UNIX on the market. In September 1991, Novell and AT&T's UNIX System Laboratories formed a joint venture whose charter was to create an Intel-architecture UNIX that would be equally useful in both the Internet TCP/IP and NetWare IPX/SPX worlds. UnixWare, which was officially announced in October 1992, was the result of this venture. Figure 9.4 shows a UnixWare screen.

9 • *Windows NT Versus UNIX*

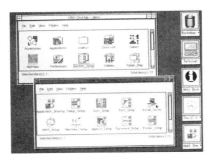

Figure 9.4. *Univel's UnixWare.*

UnixWare is equally at home in client and server environments. The software is sold in two versions: UnixWare Personal Edition, and UnixWare Application Server. Both versions offer a graphic user interface, the ability to act as clients on both TCP/IP and IPX/SPX networks, graphical installation and system administration utilities, and the Veritas high-reliability file system.

Both versions can run DOS applications under UNIX as an emulator, and both support an optional DOS/Windows emulator. The Personal Edition is designed to act as a client only, and the Application Server can simultaneously be both a UNIX server and NetWare client. The Application Server also supports Sun's NFS Network File System and can supply X Window applications to X server terminals across both NetWare and TCP/IP networks.

UnixWare has a high degree of binary compatibility with Xenix, SCO UNIX, Interactive UNIX, and System V applications. At its introduction, Univel demonstrated SCO UNIX and Xenix shrink-wrapped applications running on UnixWare without any modification or recompilation. If this demonstration was indicative of UnixWare's compatibility, it indicates that System V Release 4.2 might finally be the Rosetta stone of UNIX compatibility that the computer industry has been seeking for years.

Windows NT: The Next Generation

In January 1993, Novell acquired USL from AT&T, and in so doing acquired all of AT&T's UNIX technology, including powerful add-ons such as the TUXEDO transaction processing system. With a unified UNIX, control over UNIX licensing and development, and the largest PC network operating system installed base, Univel and Novell are well-positioned to compete head-to-head with Microsoft for the future of desktop and network computing.

System Architecture

UnixWare is based on UNIX System V Release 4.2. It runs software that complies with the Intel Binary Compatibility Standard 2 (primarily Xenix, SCO UNIX, and System V applications) without requiring recompilation. UnixWare supports multitasking and multiuser applications and uses the same enhanced security capabilities present in System V Release 4.2, which Univel claims brings UnixWare into C2-level compliance.

UnixWare supports the Veritas Advanced File System, which supports such features as online disk configuration, disk spanning, mirroring and striping, and remote disk administration. Graphical system administration utilities support user account administration, printer installation and selection, local and remote file backup and restore, file system management, and networking management.

Graphics and GUIs

UnixWare implements a three-layer graphics environment based on the latest version of X Window, called X11R5. Above X Window is a layer called MoOLIT, which provides C-language-level support for both the OSF/Motif (Mo) and Sun OPEN LOOK (OLIT) GUIs.

Above MoOLIT is the UnixWare Desktop Manager, a straightforward GUI that can have either an OPEN LOOK or Motif look and feel at the user's discretion. The UnixWare Software Development Kit provides an API for graphical application development. UnixWare also includes Adobe Type Manager for PostScript font support on displays and printers.

Networking

As you'd expect from Novell, UnixWare's networking support is one of its strongest features. To help you understand networking under UnixWare, I'll first separate the Personal Edition from the Application Server. The Personal Edition can be a client on either TCP/IP or NetWare IPX/SPX networks, but the Application Server can be either a server or client on TCP/IP networks, and a client on IPX/SPX networks (NetWare server capabilities will be available in late 1993). Interestingly, as if to emphasize Novell's influence on Univel, TCP/IP support is an extra-cost option for the Personal Edition; it's bundled with the Application Server version.

Both versions of UnixWare can operate simultaneously on both NetWare and TCP/IP networks, in order to use both NetWare's system services and the UNIX Internet utilities. The Application Server version can simultaneously be a server on a TCP/IP network and a client on an IPX/SPX network, and it can also act as a router, which interconnects NetWare and TCP/IP networks in order to allow data and messages to be passed between the networks. By the end of 1993, Univel plans to offer NetWare for UnixWare, which will enable the Application Server to be both a NetWare server and client.

The TCP/IP option for the Personal Edition also includes support for Sun's NFS Network File System; NFS support is standard in the Application Server. The Personal Edition can also be an X Window server (meaning that it provides an X Window graphic interface to X client applications running on a file server) on an IPX/SPX network, and optionally, on a TCP/IP network as well. Application Server systems can act either as X servers or clients on both networks.

Windows NT's networking capabilities are very similar to UnixWare's, except that UnixWare emphasizes NetWare support and NT focuses on LAN Manager. NT systems can be clients on NetWare networks, but the usefulness of these NT systems is limited by the NT NetWare provider and redirector offered by Novell. NT systems can't act as NetWare servers, and NT will not have this capability for quite some time. In addition, NT does not have the ability to act as a NetWare-TCP/IP router, although it's likely that either Microsoft or a third-party software developer will offer this capability in the future.

Windows NT: The Next Generation

On the other hand, NT can act as a LAN Manager client or server, and as a server to Windows for Workgroups and DOS Workgroup Connection systems, using the NetBEUI transport protocol. NetBEUI is not supported by UnixWare, and it's unclear whether a UnixWare system can be a LAN Manager client without third-party software support. (Microsoft offers a version of LAN Manager called LAN Manager for UNIX, which includes support for NetBEUI and enables UNIX systems to act as LAN Manager clients or servers, but it's not known whether Microsoft plans to port its software to UnixWare.)

NT's TCP/IP support is quite similar to that of UnixWare. NT systems can act as either clients or servers on TCP/IP networks, and they can take advantage of the same range of Internet utilities supported by UnixWare. And, both NT and UnixWare use the same streams architecture for supporting multiple transport protocols. In fact, the same streams drivers used in NetWare will be compatible with NT. To support networks other than NetWare and TCP/IP, however, network-specific redirectors, providers, and other elements are required. In these areas, UnixWare holds an advantage over Windows, due to UNIX System V's long head start on network support.

Development Tools

The UnixWare Software Development Kit includes a C compiler, linker, and debugger. In addition, it includes software packaging tools necessary for creating international applications and NetWare API libraries for clients and servers.

A set of GUI tools provides an Application Builder, X Window development package, MoOLIT development package, Desktop Manager API, and the Windowing Korn Shell. The Driver Development Kit supports streams and device driver software development. The MTF Development Tools enable C language programmers to develop OSF/Motif-compatible graphical applications. In addition, many third-party software publishers are marketing development tools for System V Release 4.2, most of which can be used with UnixWare.

Decisions, Decisions

It's not enough to understand the differences between Windows NT and UNIX. You also need to know the differences between the different flavors of UNIX in order to make an informed decision. The following sections contain brief descriptions of the four UNIX variants examined in this chapter.

NeXT NeXTSTEP

- An excellent application development environment; a true object-oriented operating system
- Good connectivity with other desktop operating systems
- Limited compatibility with other UNIX variants
- Primarily a client operating system
- This company is struggling, both technically and financially, and its long-term viability is in question

SCO UNIX

- A market leader in desktop UNIX
- A good supply of third-party applications
- Based on an older version of UNIX: System V, Release 3.2—superseded by more current competitive versions
- Usable as either a client or server; it's probably stronger as a client

Windows NT: The Next Generation

Sun Solaris

- A version of UNIX from the world's leading RISC workstation vendor, but when will they deliver?
- Excellent networking support
- Good graphics development tools
- Solid client and server performer

Univel UnixWare

- Based on UNIX System V Release 4.2, the most recent version
- Unsurpassed networking support, especially for mixed TCP/IP and NetWare networks
- Good GUI development tools
- Solid client and server performer; separate versions for clients and servers

Table 9.1 compares the key features of the four primary PC UNIX variants and Windows NT.

Table 9.1. Windows NT compared with four PC-based UNIX variants.

Feature	NeXTSTEP Rel. 3	SCO UNIX Rel. 4	Solaris 2.1	UnixWare	Windows NT
Operating System Base	Mach/BSD 4.3	System V Release 3.2	System V Release 4	System V Release 4.2	Mach/Windows
Multitasking	Yes	Yes	Yes	Yes	Yes
Multiuser	Yes	Yes	Yes	Yes	Yes
Symmetric Multi-processing	No	No	Yes	Yes	Yes

9 • Windows NT Versus UNIX

Feature	NeXTSTEP Rel. 3	SCO UNIX Rel. 4	Solaris 2.1	UnixWare	Windows NT
Virtual Memory	Yes	Yes	Yes	Yes	Yes
C2-Level Security	No	No	Optional	Optional	Yes
Graphical User Interface(s)	Workspace Manager	OSF/Motif	OPEN LOOK	OSF/Motif, OPEN LOOK, Desktop Manager	Windows NT/ 3.X GUI
X Window Version	Not Applicable	X11 Release 4	X11 Release 4	X11 Release 5	Not Applicable
DOS Emulator	Optional (SoftPC)	Optional	Optional (SoftPC)	DR DOS 6.0	Yes
Runs 16-bit Windows Real Mode Applications	Optional (SoftPC)	No	Optional (SoftPC)	Optional	Most
Runs 16-bit Windows Enhanced Mode Applications	No	No	No	No	Yes
Runs 32-bit Windows Applications	No	No	No	No	Yes
Runs OS/2 Applications	No	No	No	No	1.X Character Mode Only
POSIX Compatible	No	Yes	Yes	Yes	Yes
System V Binary Compatible	No	Yes	Yes	Yes	No

continues

Windows NT: The Next Generation

Table 9.1. continued

Feature	NeXTSTEP Rel. 3	SCO UNIX Rel. 4	Solaris 2.1	UnixWare	Windows NT
Networking Support	TCP/IP, IPX/SPX (client only), NFS	TCP/IP, NFS	TCP/IP, NFS	IPX/SPX, TCP/IP, NFS	NetBEUI, TCP/IP IPX/SPX (from Novell)
Client or Server Orientation	Client	Both	Both	Client (Personal Edition), Server (Application Server)	Both (probably separate versions for client and server)

Making any direct comparisons between Windows NT and the most important PC UNIX variants is difficult. NT has an enormous amount of power and functionality, but until Microsoft delivers it to end users and works out the bugs, NT's power is only a promise. UNIX is a robust, time-tested operating system that, with NeXTSTEP, demonstrates the latest thinking about operating system design.

Windows NT was designed to provide UNIX's functionality without carrying around UNIX's endless commands, shells, and GUIs. NT also provides a more standardized application development platform, with one GUI and API. However, versions like UnixWare are beginning to suggest that UNIX vendors can set and enforce application programming standards.

For Windows users who are outgrowing their existing systems and want to move to client/server computing, the choice between Windows NT and UNIX is not an easy one. Migrating to Windows NT is the path of least resistance, but it's not automatically the right choice in all cases. One area in which NT holds a sizable advantage is in the availability of a wide variety of (relatively) inexpensive applications, due to NT's ability to run most existing DOS and 16-bit Windows programs. These applications won't be able to take advantage of NT's many new features, but they're available right now

and can provide a migration path to true 32-bit NT-specific versions in the future.

On the other hand, users who need applications that can take advantage of preemptive multitasking, multiprocessing, and other advanced features will find few, if any, NT versions to choose from. Far more of these "mission-critical" applications are available for UNIX than for NT, now and in the near future.

Networking users need to consider their existing and future network architectures before choosing between NT and UNIX. LAN Manager users will find NT to be a far more hospitable client or server than UNIX, while NetWare users may have difficulty integrating NT systems into their existing networks. UNIX (UnixWare, at least) will work seamlessly in NetWare networks, either as a client or, in the near future, as a server. In short, potential NT users owe it to themselves to evaluate the options offered by UNIX before making a choice.

10

Making the Choice: Windows NT or Not?

Windows NT: The Next Generation

This chapter examines four of the key criteria for selecting an operating system and evaluates DOS-based Windows, OS/2, UNIX, and Windows NT on each factor. Some additional tips that you can consider when making your decision about an operating system are also covered.

The Decision Dilemma: Four Criteria for Action

The choice of which operating system to use, whether for a single PC or an entire enterprise, is one of the biggest computer decisions you'll ever need to make. The operating system you select will dictate your choices in the following areas:

- Compatible hardware and hardware requirements
- Available applications and utilities
- Development tools
- Availability of technical personnel
- Support and end-user training

The initial cost of acquiring computer hardware and software is a small fraction of the total cost of a computer system. Human costs, such as support, training, and ongoing application development, make up the biggest share of the expense. After users, developers, and support personnel are thoroughly familiar with an operating system and a set of applications, the costs of training them to use and support a new operating system—along with the costs of lost productivity while they learn—are staggering. That's why it's so critical to make the right choice about an operating system, and more importantly, why it's essential to test and phase in an operating system, instead of attempting to convert every computer at once. Several criteria are useful when evaluating an operating system—and computer systems in general—to determine if the system meets your needs. This chapter looks at the four most important criteria that relate to how the operating system works now. Chapter 11, "The Future of Windows NT," examines three more

criteria relating to how you can protect your operating system investment in the future.

The following four factors are examined in this chapter:

- Functionality
- Reliability
- Interoperability
- Compatibility

DOS-based Windows, OS/2, UNIX, and Windows NT are discussed in the following sections. Each system may or may not meet your requirements within the framework of these factors.

Functionality

Perhaps the most important factor in selecting an operating system is its functionality—what does the operating system do, and does it work as advertised? Currently, with more than 100 million PCs installed worldwide, the demand for new applications or uses for computer systems (such as multimedia and voice mail) is dwarfed by the need for more efficient, more productive, and faster ways of doing existing jobs.

To the extent that they've been tested and proven in the marketplace, DOS, Windows, OS/2, and UNIX all work. Within limits, they do what their developers say they'll do. Problems arise, however, when they are misapplied to applications or when their capabilities are stretched to the limit. An excellent example of an operating system whose functionality has been pushed, pulled, and stretched far beyond its original design is DOS.

DOS and Windows

In the beginning, DOS was an operating system designed to be used by one user on a computer with no more than 640K of memory. A five- or ten-megabyte hard disk was all that most PC buyers could ever afford. Over the

Windows NT: The Next Generation

years, users demanded more and more from their computers, and DOS struggled to keep up. Hardware and application designs have always run at least one step ahead of DOS, which forced developers to come up with creative, and often partially incompatible, methods of extending DOS to do the job. The following list is just a portion of the new capabilities (both software and hardware) that challenge DOS:

- More memory for bigger programs
- More mass storage for larger, and more, files
- Faster processors, able to do more in less time
- Detailed displays for new applications such as desktop publishing
- Powerful, high-resolution printers and other output devices
- Easier-to-use, graphics-oriented programs
- Software for displaying and printing text and graphics of near-typeset quality
- A bewildering array of peripherals for an equally bewildering array of applications
- Multitasking to support more users and more programs at one time
- Networking and communications
- Portability (portable computers)

There are many more examples, but you get the point. Through the years, DOS has been asked to do more than it was ever designed to do. The DOS and Windows combination, maligned because its performance and reliability often leave much to be desired, can be seen as nearly miraculous in comparison to the original DOS and PC.

DOS is still the most popular operating system in history, and 16-bit Windows is the fastest-growing operating environment, but both are showing their age. Windows has sometimes been described as a beautiful new structure built on a crumbling foundation—the reflective glass and high-speed elevators can't disguise the fact that the pipes leak, the heat doesn't always work, and the building is beginning to lean.

As noted in Chapter 1, "The Road to Windows NT," by the mid-eighties, the limitations of DOS were evident to many people, including Microsoft's senior managers. They knew that DOS's architecture was too limited to handle the tasks that it would be asked to perform in the future. Microsoft and IBM designed OS/2 as their first attempt to escape the limitations of DOS while maintaining compatibility with DOS applications. Although OS/2 didn't break any new architectural ground, it took advantage of the capabilities of Intel's 80286 and 80386 processors in ways that DOS could not.

OS/2

In many ways, OS/2 is the true precursor of Windows NT, although OS/2's architecture differs greatly from that of NT. OS/2 1.0 eliminated the segmented memory addressing that continues to plague DOS programmers and introduced virtual memory—although its original limits of 16M of physical memory and 48M of virtual memory look downright anemic compared to the gigabyte capacities of OS/2 2.1 and NT.

OS/2 implements what was originally called memory isolation (IBM now calls it Crash Protection), which ensures that programs cannot modify the memory of other programs without permission and isolates user programs from the operating system so errant applications can't crash the entire system. (NT's protected subsystems and virtual memory manager provide a more advanced level of protection than OS/2 1.0 originally did, but the goals underlying both operating systems are the same.)

Unlike DOS, which allows applications to interact directly with hardware and bypass any safeguards built into the operating system, OS/2 forces most applications to access the computer's hardware through the operating system and places strict limits on the few remaining programs that have to talk directly to hardware. OS/2 also takes control of parceling out access to the system's peripherals. In DOS, any program can grab control of any peripherals and keep control for as long as it likes, even if it means crashing the entire system.

OS/2 1.0 introduced support for multitasking, which prior to that time had been impossible under DOS without a third-party system extension such as DESQview. OS/2 1.0 also introduced a system kernel, a standard API,

Windows NT: The Next Generation

and replaceable device subsystems that allowed application developers to customize the system. Compared to the 32-bit architecture of OS/2 2.1 and the more advanced architecture of Windows NT, OS/2 1.0 was fairly crude, although it gave many PC users their first taste of industrial-strength computing.

The failure of OS/2 to find a wide market was due not to the operating system's design, but to its usability. In its original incarnation, OS/2 didn't live up to its hype. It needed eight megabytes of RAM during an era when most PCs had only one or two megabytes, and it was excruciatingly slow. Many DOS applications ran afoul of OS/2's memory isolation scheme and its hardware access control features—they wouldn't run without significant modifications.

The Presentation Manager GUI that was promised at the time of OS/2's announcement didn't ship for 18 months, and development tools were very slow to come to market. LAN Manager, the OS/2-based network operating system, was very unstable when it first shipped. OS/2 1.0 is an excellent example of an operating system that flunked the functionality test. It did most of what Microsoft and IBM claimed it would do, but not in a way that satisfied customers' needs or expectations. Critical features that were promised to users and developers were not delivered when they were needed.

OS/2's slow, disappointing start, combined with the launch of Windows 3.0 (whose enormous sales greatly exceeded even the most optimistic forecasts), led directly to Microsoft's refocus on DOS and Windows, which further eroded OS/2's market support. OS/2 2.1 has overcome almost all the limitations of Version 1.0. The operating system is generally very reliable and runs most DOS and Windows 3.0 applications, with Windows 3.1 support nearly complete.

OS/2 is now a full 32-bit operating system that supports both multitasking and multithreaded operation, and its memory and operating system protection features have been greatly expanded since Version 1.0. The Workplace Shell, OS/2 2.0's GUI built on top of the Presentation Manager, is considerably closer in its design and implementation to the Apple Macintosh than is the Windows Program Manager, and many users strongly prefer the OS/2 user interface to that of Windows.

Technology has caught up to OS/2, and the dramatic declines in PC prices over the last few years and advances in hard disk and display technology have brought the cost of an OS/2-compatible system down to an affordable level. The functionality of today's OS/2 equals or surpasses that of the Windows environment by a wide margin, yet 16-bit Windows outsells OS/2 by close to ten-to-one. In short, OS/2 is an excellent example of a situation in which early decisions to ship an operating system without some essential functionality and performance continue to put a damper on market acceptance, although the product's initial deficiencies have long since been remedied.

UNIX

UNIX has always been an extremely powerful and flexible operating system. Unlike the other desktop operating systems, UNIX was designed from the beginning to be a multiuser operating system and (by definition) also a multitasking operating system.

As noted in Chapter 9, "Windows NT Versus UNIX," members of the broad family of UNIX variants incorporate multitasking, multithreading, and multiprocessing, with full 32-bit operation, linear memory addressing, virtual memory, extensive networking support, access control and system integrity security, multiple APIs, platform portability, and more. UNIX (or more precisely, the range of UNIX variants) is, and has been for a long time, a true industrial-strength operating system.

The problem with UNIX has never been lack of functionality. UNIX's big drawback in the PC world is usability. Remember that UNIX, in the form of Microsoft's XENIX, made it to the desktop just a few years after DOS.

If technical specifications were the most important thing, UNIX should have mopped the floor with DOS, but it didn't, for several reasons. First, UNIX was big. It required 4M to 8M of RAM when DOS was running in 640K, and it required many megabytes of storage when big hard disks were extremely expensive. Most importantly, UNIX was incredibly cryptic. UNIX could do almost anything, but to use it, users had to memorize (or look up) bewildering commands whose names and syntax (which meant something to their creators long ago) were almost impossible for mere mortals to understand.

Windows NT: The Next Generation

In short, UNIX scared people away. In fact, UNIX would have all but died on the PC platform by the mid-eighties if it wasn't the best multiuser environment on the desktop. (Not to take anything away from the DOS clones and add-ons that provide multiuser capabilities to DOS, but UNIX is far more robust.)

As long as they were willing to forego most PC graphics, multiple users could share a single UNIX PC with very inexpensive ASCII terminals. No networks were required. The cost per user for hardware could drop from several thousand dollars, when everyone had their own PCs, to under a thousand dollars. That's what kept XENIX, and UNIX, in the running on the desktop throughout the eighties.

Now, of course, UNIX supports GUIs that present a graphical face to users. As UNIX has become friendlier, PC users have become more sophisticated about networks and directories. With X Terminal, the UNIX standard API for creating distributed graphic applications, and two popular user interfaces, OSF/Motif and Sun OPEN LOOK, UNIX's usability for average users finally matches its functionality. As Microsoft educates customers about the extensive system hardware requirements of Windows NT, the old bias against UNIX as a system resource hog is likely to fade away. In this new era, at least UNIX and NT's basic functionality are quite evenly matched.

Windows NT

What of Windows NT? The first half of this book explored NT's functionality in detail. Suffice it to say that NT is also an industrial-strength system—a worthy successor to DOS and 16-bit Windows that goes OS/2 one better with additional features, such as greatly improved security and multiprocessing support. NT was designed to provide virtually all the functionality of UNIX (the biggest exception being NT's lack of multiuser capabilities), better interoperability with the DOS-based Windows and NetWare worlds, and a more understandable command set designed from the ground up with a GUI in mind.

The fact that NT is a new operating system, however, is a double-edged sword. On one hand, NT doesn't carry the baggage that DOS and UNIX have

picked up over the years in the form of system extensions, new commands, and new functions, many of which were originally developed to remedy real or perceived flaws in the basic operating system.

To maintain compatibility with these extensions, DOS and UNIX have had to make some serious compromises in the form of performance, size, or compatibility. On the other hand, DOS and UNIX are seasoned operating systems; DOS has been around for more than a decade, and UNIX has been out for almost a quarter-century. Both operating systems have had plenty of time to address bugs and their most glaring deficiencies.

NT is new, and any entirely new operating system, especially one as complex as NT, needs a significant amount of "shakedown" time to identify and fix its problems. When NT ships to customers, it will probably not meet all the functionality targets and promises made by Microsoft in the summer of 1992, when NT's first software developer kits were distributed.

NT, for example, will require more memory than the 8M that Microsoft originally indicated. The current beta version is much too slow and it is limited to systems with less than 12M of RAM (developers are encouraged to use 16M or more). The virtual DOS machines used for DOS and 16-bit Windows emulation continue to be incompatible with a significant number of applications, and the performance of programs running under them lags far behind equivalent PCs running DOS and 16-bit Windows directly. (Performance problems are, at least in part, due to Microsoft's decision to use a DOS emulator for running DOS and 16-bit Windows applications. An emulator "clones" the PC's hardware and operating system entirely in software and is thus inherently less efficient than DOS running directly on a comparable Intel 80x86-family processor.)

Other functionality issues are tied to more fundamental design decisions. NT's OS/2 protected subsystem supports only character-mode applications, and Microsoft hasn't indicated that it plans to support graphical OS/2 applications or the Workplace Shell. Unless Microsoft reverses this decision, or a third party designs an OS/2 API that relieves this constraint, NT's OS/2 compatibility features will be limited or useless for many applications. The POSIX subsystem provides compatibility with many UNIX programs written for POSIX compliance, but the POSIX standard is evolving rapidly. Will

Windows NT: The Next Generation

Microsoft give high priority to updating and improving the POSIX subsystem, or will it pay more attention to the core functionality of NT and compatibility with 16-bit Windows?

On paper, NT is a dream operating system—powerful, flexible, easy-to-use, and compatible. It's still too early to tell how NT will perform in the real world, however, and it's impossible to know how much of NT's functionality will need to be postponed or abandoned in order to meet Microsoft's release schedule. The real test for Windows NT will come six months to a year after its initial release. If it performs as originally projected, and if it has the full functionality promised by Microsoft, then and only then will NT's functionality promises be fulfilled.

Reliability

The reliability of an operating system is a measure of how often the following things happen (or are likely to happen):

- An application crashes, but the operating system continues to run.
- An application interferes with the operation of another program, causing one or both to crash.
- An application crash brings down the entire operating system.
- The operating system crashes, due to no fault of the applications.
- An application reads from or writes to a file that it's not supposed to access or performs the wrong operation on an accessible file, resulting in either compromised security or corrupted data.
- A power failure or another catastrophic hardware failure corrupts programs and data, making it difficult or impossible to recover.
- Unauthorized users or programs penetrate the system, defeat access control security, and may destroy system integrity.

DOS and Windows

DOS was designed for a single-user, single-tasking world, with no networks or modems—one user, one computer. As a result, the reliability of DOS, and to a slightly lesser extent, of 16-bit Windows, leaves a lot to be desired.

If Enter is the most popular key on a DOS keyboard, the second most popular choice probably is the Ctrl-Alt-Del combination that reboots the system. An application crash on a DOS system almost always crashes the operating system as well. Even though DOS is not a multitasking operating system, it supports utilities called terminate-and-stay-resident programs, or TSRs. Conflicts between TSRs and applications, and between TSRs themselves, are common and often turn the process of determining exactly why a DOS system repeatedly fails into a nightmare. There are no integral access security features, and only a handful of file security safeguards. For the most part, DOS applications can do whatever they want to memory and files. To a large extent, this is what has made DOS PCs so vulnerable to viruses and computer hackers.

Windows 3.1 has added some rudimentary safeguards against application crashes and memory protection violations. Today, it's more likely that Windows will continue running after an application crash, and users often have the option of either terminating a hung application or rebooting the entire system.

Thanks to additional safeguards built into Windows 3.1, DOS can now often survive Windows crashes. In addition, third-party utilities and system extensions provide some measure of access control and recovery in the event of power failure or hardware crashes. Nevertheless, DOS and Windows's system reliability still leave a lot to be desired for critical applications such as banking and financial transaction processing, which is one reason why so many major corporations and government organizations continue to rely on mainframe computers. Mainframes, while they're rapidly becoming obsolete in a world of client/server networks and distributed computing, run operating systems designed and proven to be reliable for transaction processing.

Windows NT: The Next Generation

OS/2

OS/2, on the other hand, was designed to provide a more stable platform than DOS-based Windows for application development and execution. OS/2 protects each application's memory from incursions by other programs and isolates the operating system from applications, so it's difficult for any single application to crash the entire system.

OS/2 has several holes, however, mostly involving security. Neither OS/2 nor the high performance file system (HPFS) provide much in the way of access security, so it's relatively easy to penetrate an OS/2 system. IBM does provide a combination password protection/screen saver utility, but it simply limits access to a single system, not to individual system components or the file system. Penetrating the system is as easy as typing on the keyboard of an unlocked system. (IBM provides an enhanced version of HPFS for LAN Server, its proprietary version of LAN Manager, which enhances OS/2's access security and performance.)

After you get past the initial password, there are few safeguards against security violations. Applications can read and write files on the hard disk with impunity. As with Windows, it's possible to install third-party utilities and system extensions that add security features, but adding these new features runs the risk of causing incompatibility problems with the system and other applications.

Although IBM has tried to keep up with the latest thinking about networking, communications, and interoperability and the burdens that these capabilities place on system integrity, it's also clear that OS/2's fundamental architecture is still stuck in the "one person, one machine" mode. IBM claims that OS/2 is an industrial-strength operating system, but it clearly needs more security horsepower to compete with UNIX and Windows NT. This may be one reason why IBM is working on a microkernel operating system that will provide UNIX functionality, run OS/2 applications, and comply with the U.S. Government's C2 level of security.

UNIX

Unlike the desktop PC model around which Windows and OS/2 were designed, UNIX has always followed the "several users, one machine" model. UNIX was designed from the beginning to be a multiuser, multitasking operating system, so memory protection and access control security have been a part of the operating system for many years. A faulty application rarely crashes the entire system, but it's not terribly difficult for a UNIX programmer to penetrate security and modify key operating system files.

For example, one programmer used a well-known flaw in UNIX's security system to have remote systems electronically mail their encrypted password files to him. He then used a widely available technique for decrypting the passwords (by applying the fact that most people use their own names, the name of a relative or loved one, commonly used words, or telephone numbers as their password). After he successfully cracked one or two passwords, he was able to decrypt all of them, including the system administrator's password. By so doing, he obtained unlimited access to the system. Most UNIX vendors have beefed up their software's security capabilities. Sun, for example, sells an add-on for Solaris that implements full C2-level security, which is equivalent to NT's proposed capabilities. Be aware that you might need to buy additional software to get the best possible system security and reliability.

This story shouldn't be seen as a reason not to use UNIX, but rather as a warning that UNIX system administrators must be vigilant. Unlike Windows, OS/2, and NT, the source code of UNIX has been distributed worldwide and studied by tens or even hundreds of thousands of programmers. The source code of any operating system is the key—anyone who understands how an operating system works, down to the individual instruction level, can identify and take advantage of opportunities to penetrate, modify, and perhaps even destroy the system. After a flaw in system security or integrity is identified, it's essential that UNIX administrators fix the problem immediately. If it isn't fixed, they run the risk of major, and possibly catastrophic, problems.

The other key area that has, until quite recently, been a major thorn in the side of UNIX users is power-fail recovery. When I was a UNIX systems marketing manager five years ago, I remember constantly reminding DOS users who were moving to UNIX to never turn off their computers' power before first running the shutdown program. As a multitasking system, many processes are constantly running under UNIX, including processes that are normally invisible to the user. These processes include the virtual memory manager, which intermittently writes, or flushes, pages of data from RAM to the hard disk. The latest version of all or a portion of a file might exist only within RAM until it's flushed to the hard disk for permanent storage.

If the power fails before this process completes, or if the user simply turns off the power, the file updates held in RAM are lost. In addition, other disk-related processes are also likely to be interrupted by a power failure. For the most part, UNIX systems can recover from these failures with minimal data loss, but it's a constant area of concern. As a rule of thumb, for both UNIX and NT systems, a good uninterruptible power supply is one of your best investments in system reliability (along with a hard disk backup device). Most UNIX systems can "talk" to an intelligent UPS device and automatically run the shutdown process, which flushes all pending information to the hard disk, closes all running applications, and enables power to be turned off safely.

Windows NT

NT has robust access control and system integrity maintenance features. These features provide full C2-level security. In addition, they prohibit one application from interfering with another, and they insulate the NT executive from the protected subsystems and the subsystems from client applications. In theory, no application can crash or modify a subsystem, and no application or subsystem can crash the executive.

NT includes fault-tolerant features that require additional software on other operating systems. NT supports disk striping with parity and mirroring, which enables the system to continue running in the event of a disk drive or controller failure. NT can also control and communicate with a UPS and, like UNIX, it can execute a safe shutdown before power fails entirely. These

features have not been tested in extensive real-world applications, however, so their robustness and reliability under a variety of conditions remain uncertain.

Over time, it's likely that flaws in NT's security and memory protection schemes will be identified and exploited. Chapter 4, "A Quick Walk Through Windows NT," looked at NT's administrative tools, including the Registry Editor, and noted that it could view and modify almost any system parameter. Microsoft has indicated that the Registry Editor might be removed from commercially available versions of NT, but it's clear that if Microsoft could write it, outside programmers will eventually be able to create their own versions. Anyone with administrator-level permissions can wreak havoc on the system with the Registry Editor.

Chapter 6, "Networking with Windows NT," discusses the concept of trusted domains. When one domain of systems is trusted by another, the trusting domain takes the access control permissions of the trusted domain as the "gospel truth."

If someone can penetrate the access control system of a trusted domain controller, he or she should, at least theoretically, be able to access all other systems within the domain, as well as those in other trusting domains. Thus, NT system administrators must take special care when assigning trust relationships; trust always must flow from less-sensitive systems to more-sensitive ones, not vice versa. In this way, penetration of a relatively unimportant domain does not provide access to more important, and thus more closely guarded, domains.

In short, the reliability and security of Windows NT systems look good, but their real-world performance remains to be seen. For customers seeking to implement high-reliability applications under Windows NT, now is the time to begin pilot tests to gain experience and shake out problems. It's not the time, however, to jump directly to a full production system. It will take at least a year to identify, acknowledge, and either fix or work around NT's hidden flaws.

The safest route to take is to spend a year writing, debugging, and testing your applications. If you can't wait that long, consider adopting a platform like UNIX or OS/2 that has been in the field longer and is likely to be more robust.

Windows NT: The Next Generation

Interoperability

No man is an island, and increasingly, no computer is one either. It's essential that otherwise incompatible computer systems be able to share data with a minimum of conversion and manual intervention. The following sections look at each operating system to determine how it works with others and examine some options for maximizing your existing system investment.

DOS and Windows

DOS and Windows users have a variety of options available for interoperability. Obviously, DOS and Windows systems can be linked by communications software and hardware to a variety of other systems:

- They can act as terminals to mainframes and minicomputers such as IBM's AS/400 by emulating 3270 or 5250 terminals, or to non-IBM systems by emulating serial terminals like Digital's VT220.

- By adding appropriate software and network interfaces, they can act as X Terminals to UNIX systems, which makes them capable of remotely running graphic UNIX applications and using UNIX GUIs.

- DOS and Windows systems can also attach to the Internet and UNIX networks by running a TCP/IP protocol stack via the Single-Line Internet Protocol (SLIP).

- By attaching to a NetWare network, they can share the files and peripherals of a network server. (The same capabilities are available with VINES, as well as peer-to-peer networks such as LANtastic and WEB.)

- Windows for Workgroups (WFW) systems can form peer-to-peer networks to share data and peripherals, and DOS systems can connect to these networks as clients. WFW systems can in turn act as clients to an NT server.

Software and hardware that allows DOS or Windows systems to connect to almost any other computer or network is available, but the limitations of such approaches are obvious. DOS and Windows systems are almost always constrained to the role of clients, or terminals, rather than servers. Thus, the flow of data is usually lopsided—from the server or host system to the client, rather than from the client to the server or host system.

OS/2

Most DOS and Windows connectivity software and hardware also works under OS/2. In addition, OS/2 has extensive links to the IBM mainframe world. The OS/2 Communications Manager supports connections to SNA networks in which the local OS/2 system emulates a 3270 terminal. The Communications Manager also links OS/2 systems to X.25 packet-switching networks and supports a TCP/IP protocol stack for connection to the Internet and UNIX networks. Asynchronous ASCII communications to non-IBM systems are also supported.

IBM and Novell have worked together for several years to provide tight integration between IBM's PCs and NetWare, and later this year, IBM and Novell will jointly announce NetWare 4.0 for OS/2. Figure 10.1 illustrates how NetWare and OS/2 work together.

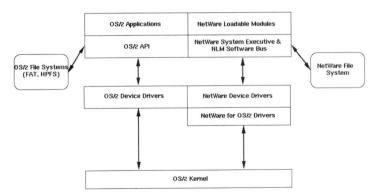

Figure 10.1. An OS/2-NetWare 4.0 block diagram, showing how NetWare is implemented as a parallel operating system on top of the OS/2 kernel.

Windows NT: The Next Generation

OS/2 also forms the backbone of IBM's LAN Server network operating system. LAN Server provides a client/server networking environment for OS/2 and DOS-based systems. OS/2 PCs can act as either clients or servers in such a network. As discussed earlier, the advanced version of LAN Server adds local server security and support for disk mirroring and duplexing to OS/2.

OS/2 systems have the horsepower to act as servers as well as clients. Their interoperability capabilities are very similar to that of DOS and Windows, with the added advantages that multitasking and multithreading provide for maintaining multiple, simultaneous communications links.

UNIX

UNIX systems have exceptional interoperability features, due in large part to the fact that they've been available for so long and have had to connect to every conceivable computer system and network. UNIX systems are commonly used as both servers and clients and as both hosts and terminals. The following types of connectivity are among the options available with various forms of UNIX:

- Support for an enormous variety of ASCII terminals and character-oriented asynchronous protocols.

- 3270 emulation and support for SNA networks.

- X.25 packet-switching networks.

- Networking, via the Internet TCP/IP protocol. Chapter 9 contains more detail about UNIX networking, but for now, keep in mind that TCP/IP is the *lingua franca* that ties together tens of thousands of educational, governmental, research, and business computers on the worldwide Internet. UNIX systems commonly support distributed file systems, such as the Networked File System (NFS), while permitting remote computers' file systems (UNIX, NetWare, OS/2, and others) to be accessed as if they all reside on the local system. Novell's UnixWare includes support for NetWare IPX/SPX protocols in its kernel, which allows a single UnixWare system to simultaneously act as a client or server on both TCP/IP and NetWare networks.

- X Windows, a standardized library of graphic primitives and functions that can be used to develop graphical networked applications.

UNIX systems provide excellent interoperability with mainframe, minicomputer, workstation, and PC systems. Unlike Windows NetWare servers that primarily share file systems and peripherals, UNIX platforms are equally well suited for situations in which the UNIX system acts as a file, communications, or application server.

Windows NT

Windows NT's interoperability features are something of a cross between DOS-based Windows and UNIX. NT can act as a client, run most DOS and 16-bit Windows connectivity software, and support virtually all PC networking and communications hardware. NT also is a full-server operating system and can support networks with DOS and Windows for Workgroups clients, as well as multiple NT clients and servers. NT comes with support for both NDIS (LAN Manager/LAN Server) and TCP/IP network protocols, and with the addition of LAN Manager for Windows NT, it will support complex networks with multiple client/server domains.

There are two big question marks about NT's interoperability, however. The first is that Microsoft is relying on third parties to support a variety of protocols and network architectures, including DECnet and AppleTalk. Because Digital Equipment Corporation (DEC) is a major proponent of Windows NT for its new line of computers based on the Alpha processor, it's likely that DECnet support will be available soon. AppleTalk is another matter. Apple and Microsoft continue to have a strained relationship. It will take some time for Microsoft and third parties to develop support for other, less-used protocols.

The other, larger interoperability question mark is support for NetWare. Novell has withdrawn Microsoft's license to include Novell's IPX/SPX code with Windows NT because Novell claims that its license covers only the immediate 16-bit Windows product line, not NT or Windows for Workgroups. Novell has demonstrated and has indicated its willingness to distribute a NetWare redirector for NT, but this would allow NT systems to be only clients on a NetWare network, rather than servers. Microsoft has indicated it

Windows NT: The Next Generation

will independently develop its own NetWare provider, redirector, and transport protocols if it can't come to a new licensing agreement with Novell.

As far as NT's interoperability is concerned, the following statements summarize the current situation:

- If your application is to use NT as a network client, or as a terminal to a serial or SNA (Systems Network Architecture) communications link, you'll have no problem finding the hardware and software you need to make it work.

- NT is also well suited to act as a server or client in a LAN Manager or Windows for Workgroups network, and although IBM will in all probability discourage it, NT systems will likely interoperate very well on LAN Server networks.

- NT offers out-of-the-box interoperability with TCP/IP networks, and many users will actually find it easier to configure NT systems for Internet environments than it is to configure UNIX systems.

- NT will probably work well as a NetWare client using Novell's own redirector, but don't expect NT to be able to act as a NetWare server anytime soon. If Microsoft and Novell can't come to a licensing agreement, Microsoft will have to reverse-engineer Novell's software—without violating any of Novell's related patents and copyrights—to offer full interoperability. It could take a year or more for Microsoft to release the required software.

- If you need to connect to anything other than a Microsoft/IBM NDIS, UNIX TCP/IP, or Novell IPX/SPX network, don't hold your breath. You need to investigate who will actually provide the software and hardware needed to make the connection and find out their release schedules before committing to NT.

Compatibility

Compatibility refers to the ability of an operating system to run a wide variety of existing software applications, without requiring the applications to

first be extensively modified. If the specific application you need isn't available for the operating system you select, you'll need to either modify and recompile an existing application (which is well-nigh impossible in an era of shrink-wrapped software) or write a new application from scratch, which is an expensive, time-consuming process.

The bigger an operating system's library of available applications is, the more likely it is that you'll be able to find the software you need to meet your requirements. In addition, because custom programming may not be required, your computer system can be fully operational faster, and at less cost, than if you select an operating system with few available applications.

DOS and Windows

DOS and Windows possess the largest base of applications in the world. There are DOS programs for virtually every horizontal or vertical application, plus thousands of utilities, drivers, and other programs that add functionality to the operating system. 16-bit Windows has only a fraction of the number of available applications that DOS supports, but the number and quality of available applications are growing by leaps and bounds.

For DOS users, however, the party is just about over. Very little new application development is going on for DOS because most software developers target the faster-growing Windows environment or shift to development tools that enable them to simultaneously develop Windows, OS/2, UNIX, and even Macintosh applications. Many DOS applications have gone into maintenance mode, meaning that although bugs are continuing to be fixed, they're not being updated with major new features.

The 16-bit Windows market is growing rapidly, but even there, the opportunities for powerful new software applications are limited because of Windows' dependence on DOS. As the Win32s API is more widely distributed and the bugs that creep into any new piece of software are fixed, application developers will begin to move their 16-bit applications to a 32-bit form in preparation for an ultimate move to full NT compatibility.

Windows NT: The Next Generation

In short, even though new DOS development is tapering off, neither DOS nor 16-bit Windows is going away, and users can be assured of a huge library of compatible applications for the foreseeable future. If you're planning new development or new applications, however, it makes more sense to go directly to 16-bit Windows, or even to the Win32s 32-bit API, after its quality, functionality, and reliability are confirmed in the marketplace.

OS/2

OS/2 is obviously compatible with all past and present OS/2 applications, as well as most DOS and Windows 3.0 applications. A version that offers Windows 3.1 compatibility is about to be released, but the fact that Microsoft had Windows 3.1 in the market for almost a year before IBM was able to support it raises some significant questions.

By the end of 1993, IBM will be on its own for DOS and Windows development. Microsoft plainly views IBM as a competitor instead of the strategic partner that it once was, and history indicates Microsoft almost never includes competitors and potential competitors in its beta testing programs. As a result, competitors are forced to play catch-up. For example, Microsoft refused to allow Novell to beta test Windows 3.1. As a result, the DR DOS design team could not support Windows 3.1 in DR DOS 6.0. Additionally, some Windows 3.1 code makes it difficult to work with DR DOS.

If Microsoft plays hardball with IBM, it's entirely conceivable that IBM's PC DOS and Microsoft's MS-DOS will begin to diverge, and it's even more likely that OS/2's support for DOS-based Windows will remain at least six months to a year behind Microsoft's latest version. Keep in mind, however, that OS/2 has a feature called dual boot capability, which allows the user to select which operating system (DOS or OS/2) to run when the computer is turned on. Thus, OS/2 users can run any DOS or Windows applications that are incompatible with OS/2 by executing them under the native DOS operating system. This feature requires that the hard disk have a separate partition for DOS and DOS/Windows applications. IBM has not indicated whether or not it plans to reproduce the Win32s API under OS/2, although IBM officials have indicated they don't currently plan to support NT applications under OS/2.

10 • Making the Choice: Windows NT or Not?

To date, most third-party OS/2 applications have been developed by organizations for their own internal use, and a quick look at the roster of available OS/2 applications indicates it has far fewer choices in most categories than 16-bit Windows does. However, OS/2's application base has been growing rapidly, and the longer Microsoft delays shipping NT, the more time allowed for OS/2 applications to be developed. For now, OS/2 users who require a high degree of Windows compatibility can expect that their Windows 3.1 applications will be supported very soon, but in the long run it may be difficult for IBM to keep up with Microsoft as it integrates full operating system capabilities into Windows.

UNIX

UNIX's compatibility is a controversial subject, due to the many UNIX variants available on the market. There are two primary schools of thought. The first says that UNIX provides a high degree of compatibility as long as you're willing to recompile source code for different UNIX platforms. The second school of thought says that shrink-wrapped applications are the only true measure of compatibility—there are precious few off-the-shelf UNIX applications.

As explained in Chapter 9, UNIX System V Release 4 marked the great unification of UNIX. AT&T/USL UNIX System V, SCO/Microsoft XENIX, Berkeley BSD, and Sun UNIX were combined into a single version of UNIX that was highly source-code compatible with the four constituent UNIX flavors. An application written for any of the four flavors could be recompiled under System V Release 4 and would, with minor modifications, run properly.

Since the release of System V Release 4, most UNIX vendors have adopted the USL version as their core functionality and added additional capabilities in the form of commands, utilities, and applications. A few major exceptions remain, of course, including OSF/1, which was specifically written to avoid using USL's code, and flavors like NeXTSTEP, which are based on Carnegie-Mellon's Mach operating system.

The high compatibility school of thought is correct if your application is written to conform to the System V Release 4 specification or POSIX, if source code is available to you for recompilation on your system, or if your

341

Windows NT: The Next Generation

software vendor has already ported the application to your system. However, if your application is written to access UNIX at the kernel level, where there are significant differences among most UNIX variants, be prepared for lots of software rewriting and testing. If you're using or wish to port to OSF/1 or NeXTSTEP, the same warning applies.

The second school of thought argues that you're not compatible if you can't take a UNIX application out of its box, install it, and run it on a variety of different UNIX-based systems. Few UNIX systems or applications can meet this criteria, but two developments are helping to improve the situation.

The first is the Intel Binary Compatibility Standard 2 (iBCS2), which enables the latest version of System V, Release 4.2, to run XENIX and SCO UNIX binaries without recompilation. Univel has successfully demonstrated several SCO UNIX binary applications running without recompilation or modification under UnixWare. The other development is OSF's nascent Application-Neutral Distribution Format, or ANDF, which enables a single application binary to run on many different, and otherwise hardware-incompatible, systems.

Some UNIX vendors also offer DOS and Windows compatibility through an emulator. Insignia Systems, the company that designed the NT virtual DOS machine for Microsoft, markets a DOS emulator called SoftPC, which runs under NeXTSTEP and some other UNIX variants. SoftPC emulates the entire DOS software and PC hardware environment on the targeted computer. Recently, Insignia added Windows 3.1 compatibility to its high-end version of SoftPC.

DOS emulators for UNIX are also available from Locus Computing and other companies. Emulators are always inefficient because they must duplicate an entire operating system and hardware platform in software, and they add to the system's cost. However, fast RISC processors and Intel's Pentium have sufficient power to run DOS applications, and possibly even 16-bit Windows applications, with adequate performance. The bottom line for UNIX compatibility includes the following:

- ■ If you have access to the source code of the UNIX application that you wish to run, or your software vendor has already compiled its application for your hardware and version of UNIX, you should have few compatibility problems. (If your chosen application runs on top of a UNIX GUI, such as OSF/Motif or OPEN LOOK, you must make sure that your UNIX variant supports the required GUI, and that you've installed a copy of the GUI software.)

- If your pre-compiled application is compatible with Intel's Binary Compatibility Standard and you're running SCO UNIX or System V Release 4.2, compatibility will not be a problem.

- If you don't have access to source code and your application vendor doesn't support either your specific hardware platform or flavor of UNIX, you could have major compatibility problems.

- If your flavor of UNIX supports a DOS emulator, you can run many DOS, and possibly even 16-bit Windows, applications. Because no emulator is a perfect duplicate of the original system's hardware and software, however, be prepared for significant incompatibility and performance problems.

- Don't expect OS/2 applications to run under any version of UNIX other than the microkernel OS under development at IBM, and don't expect native NT applications to run under any UNIX flavor whatsoever for a very long time.

Windows NT

Windows NT will be compatible with the majority of DOS and 16-bit Windows applications through the virtual DOS machine (VDM) and Windows on Win32 (WOW) emulators, respectively. (Like OS/2, NT includes a dual boot capability, so that DOS and Windows applications that are incompatible with the NT VDM or WOW can still be run by the native DOS operating system. The choice of which operating system to run is made whenever the computer is turned on.) OS/2 character-mode programs will run under the OS/2 protected subsystem, and POSIX-compatible applications will run under the POSIX subsystem. Obviously, NT will be compatible with its own native applications, but there will be only a handful of applications available when NT first ships. The biggest question marks are OS/2 and POSIX compatibility.

Windows NT: The Next Generation

Microsoft is committed to offering only one graphic user interface for all the supported NT subsystems, which means in effect that neither the OS/2 Workplace Shell nor UNIX X Window-based GUIs like OSF/Motif and OPEN LOOK will be supported directly by the operating system.

With more and more application developers turning to graphic interfaces, fewer and fewer OS/2 and POSIX applications will be supported by NT, and the value of these subsystems will decline unless Microsoft either changes its mind and adds full graphic support or third parties step in and write replacement subsystems that bypass the Win32 API and create their own user interfaces.

Current LAN Manager users will either have to adopt NT, because Microsoft will phase out support for the OS/2 version of LAN Manager after NT is available, or switch to IBM's LAN Server in order to maintain OS/2 compatibility. Compatibility with other network operating systems, including NetWare and VINES, is still a question mark, and NT users should expect ongoing compatibility problems as the Novell/Microsoft rivalry intensifies.

The following list contains a few points to keep in mind when considering NT's application and network OS compatibility:

- If you're already using DOS and 16-bit Windows, most of your applications will run under NT without modification, although they may run more slowly than you'd prefer due to Microsoft's use of emulators.

- If you're developing applications that need to run under both 16-bit Windows and Windows NT, writing your applications to conform with the functional subset defined by the Win32s API is the best way to ensure compatibility.

- If you must support OS/2 applications, NT may not be the way to go because it supports only character-mode applications; Microsoft has indicated that it won't support the OS/2 Workplace Shell.

- If UNIX/POSIX support is essential, test NT's capabilities thoroughly before you make a commitment to the operating system. Again, Microsoft's POSIX implementation is likely to be a bare-bones, character-oriented version that will not take advantage of UNIX graphic user interfaces.

- If you're currently using LAN Manager, you should start making some critical decisions. You can stay with LAN Manager, which will eventually require you to switch from OS/2 to Windows NT, you can switch to IBM's LAN Server, which is largely compatible with LAN Manager and runs under OS/2, or you can switch to NetWare, another network operating system, or UNIX.

- If you require NetWare compatibility, you might want to let the dust settle between Novell and Microsoft before moving to NT. For the time being, NT will be only as compatible as Novell will let it be, and it's not in Novell's strategic interest to support NT as a server. If client compatibility is all you need, however, the risks involved in adopting NT are much smaller.

Some Final Thoughts

In addition to everything I've said about the criteria for choosing an operating system, you should consider a few additional points if you're thinking about migrating to Windows NT:

- If you're moving up from DOS-based Windows and you want to maintain a high degree of compatibility, your choices are OS/2 and Windows NT. For DOS applications, both operating systems will offer a similar degree of compatibility and performance. But the added complexities of Windows, combined with the schism between IBM and Microsoft, suggest that NT will probably be compatible with future versions of DOS-based Windows significantly sooner than OS/2. Existing Windows users will also find the NT user interface and development environment much more familiar than that of OS/2.

- If your organization is already committed to OS/2, you should carefully consider the incremental advantages of NT before making a change. If you don't need immediate POSIX support or multiprocessing, consider staying with OS/2 for the next year (IBM's forthcoming microkernel OS will offer these features and maintain full compatibility with OS/2). The delay will also give NT a chance to stabilize and reduce your development headaches.

Windows NT: The Next Generation

- If you're already using UNIX, there are few advantages to moving to NT unless you need DOS or Windows compatibility (and access to the huge library of 16-bit Windows applications), as well as limited OS/2 support. All the other features of NT are already available in one or more flavors of UNIX. For PC users, Novell/Univel's UnixWare, SCO UNIX, and SunSoft's Solaris should be given careful consideration. For organizations with a mixture of Novell and UNIX networks, UnixWare is the obvious choice.

No matter what your situation, there are few compelling reasons to jump headfirst into NT. From the time NT is first released, it will take Microsoft six months to a year to fully stabilize the operating system and resolve most of the bugs. Use that time to test NT, design and develop your applications, and gain experience. When NT is stable and more reliable, you'll be ready to install pilot applications, and you may even be ready to move from pilot to production. With luck, NT will work as advertised, but be sure that you're ready for any contingency.

The Future of Windows NT

Windows NT: The Next Generation

This chapter looks at the future of Windows NT from a product and a market perspective, examines moves being made by competitors, and offers some market forecasts and perspectives from respected industry analysts.

Windows NT: Meeting the Market

Current and potential competitors of Microsoft, including IBM, Novell, Sun, SCO, NeXT, and others, have been going through significant strategic turmoil in an effort to take the high ground away from Windows NT. Thousands of Windows developers have had to begin thinking hard about how they will migrate to the new 32-bit world. It's also probably safe to say that thousands of UNIX developers have had nightmares about a potential flood of inexpensive workstation-level Windows programs, which could drive UNIX application prices down from thousands of dollars to hundreds of dollars in a year or two.

From the stories being circulated by Microsoft, NT is the apex of operating system design—the software that no self-respecting enterprise will be able to do without. On the other hand, the OS/2 and UNIX communities have their own stories to tell.

IBM points to the fact that it has sold more than one million copies of OS/2, a 32-bit multitasking operating system that has a graphic user interface and compatibility with DOS and 16-bit Windows. UNIX advocates argue that there's nothing that NT can do that UNIX doesn't already do better, and that UNIX has the advantage of almost 25 years of experience. They point out that NT is a totally new, untested operating system.

Users and potential users have a different perspective. For them, Windows NT represents both an opportunity and a threat. Windows NT has the power to enable DOS and 16-bit Windows users do things that they've either only dreamed about, or were able to do only by purchasing and integrating a raft of third-party software.

If you want a true network server running Windows exclusively, Windows NT has got it. If you want an engineering workstation with full UNIX network interoperability, NT has that, too. How about a true multiuser bulletin board system with the Windows GUI? You can do it with NT.

11 • The Future of Windows NT

On the other hand, although NT looks and feels much like 16-bit Windows, it's an entirely new operating system. The cost of adopting a new operating system—in lost work time, system downtime, and training—dwarf the initial cost of new hardware and software. What if NT doesn't work as advertised? After all, Microsoft has less than a sterling reputation for getting new software right the first time. (In fact, the axiom used to be, "Never buy a Microsoft product before it reaches Version 3.0.") It is known that Microsoft intends to introduce Windows NT as Version 3.1 instead of Version 1.0 to bring it in line with the current shipping version of Windows for DOS. Whatever Microsoft chooses to call it, in reality it will be the first commercially released version of NT. Purchasing the first version of anything, whether an operating system or an automobile, implies some risk. For a new operating system, risk factors are involved, including the following:

- Functionality: will the operating system work as the vendor says it will?

- Reliability: will it run reliably under real-world conditions; will it maintain data integrity?

- Interoperability: can I get it to work harmoniously with my currently installed hardware and software?

- Compatibility: will it run my existing applications?

- Application availability: will I have a wide choice of application software; will the applications do what I need them to do?

- Longevity: will the operating system and its vendor stay in the market for a long time; will the software be updated and maintained?

- Competition: is there another operating system that does more things better than the one under consideration?

Chapter 10, "Making the Choice: Windows NT or Not?" looked at Windows NT's functionality, reliability, interoperability, and compatibility. This chapter focuses on application availability, longevity, and competition.

Windows NT: The Next Generation

Application Availability

There are two categories of application programs: horizontal and vertical. Horizontal applications are programs that are used by many different people for many different things. Databases, spreadsheets, word processors, and desktop publishing programs are good examples of horizontal applications because they can be widely used by a variety of businesses, government departments, schools, individuals, and so on.

Vertical applications are applications that have direct applicability to only one or a handful of businesses or organizations. A pharmacy management package is a vertical application, as is a hotel reservation system or a medical billing package. All of these programs may be useful to thousands of users, but they are useless outside a specific application area. The pharmacy package, obviously, is of no use to a hotel.

Beyond these broad categories, there are others. For example, engineering and scientific applications usually require lots of processing and graphics power and can't be run on anything less than a high-end PC or a RISC workstation. Most of these applications run under UNIX or on a mainframe running a proprietary operating system.

A good rule of thumb for determining whether to go with an operating system is the number and type of applications available for it. It is important to determine exactly what you want to do with your computer system, and then pick the operating system that makes the most sense for your needs.

DOS and Windows Applications

If you simply look at the sheer number of available applications, DOS is the winner, hands-down. DOS applications to do virtually anything you could imagine are available. However, DOS is extremely limited, and frankly, you probably wouldn't be interested in this book if you could do everything you want to do with DOS. So, for the time being, set DOS aside, except in relation to its critical role in standard Windows.

Windows has the fastest-growing array of horizontal applications in the computer industry. Every major DOS and Macintosh software vendor has

11 • The Future of Windows NT

already made the move to Windows or is working on it. More importantly, a price war has broken out in the Windows marketplace that shows no signs of subsiding. Some of the most popular Windows applications started in the Macintosh world because the Mac was the first widely popular GUI environment. Yet today, the Windows versions often sell for less than half the price of the Macintosh versions.

Competition is the reason for this price disparity. Microsoft, Lotus, Borland, WordPerfect, Aldus, Adobe, Micrografx, and others are fighting for dominance of their application categories, and the consumer is the winner. With introductory price offers, software upgrades, and "sidegrades" (low-priced offers to users of competitive products), users are becoming accustomed to paying no more than $199 for any major horizontal application.

Volume users who need 50, 100, or more copies of applications are being offered site licenses and network licenses at extremely attractive prices. Microsoft, Lotus, and Borland are all offering incentives to customers who commit to their entire suite of Windows applications. More and more computer vendors are bundling applications with new systems at little or no cost to the end user. In short, the Windows horizontal application market is a war zone, and no truce is in sight!

OS/2 Applications

The OS/2 library of horizontal applications is also growing, although at a slower pace. The competitive fury of the Windows market hasn't touched the OS/2 arena yet. There are fewer players, and their products are more expensive than their Windows equivalents. OS/2 horizontal applications aren't as widely available as Windows products. Most computer dealers and mail order outlets don't carry them, although they're usually available by direct order from the vendors.

UNIX Applications

The UNIX world is considerably different. Unlike the Windows and OS/2 markets, there is no single standard UNIX version. Users have to order applications for a specific flavor of UNIX.

Windows NT: The Next Generation

Chapter 9, "Windows NT Versus UNIX," discussed UNIX at length. For the purposes of this discussion, keep in mind that no standardization means no "shrink-wrapped" software—no UNIX software that can be put on a retailer's shelves and sold in high quantity.

No standardization, low quantities of sales for each UNIX variant, little competition, and high costs for supporting software running on many different platforms has historically added up to high-priced software. Although Windows horizontal applications sell for a few hundred dollars, equivalent UNIX applications may sell for many hundreds or even thousands of dollars. Even though many UNIX applications provide some features, such as tight integration with a database or other applications, that are missing in their Windows counterparts, these features rarely justify the often enormous price difference customers must pay for UNIX.

Vertical applications are another matter. By their nature, vertical applications appeal to a small set of potential users, and software vendors can't sell mass quantities of any one program. Because the skill and knowledge required to develop, market, and support a vertical application can be quite specialized, there is usually not as much, or as intense, competition between vertical application developers as there is in the horizontal arena. Compared to their horizontal brethren, vertical developers are smaller companies that are less able to spread operating costs across a wide product line. As a result, vertical applications tend to be much more expensive and less widely available than horizontal ones.

Of UNIX, Windows, and OS/2, UNIX is the most mature platform for vertical applications, and it probably still has a lead over Windows in the quantity of applications available, although Windows is quickly closing the gap. Windows is currently the platform of choice for most new vertical applications, but for multiuser applications, it's still easier to use a UNIX system with multiple serial connections than it is to configure a network with multiple Windows PCs—although the wide availability of peer-to-peer LAN packages for Windows is closing that gap as well. In engineering and scientific applications, however, UNIX has a wide lead in applications and developers that Windows will be hard-pressed to overcome.

OS/2 is finding its greatest success as a platform for development of vertical applications, especially applications that are designed for use within one company, agency, or organization. Major customers who have

historically been solid IBM users were the first, and have remained the primary, market for OS/2 applications. If you're developing your own applications for in-house use, OS/2's strengths may well outweigh the lack of available third-party applications.

Windows NT Applications

Where does Windows NT fit into all this? NT is a new operating system, so there are very few applications (either vertical or horizontal) available for it. Lots of software developers have committed to release NT applications, but some of the major players, such as Lotus and WordPerfect, have held off their support for NT primarily for competitive reasons. NT hasn't been tested in the furnace of the marketplace—they don't know how it will perform in the real world.

On the other hand, NT will run most DOS and 16-bit Windows applications. According to *UnixWorld* magazine's February 1993 issue, many UNIX developers, including those with complex engineering and scientific applications, are actively porting their applications to NT. It's not terribly difficult to move a 16-bit Windows application to the 32-bit NT world, although taking full advantage of NT requires a lot more work. Quite a few 16-bit applications are likely to come over to NT very quickly in order to take advantage of 32-bit addressing, preemptive multitasking, and the other NT features that require little or no application rewriting.

NT's application development momentum will depend to a great extent on the quality and completeness of its first release. When OS/2 was first released, it was crippled by sluggish performance, high demand for storage and memory, and the total absence of a promised GUI. Over the next few months and years, developers and end users waited for all of OS/2's promised features to be delivered, and many people simply gave up and adopted other operating systems and environments. IBM and Microsoft worked hard and spent enormous amounts of money to promote OS/2 as a serious application platform, but neither company could overcome OS/2's poor start.

It's still too early to tell exactly how Windows NT will perform when it's released, but it's likely that the first release of NT will not be as fast or as memory-efficient as Microsoft or its customers would like. On the other hand, Microsoft has been distributing NT development tools since July 1992, and

Windows NT: The Next Generation

to date more than 40,000 copies of the SDK have been sold. By the time NT is finally released and shipped to customers, developers will have had almost one full year of experience with the operating system. The more experience developers have with an operating system, the better and faster they can create applications. NT's beta program is proof that Microsoft learned some important lessons from the OS/2 debacle. The following list presents a few assumptions you can safely make about application availability for Windows NT:

- If you need to rely on third-party applications, both horizontal and vertical, plan on using 16-bit Windows applications with NT, at least for the first year. It will take at least that long for a good variety of applications to become available in 32-bit versions, and it may take another 6 to 12 months before a large number of applications that take full advantage of NT are available. Contact your software suppliers. If you have a good working relationship with them, they should be willing to fill you in about their plans and schedules to support NT. Make them partners in your efforts to evaluate and implement NT systems.

- If you're developing your own applications, or you're contracting with outside developers to create custom applications, it's safe to begin pilot development with the versions of NT available right now, but don't rush. The first released version of NT is likely to be a "final beta" version that needs performance tuning, optimization, and debugging. Unless you have a critical need for an application, give Microsoft time to fine-tune and fully debug NT. It may take 6 months to a year for Microsoft to get everything right, so set your application piloting and implementation schedules accordingly. If Microsoft gets its work done in less time, you can accelerate your schedules.

Longevity

The amount of money that you (as a user, developer, or both) initially spend on purchasing, developing, and installing an application will be dwarfed over the years by the amount you spend training people to use the application, supporting the users, and upgrading the application.

11 • The Future of Windows NT

As any software developer can tell you, one of the most wrenching and expensive experiences you can have is moving an application from one operating system to another. No matter how easy and painless the transition is purported to be, it usually turns out to be neither painless nor easy. For these reasons, it's essential to choose an application platform that's going to be around for a while. You need an operating system that will not only last for the expected lifetime of your application, but one that also will be upgraded and supported.

UNIX Outlook

Of all the operating systems discussed, UNIX, at almost 25 years, is the oldest. Almost two generations of computer scientists, software engineers, programmers, and other computer professionals cut their teeth on UNIX systems in colleges, universities, businesses, and government. UNIX is the standard operating system for much of the U.S. government and most European governments. It's also the standard operating system of the engineering and scientific worlds. Every RISC workstation vendor offers a version of UNIX, as do most file and application server vendors.

UNIX is well-established, has momentum in the RISC world, and is well-understood by hundreds of thousands of computer professionals. In one form or another, UNIX will survive and even thrive for many years. As a practical matter, however, it's not the survival of UNIX in general that's as important as the survival of the particular UNIX variant you select as your application platform. Literally dozens of different UNIX flavors are on the market, including dozens of versions available from U.S., Canadian, European, and Far Eastern hardware vendors, as well as from a variety of small North American software vendors. They're all UNIX, but they often have subtle (and not so subtle) differences—a faster file system for better performance, additional hardware-specific features, a unique user interface or software development system. Whatever the differences, they're often enough to prohibit easy software portability from one flavor of UNIX to another.

In early 1993, UNIX Systems Laboratories, formerly a company partially owned by AT&T, was purchased by Novell. The impact of Novell's acquisition on UNIX remains to be seen. Some industry analysts saw the purchase

Windows NT: The Next Generation

as a plus because AT&T is a computer hardware vendor and many UNIX licensees have been concerned for years that AT&T had an advantage by simultaneously being a competitor and the licensor of a core technology like UNIX.

Novell, as a software-only company, is not perceived as a competitor for hardware companies. Some analysts think Novell doesn't have the financial and technical resources to back UNIX as effectively as AT&T did for years, and they suggest that the acquisition might jeopardize the long-term future of UNIX. Obviously, the jury is still out, but the fact that so many companies have a stake in UNIX suggests that the success or failure of any one company will not have a big impact on its future.

OS/2 Futures

OS/2's inception dates to 1987-1988, and although it was originally a joint Microsoft/IBM production, today OS/2 is solely under IBM's control. As of September 1993, IBM will lose its rights to future versions of Microsoft's software. This means that IBM will be solely responsible for duplicating DOS' and Windows' future functionality in OS/2. For the millions of customers who have standardized on Windows applications such as Microsoft Word and Excel, Borland Quattro Pro for Windows, or WordPerfect for Windows, this is a critical issue.

Application developers are far more likely to maintain compatibility with future versions of Microsoft Windows than they are with future versions of IBM "Windows" under OS/2. If OS/2's Windows compatibility begins to drift away from that of the core Microsoft product, or if IBM can't keep up with Microsoft's rate of product development and upgrading, users of Windows applications under OS/2 could be in trouble.

IBM is still the world's biggest computer company, but it has fallen on hard times in the past few years, culminating in a loss of almost $5 billion in 1992. Since the late-eighties, IBM has invested in, experimented with, developed, or co-developed an array of operating systems, most of which the company eventually relegated to specialty applications, dropped, or merged with other projects (Go's PenPoint and CIC's PenDOS for pen computing applications, Novell's DR DOS, Patriot Partners, and Taligent, for example). The

11 • The Future of Windows NT

company is now developing a microkernel-based operating system based on AIX, which will also be able to run OS/2 applications.

But OS/2 is not a passing fancy for IBM. The company has stuck with it, even while dropping or downgrading the roles of other operating systems. Nevertheless, IBM doesn't have a good track record for strategic consistency in the nineties. The positioning of Taligent versus IBM's new AIX-based operating system, for example, hasn't been made clear. At first glance, they both seem to cover the same application areas and hardware platforms. Could IBM take a strategic turn, or hit an even deeper financial rut, that would cause it to lessen its commitment to OS/2? Unlike UNIX, if IBM decides to turn its back on OS/2 in the future, there are no alternate vendors (other than Microsoft) with a compatible operating system. In short, OS/2's longevity is intimately tied to IBM's fate.

Windows Forecast

Microsoft Windows, if you count Windows 1.0 and 2.0, has been around since the mid-eighties. The DOS platform that Windows is based on is more than a decade old and extremely well established. Like OS/2, however, only one company controls the fate of Windows: Microsoft.

The future of the DOS and Windows combination is unclear, but it's very clear that Microsoft plans a future version of Windows, in addition to Windows NT, that includes full operating system functionality and thus eliminates the need for a separate copy of DOS. Other rumored Windows variants include NT Lite, a slimmed-down version of NT for client use on smaller PCs, and future generations of NT, including an object-oriented version code-named "Cairo."

If there's one word that describes Microsoft's product development approach, it is persistence. Windows 1.0 was at best a toy GUI, and Windows 2.0 wasn't much of an improvement. Even though IBM put tremendous pressure on Microsoft to drop Windows and focus on OS/2, Bill Gates persisted until Windows 3.0 finally broke through to become a spectacular success. In networking, Microsoft has been trying to come up with a winner since the MS-NET days of the mid-eighties, and LAN Manager is still a poor also-ran compared to Novell NetWare. Nevertheless, Microsoft hasn't given up, and

Windows NT: The Next Generation

now both Windows NT and Windows for Workgroups are positioned to again assault Novell's leadership position. (To be fair, Microsoft has abandoned its share of products, from communications software to an early database management system. However, when Microsoft considers a product or market area to be strategic to its long-term success, it pursues its efforts in these areas with enormous tenacity.)

What does this mean for Windows NT? Even if the first version of NT is a failure, which is unlikely, Microsoft won't give up. Gates and company will go back to the drawing board and come up with a new version of NT. From an end user's point of view, this means that NT will continue to be sold and supported for several years, although third-party applications would be scarce. From a developer's point of view, however, it might mean that each new version of NT would require big application changes to conform to Microsoft's latest model of what's needed to make NT successful.

The fact that Microsoft is the only supplier of Windows NT carries with it some vendor risk. On the other hand, Microsoft has the financial and technical resources to stick with NT for a long time. Very few software vendors have the resources and tenacity of Microsoft. It's likely that Microsoft will keep working on NT until it's a market success.

Competition

Dozens of operating system vendors in the marketplace are selling everything from specialized systems for pen computers to networked operating systems for enterprise-wide applications. For an operating system vendor to thrive, not just survive, it must excel on these four criteria:

- ■ Financial Resources. Does it have the financial resources to invest in long-term product development, marketing and support, as well as to survive a competitive onslaught?

- ■ Technical Capabilities. Does it have the engineering and programming talent needed for long-term, high-quality product development, and does it have the product and customer support organizations required to meet end user, developer, and OEM (manufacturer) needs?

11 • *The Future of Windows NT*

- Marketing Capabilities. Does it have the proven ability to successfully identify customer needs, shepherd products that meet these needs through their development organizations, and successfully market the finished products?
- Management Resources. Is its management team experienced, and does it have a track record of success in the operating system market or in related markets?

In 1992, three vendors rose above the pack to become the biggest and most likely to succeed: IBM, Novell, and Microsoft.

IBM

IBM's future in desktop/network operating systems has an enormous amount riding on the success or failure of two unreleased platforms: the microkernel OS and Taligent, a joint development of IBM and Apple.

IBM's microkernel OS is based on its existing AIX version of UNIX and the Mach UNIX derivative designed by Carnegie-Mellon University. Mach was one of the first implementations of a microkernel OS, and many of its design concepts have been adopted by NeXT Computer for NeXTSTEP, Microsoft for Windows NT, IBM, and others. (Richard Rashid, one of the chief architects of Mach at Carnegie-Mellon, is now working on Windows NT at Microsoft.)

Microkernel

A compact, efficient set of core operating system functions. Microkernels are a response to the growth of the UNIX kernel over the years to include greater and greater levels of functionality at the expense of size and performance.

In the forthcoming microkernel OS, IBM plans to implement a client/server architecture similar to NT's user mode design, in which application

Windows NT: The Next Generation

clients "talk" to their equivalent subsystem APIs. IBM's architecture would support OS/2 as a protected subsystem on top of the AIX microkernel. In addition, AIX native programs would have their own subsystem, as would DOS and 16-bit Windows. (AIX would include POSIX compatibility, so a separate POSIX subsystem wouldn't be necessary.)

The multithreaded, multitasking, and multiprocessing capabilities of AIX would be fully supported and extended by the microkernel OS. The microkernel OS is intended to run on Intel, IBM, and Motorola processors, specifically Intel 486 and Pentium CPUs, IBM's RS/6000 RISC processor, the AS/400 minicomputer/server, and the forthcoming IBM/Motorola PowerPC, which will be used by Apple, IBM, and other vendors.

The second new operating system will be from Taligent, a joint venture of Apple and IBM. Taligent's OS will be a fully object-oriented operating system like NeXTSTEP. The object model implemented in Windows NT will be greatly extended to cover all functions of and data associated with the operating system. Like the microkernel OS, Taligent will support multiple guest operating systems, including OS/2 and Macintosh System 7.

Taligent's architecture is based on an object-oriented operating system from Apple, code-named "Pink," which was to be the next generation Macintosh OS. In addition, concepts developed by Patriot Partners, IBM's former joint venture with Metaphor, have also been integrated into the Taligent OS.

Both the microkernel OS and Taligent OS are portrayed as enterprise-wide operating systems capable of running mission-critical applications. Both are "next generation" operating systems. Why does IBM need two overlapping state-of-the-art operating systems? The primary reasons are control and security.

The microkernel OS is being developed solely by IBM designers under IBM control (unlike Taligent, which is a joint venture and is by definition the outcome of negotiations and compromises between the two partners). IBM's senior management wants to control the destiny of its future operating system, which will ultimately be the backbone of its future computer products. They don't want to repeat their experiences with Microsoft and OS/2.

11 • *The Future of Windows NT*

Taligent, on the other hand, is a strong side bet, a potential operating system marketplace winner that IBM can co-develop and market at a fraction of the cost of an internally designed and developed OS. If Taligent turns into a big winner, IBM can back away from the microkernel OS. If Taligent is a dud, IBM's financial and market exposure are limited because the microkernel OS will already be available and fully supported.

For end users and developers, IBM's strategy poses a dilemma. The cost of supporting any operating system is so high that most users and developers won't be able to afford to support both the microkernel and Taligent operating systems. How do you choose between them? In providing itself with options, IBM runs the risk of confusing the market. For example, if IBM strongly supports its own in-house microkernel OS, how strongly will it promote and support Taligent? How long will IBM stick with either operating system if their sales fall below forecasts for an extended period of time? By pursuing two different operating systems without clear product differentiation, IBM has passed some of its risks on to its customers, who must take the risk and make the choice for IBM. If a customer chooses the operating system that IBM chooses to back away from, the customer is the loser.

At this point, the best we can hope for is that IBM will clearly and forcefully explain the differences between its two upcoming operating systems and position the two systems so that the choice between them is clear for most users and developers. After IBM formally introduces one or both operating systems, users and developers should demand that IBM make an absolute commitment to market, upgrade, and support the product for several years.

Novell

The second key player is Novell. Novell is the unchallenged leader in network operating systems with NetWare, although Novell is a poor second-place finisher in the PC operating system business with DR DOS.

In December 1991, Novell and AT&T's UNIX Systems Laboratories (USL) formed a joint venture called Univel to develop a version of UNIX System V Release 4.2 with a GUI for Intel-based personal computers. (Until the recent

sale of USL to Novell, AT&T owned the core version of UNIX, as well as the UNIX trademark. Anyone who wished to use the UNIX trademark or incorporate any part of the UNIX Systems Laboratories' code in their operating system had to acquire a license from AT&T and pay substantial royalties.)

In late 1992, Univel shipped UnixWare in client and server versions. UnixWare is a complete version of UNIX that supports both the UNIX-standard Internet TCP/IP and Novell-standard IPX/SPX networking protocols. This enables UnixWare-based systems to interoperate freely with Novell networks and UNIX networks.

UnixWare-based PCs can be clients or servers on Novell or UNIX networks. In addition, UnixWare systems can act as routers, interconnecting Novell and UNIX networks. UnixWare was also written to provide a high degree of compatibility with SCO UNIX, which is the most popular version of UNIX for PCs. Most SCO UNIX applications run without modification under UnixWare.

In January 1993, Novell joined the top rank of operating system vendors by signing an agreement to acquire the UNIX Systems Laboratories from AT&T. With this agreement, Novell acquired the rights to the UNIX trademark, all the UNIX code, a family of utilities and applications that greatly extend UNIX's functionality, and control over the future direction of UNIX. Novell also cemented its domination of the networking business by adding the vast worldwide network of UNIX-based TCP/IP systems to its existing NetWare base.

More importantly, through UNIX and UnixWare, Novell obtained the operating system components necessary to go head-to-head with Microsoft. NetWare is a very powerful network operating system, and NetWare 4.0 will add extensive security and system administration features similar to those found in Windows NT. NetWare, however, was never designed to actually run application software. Instead, it provides networking support for DOS and Windows applications.

UNIX, UnixWare, and DR DOS, on the other hand, actually run applications. DR DOS is a fully-compatible replacement for MS-DOS, and UnixWare is designed to take on Windows NT and OS/2, as well as other flavors of UNIX. With the addition of UNIX, Novell can offer complete operating system solutions: UNIX and UnixWare for homogeneous UNIX networks, UnixWare

11 • The Future of Windows NT

or DR DOS and NetWare for homogenous Novell networks, and a combination for sites with PCs, RISC workstations, and various kinds of servers.

Even though Novell is in position to dominate the UNIX and networking worlds, it still has an uphill battle in trying to take UNIX to the PC. UNIX's installed base is a fraction of the Windows world, which is in turn a fraction of the DOS-installed base. Windows NT is the obvious upgrade path for DOS and Windows for DOS users because of its compatibility and common user interface. For Windows users, UNIX is a new, incompatible operating system that requires a significant amount of training to master its use. UNIX has gained a reputation over the years for being difficult to use, with a host of obscure, seemingly meaningless commands that can do almost anything if you can figure out how they work. Systems like NeXTSTEP have gone a very long way to make UNIX understandable to mere mortals, but the reputation remains.

Control of UNIX is not totally in Novell's hands. Over the years, AT&T licensed its UNIX source code to many computer vendors, software developers, and educational institutions. These licensees added features and made changes to UNIX. Some of the changes added such valuable functionality that they were eventually incorporated into AT&T UNIX itself, and others served little purpose other than differentiating one flavor of UNIX from another.

These UNIX flavors have varying degrees of compatibility with each other and with AT&T (now Novell) UNIX. It often takes significant reprogramming effort to move an application from one UNIX variant to another. Without absolute compatibility (at least at the source code level), the dream of truly open systems and a mass market for UNIX applications has remained just that, a dream.

One also has to wonder whether Novell will be more successful with UNIX and UnixWare than it has been with DR DOS. Microsoft's software licensing terms and beta testing policies notwithstanding, Novell has had little success in cracking the DOS marketplace, even though DR DOS is considered by some to be a superior alternative to MS-DOS.

On the other hand, the UNIX marketplace is much more systems-oriented than the DOS market. UNIX systems require a significant amount of installation assistance and ongoing support, and this is an area where Novell's reseller network shines (see Chapter 6, "Networking with Windows NT").

Windows NT: The Next Generation

Novell's training programs and resellers dominate the PC networking business, and their basic skills and capabilities can readily be transferred to the UNIX arena. In fact, Novell has already begun a concerted effort to recruit, train, and equip its resellers to support UnixWare.

Novell's success in the PC-centric enterprise-wide marketplace will ultimately depend on its ability to convince skeptical users that in comparison with Windows NT, UnixWare is the superior application platform and server. For most users, the move from Windows for DOS to Windows NT will be the path of least resistance.

Novell must demonstrate that UnixWare, especially in combination with NetWare, will provide performance, functionality, and compatibility that Windows NT, Windows for Workgroups, and LAN Manager for Windows NT can't match. It's a tough challenge, but given Novell's huge installed base of NetWare systems, it's a realistic goal. By holding onto the majority of its existing installed NetWare base, Novell could make UnixWare the market leader for enterprise-wide operating systems and beat back Microsoft's attempt to dethrone UNIX. No one doubts that it will be a tremendous struggle for both competitors.

Microsoft

The final key player is Microsoft. On the desktop, Microsoft absolutely dominates the operating system business. According to Dataquest, a market research firm headquartered in San Jose, California, in 1992 Microsoft's DOS represented more than 73 percent of all desktop operating system shipments. Sales of Windows are running at almost one million copies per month, and there's no end in sight. Microsoft is also the dominant vendor of Windows applications with an ever-growing product line. They've put Borland on the defensive in the database business with FoxPro and Access. In fact, networking is the only major market that Microsoft has repeatedly tried, and failed, to dominate.

Microsoft is rolling out a host of new operating system products and versions to meet almost every need. As noted in Chapter 2, "Microsoft's

11 • The Future of Windows NT

Blueprint for the Nineties," Microsoft is readying a family of Windows-based products, from Modular Windows at the low-end to Windows NT for enterprise-wide applications. DOS will eventually disappear into a future version of Windows that includes all of DOS' functionality. A streamlined version of NT, nicknamed NT Lite, will allow systems with Intel 386 and slower versions of the 486 processor to take advantage of 32-bit addressing, true preemptive multitasking, multithreading, and many of the other features of NT. A future, fully object-oriented version of Windows NT, Cairo, has been discussed in the trade press and hinted at by Microsoft itself. This version of NT will have a true microkernel architecture for better performance and an object-oriented design for faster and easier software development, as well as simple system expandability.

In a curious way, Windows NT is strategically very significant to Microsoft if it succeeds, but relatively unimportant if it doesn't. If NT is a major success, it will give Microsoft a strong position in both the networking and mission-critical systems marketplaces, neither of which have been significant sources of revenue in the past. Both of these markets also represent a major source of future revenue growth for Microsoft. The average dollar value of a network or enterprise-wide systems sale is far greater than the average value of a stand-alone PC software sale, even for a large customer with many computers.

On the other hand, if NT is a mediocre or poor seller, Microsoft has risked little but its pride. It can't lose market share in markets that it previously didn't compete in, like the enterprise-wide arena, and its current share in the networking market is so small that any revenue it earns from Windows for Workgroups and Windows NT will be an improvement. As with Windows 1.0 and 2.0, Microsoft can keep trying with new versions of NT until it gets it right.

One big stumbling block for Microsoft could be support. As noted in Chapter 6, one of Novell's most powerful weapons against Microsoft is its cadre of trained resellers who are much more experienced in installing and supporting networks.

Windows NT: The Next Generation

Again, Microsoft enters a marketplace where training, installation, and support are critical. The company learned valuable lessons from its missteps in the networking arena; today, its LAN Manager resellers are trained and certified much like Novell's. Microsoft is also a minority investor in SCO, and it has had many opportunities to study how SCO and SCO's resellers support their customers. Since mid-1992, Microsoft has been working to put in place a network of trained, knowledgeable NT consultants, custom developers, and resellers.

Clearly, Microsoft has the technical, financial, and marketing resources to compete with any computer company in the world. However, with so many irons in the fire, so many operating system versions and new applications under development, and increasing competitive and governmental pressure, can it stay focused on Windows NT? To date, Microsoft has done more things right than any other software company in history, but as IBM and Digital Equipment proved, invincible competitors can become also-rans at a frightening pace. Microsoft's fate, and the fate of Windows NT, are yet to be determined.

Forecasts

No future outlook would be complete without a forecast or two. Keep in mind that most market forecasts, especially for unreleased products, are significantly less accurate than tomorrow's weather forecast. No matter what the market prognosticators predict, it's a good idea to keep a raincoat, umbrella, and snowshoes ready, just in case.

In mid-1992, Chris LeTocq, a senior analyst at InfoCorp Software Service, took an interesting approach to forecasting the future of the Microsoft family of operating systems, APIs, and IBM's OS/2. Instead of forecasting the sales of each operating system environment, he forecasted the sales of applications for each environment. Users purchase operating systems in order to run applications, and the number of applications running on an operating system is a good indicator of the OS's real market success. Figure 11.1 shows InfoCorp's forecast.

11 • The Future of Windows NT

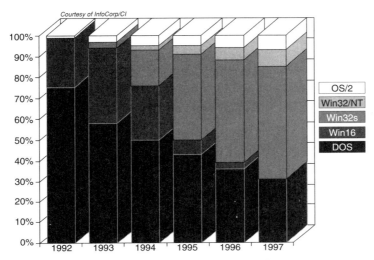

Figure 11.1. *Worldwide application software sales by operating system environment.*

It's important to note that InfoCorp breaks the Windows NT market into two categories: the Win32s API, which enables 32-bit Windows applications to run under 16-bit DOS/Windows, and Win32/NT, the environment that provides developers and users with full access to all the features of Windows NT (at the expense of compatibility with Win32s). The forecast indicates that by 1995 virtually all 16-bit Windows applications will have shifted to the Win32s API. What's more interesting is that LeTocq projects that it will be 1997 before native NT applications overtake OS/2, and even then, native NT applications will comprise only 8 percent of total application sales. This indicates that most Windows developers will take the path of least resistance and move their applications, more or less intact, to Win32s without rewriting them to take full advantage of NT. It also suggests that it could be a long time before a "critical mass" of native NT applications becomes available.

Other market researchers have forecasted each operating system's share of the desktop marketplace (see Figure 11.2).

Windows NT: The Next Generation

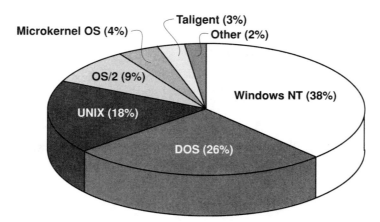

Figure 11.2. *Projected 1996 worldwide sales of operating systems (in units).*

This forecast indicates that Windows NT (including NT Lite and Win32s) will become a dominant operating system, followed by a future version of DOS (probably an integrated Windows OS capable of running most Win32s applications), UNIX, OS/2, and others. It suggests that DOS will slowly fade away as NT gains strength, and that UNIX will be a reasonably strong, though second-tier, contender. Future operating systems like Taligent OS and IBM's microkernel OS will just be beginning to make serious market inroads by 1996. Most OS/2 users and developers will be faced with the decision of whether to stay with OS/2 or port their applications to another operating system such as Taligent or the microkernel OS.

Again, take these forecasts with a grain of salt. They should be just one factor in your decision-making process. Use the preceding criteria to determine if NT, or any operating system, is right for your application and computer environment.

Conclusion

Any book that purports to tell you everything you need to know about an operating system, or about anything else for that matter, is missing the most

11 • The Future of Windows NT

important factor of all: you. Your unique applications, users, systems, organization, and personal preferences are by far the most critical factors in your decision-making process. You need to weigh every piece of advice and information against your own knowledge and experience.

Is Windows NT a powerful, easy-to-use operating system with excellent communication capabilities, interoperability, and extensive compatibility with other operating systems? From the beta version of the software, it appears this is true.

- Is Windows NT reliable? It's impossible to say for sure, but Microsoft has made a good start.

- Can Microsoft and its resellers support NT? Microsoft claims that its support system is falling into place, but the jury is still out.

- Will lots of applications be available for NT? Many software vendors have voiced support for the operating system, but the proof will come once NT starts shipping in quantity.

- How about development tools? Microsoft has already released a suite of development tools, and more are on the way from other vendors.

Is Windows NT right for you? You're the most qualified person in the world to answer that question. I hope that this book has given you some insight into NT and at least some of the information you need to determine if and when you want to investigate NT further.

A Glossary

Windows NT: The Next Generation

access control list (ACL)
> The list of access control protections attached to all NT system objects.

ACL
> *access control list.*

address
> The location of a single byte of information in the computer's memory or mass storage. An address can be physical—point to a specific byte of data in a specific physical location in memory or on disk—or virtual—point to a logical (software-based) address that the operating system then maps to a specific physical address. Windows NT uses virtual addressing to provide each application with 4G of address space (of which 2G are reserved for the operating system.)

API
> *application programming interface.*

application programming interface (API)
> A library of routines and services used by application programmers to avoid having to directly access low-level operating system functions.

asymmetric multiprocessing
> A form of multiprocessing that dedicates one processor to run the operating system while other processors run user applications (see *symmetric multiprocessing*).

asynchronous I/O
> A form of input/output in which an application issues an I/O request and then continues execution while the I/O request is filled.

authentication
> The process of verifying a system user's identification for access control. NT uses a combination of user names and passwords to provide authentication.

bits per second (bps)
> A measure of data transfer speed between two devices, generally over a communications line such as a phone line. To roughly measure the

A • Glossary

speed of data transfer in characters per second (each character being one byte long, with additional bits needed for the communications process), divide the bps figure by 10, so a 2400 bps modem transfers 240 characters per second.

bps

bits per second.

C2 security

The controlled security access level of security specified by the National Computer Security Council, a department of the U.S. National Security Agency (NSA) that is responsible for establishing standards for computer security for the U.S. government. C2 systems must require individual user logon with password authentication, along with a means of auditing (recording and tracking) system security events.

Cairo

Microsoft's code name for its new object-oriented operating system, scheduled for release in 1994/95.

Chicago

Microsoft's code name for a new 32-bit operating system that will provide most of the functionality of Windows NT, except for NT's server networking features.

CISC

complex instruction set computer.

client/server networking

A form of networking in which programs and data files shared between several computers reside on a larger computer called a server, and the computer using the shared data and programs are called clients. Clients may both share the resources of and execute applications on a server. Peripherals, such as printers and modems, may also be shared. A shared printer with memory for storing files waiting to be printed or connected to a computer with file storage is called a print server; a shared modem or set of modems is called a communications server.

Windows NT: The Next Generation

compiler
> A computer program that converts other computer programs written in a high-level language such as C or Pascal into low-level machine language instructions for a specific processor.

complex instruction set computer (CISC)
> A processor that has an extensive set of hardware-based operating instructions. Intel's x86 and Motorola's 680x0 families of CPUs are examples of CISC processors.

cooperative multitasking
> See *nonpreemptive multitasking*.

DDE
> *dynamic data exchange.*

DLL
> *dynamic link library.*

domain
> A group of network clients and servers that share a single security access control database.

DOS protected mode interface (DPMI)
> A DOS extender specification that enables DOS extended (XMS-compatible) programs to cooperatively run under 16-bit Windows without crashing the system.

DPMI
> *DOS protected mode interface.*

dynamic data exchange (DDE)
> A Windows feature that allows simultaneously running application programs to exchange data, even as the data changes.

dynamic link library (DLL)
> A set of API routines that applications call to access operating system functions, in lieu of embedding the operating system instructions directly in the application during compilation.

EA
> *extended attributes.*

A • *Glossary*

EMS
Expanded memory specification.

enterprise-wide network
A network that connects all of a company's computers in all locations and runs its *mission-critical applications.*

EtherNet
A *local area network* architecture originally developed by Xerox Corporation and subsequently standardized by the IEEE as the 802.3 standard.

expanded memory specification (EMS)
A memory management technique originally developed by Lotus, Intel, and Microsoft that allows DOS to work with up to 32M of additional memory. Unlike XMS, which requires an Intel 286 or greater processor, EMS runs on any Intel processor from 8088/86 on up.

extended attributes (EA)
Attributes, such as the name of a file's creator and other variable information, not normally stored within the OS/2 *HPFS* file directory.

extended memory specification (XMS)
A memory manager that allows DOS programs running on personal computers based on Intel 286 or greater processors to use extended memory.

extensibility
The capability of adding new features and functions to an operating system or application program without needing to modify the original software.

FAT
file allocation table.

fault tolerance
The ability of a computer system, both hardware and software, to tolerate and recover from system failures, such as hard disk crashes, power failures, memory errors, and other problems.

Windows NT: The Next Generation

file allocation table (FAT) file system
> The native DOS file system, named after DOS's file allocation table file directory scheme.

file server
> A computer, with a large-capacity hard disk, that is attached to a LAN and stores files used by other computers attached to the same network.

graphical user interface (GUI)
> A software program that enables users to interact with a computer by using a mouse or keyboard to manipulate graphical objects (files, printers, and so on) instead of typing commands.

GUI
> *graphical user interface.*

HAL
> *hardware abstraction layer.*

hardware abstraction layer (HAL)
> The lowest level of the NT operating system, which interconnects the NT kernel and I/O subsystem with the specific computer hardware that NT is running on.

high-level language
> A computer programming language with commands (code) that resemble human language, which are converted into machine language. Popular examples are BASIC, C, C++, COBOL, FORTRAN, and Pascal.

high performance file system (HPFS)
> OS/2's native file system, designed to avoid the limitations of the DOS FAT file system. HPFS supports 255-character filenames, disk directories located in the center of disks for better performance, and other features.

HPFS
> *high performance file system.*

A • Glossary

icon
A graphical symbol used to represent a file, program, or device within a GUI. For example, Windows NT application programs are represented as icons within the Windows Program Manager.

internetworking
The ability to link two or more networks with dissimilar network operating systems, network transport protocols, media types, and topologies.

interrupt
An event that momentarily halts the operating system and diverts control to a special software routine, called an interrupt handler.

IPX/SPX
Internetwork packet exchange/sequenced packet exchange, the standard network and transport layers (respectively) used by Novell's NetWare network operating system. IPX/SPX is Novell's standard transport protocol.

kernel
The most essential, or core, functions of an operating system. Kernels commonly manage the essential program execution and low-level input/output functions of the operating system.

kernel mode
The protected processor mode in which the *NT executive* runs.

LAN
local area network.

LAN Manager
Microsoft's *network operating system* that currently runs on an OS/2 server, but is being moved to Windows NT.

LAN Server
IBM's implementation of Microsoft's OS/2 LAN Manager.

local area network (LAN)
A high-speed communications link between two or more computers that allows the computers to share data and system resources.

Windows NT: The Next Generation

local procedure call
A facility, designed to mimic the syntax of *remote procedure calls*, used by *protected subsystems* to pass messages among themselves and client applications.

logon process
The NT "gatekeeper" process that ensures users are authenticated prior to gaining access to an NT system.

Mach
An operating system that was developed at Carnegie-Mellon University. Mach was originally based on the University of California's BSD 4.3 operating system, which was derived from UNIX.

machine language
A very low-level computer programming language that uses the native instruction set of a specific processor, such as an Intel 486 or MIPS 4000. Computers convert programs written in high-level languages into machine language for execution.

mailbox
A portion of main memory shared by two or more processes for the purpose of sending messages to each other. Unlike a *named pipe*, which connects one process to another process, a mailbox connects one process to several processes.

memory segmentation
A technique for memory addressing that references each byte of memory by a segment (base) number, to which an offset number is added. In DOS programs, each segmented memory location is referred to in the form of segment:offset.

microkernel
A compact, efficient set of core operating system functions. Microkernels are a response to the growth of the UNIX kernel over the years to include greater and greater levels of functionality, at the expense of size and performance.

mirrored disk set
A disk drive array in which identical data is simultaneously recorded on two drives. If one drive fails, the system can continue to operate with the data recorded on the mirror drive.

A • *Glossary*

mission-critical applications
  Computer applications that are essential to day-to-day operations of a business or governmental agency. Examples include reservation and plane scheduling systems for airlines, policy processing systems for insurance companies, and securities trading systems for brokerage firms.

modem (modulator/demodulator)
  A device that converts the digital (binary) signals used internally by computers for data storage, transmission, and processing into analog (sound) signals that can be transmitted over a phone line, cellular phone, or other device, and back again.

MS-DOS
  The standard, single-user operating system of IBM and IBM-compatible personal computers. Developed by Microsoft, MS-DOS is also marketed by IBM as PC DOS.

multiprocessing
  The use of more than one processor in a computer system. The processors are connected by shared memory or high-speed links.

multitasking
  A process whereby a computer appears to simultaneously run several tasks by giving each program a tiny slice of the computer's time and rapidly switching between each program.

multithreading
  The ability of an operating system to execute multiple threads simultaneously (see *thread*).

named pipe
  A means for enabling one process to send a message to another process, regardless of whether the target process is local or across the network.

NDIS
  network driver interface specification.

NetBEUI
  NetBIOS extended user interface, NT's primary network transport protocol and the standard transport protocol for Windows for Workgroups, LAN Manager, and IBM LAN Server networks.

Windows NT: The Next Generation

NetBIOS
> A network API that enables applications to send I/O requests to, and receive requests from, other computers on the network. NetBIOS is the standard network API for Windows for Workgroups, LAN Manager, and IBM LAN Server networks.

NetWare
> Novell's network operating system. It is based on Novell's IPX/SPX, but also accommodates TCP/IP.

network
> A system of computer hardware and software connected so that data can be transmitted between machines and end users can communicate.

network driver interface specification (NDIS)
> Microsoft's standard interface for network interface card drivers, used by Windows for Workgroups, LAN Manager, and IBM LAN Server networks.

Network File System (NFS)
> Sun Microsystems' distributed file system based on TCP/IP, for network applications.

network interface card (NIC)
> A hardware device that connects the internal bus of a computer to a local area network in order to establish a bidirectional communications link between the network and the computer.

network operating system (NOS)
> The software, running on a server, that governs access to the files and resources of the network by multiple users.

NeXTSTEP
> Operating system from NeXT Computer, Inc. Originally designed to run only on NeXT hardware, the operating system is being ported to the Intel-based PC platform.

NFS
> *network file system.*

NIC
> *network interface card.*

A • Glossary

nonpreemptive multitasking
    A form of multitasking in which the individual threads, rather than the operating system, determine when one thread relinquishes control of the system in order to allow other threads to run.

NOS
    network operating system.

NT executive
    The entire NT operating system, except the protected subsystems. The NT executive runs in kernel mode.

NT file system (NTFS)
    Windows NT's native file system. NTFS supports extensive access control, data integrity maintenance and recovery features, and POSIX compatibility. It uses the 16-bit Unicode standard for filename and attribute storage.

NT kernel
    The portion of the NT executive that manages threads, handles interrupts and exceptions, enables multiprocessor synchronization, and supports creation of user-mode objects.

NTFS
    NT file system.

object
    An instance of an NT system resource, including its properties. Files, memory, I/O devices, processes, and threads are among the many NT objects.

object linking and embedding (OLE)
    Microsoft's specification for application-to-application exchange and communication.

OLE
    object linking and embedding.

Open Systems Interconnection (OSI) reference model
    The International Standard Organization's software model for interaction between networked systems. The OSI model specifies seven layers of communication between systems.

Windows NT: The Next Generation

operating system
: A program or set of programs that provides essential services required by all other programs running on a computer. The operating system is, in effect, a "superprogram" that coordinates the activities of all other programs and provides uniform access to system resources. An operating system provides a common way of accessing system resources so that application developers can focus on writing the best possible applications without worrying about system management.

OS/2
: IBM's multithreaded, multitasking, single-user operating system. Though OS/2 was originally developed jointly with Microsoft, IBM has assumed responsibility for its development.

OSI
: *Open Systems Interconnection (OSI) reference model.*

page
: A block of contiguous virtual memory that is moved from RAM to hard disk and back again as part of the *Virtual Memory Manager's* memory management.

palmtop
: A handheld computer that typically runs applications useful outside the office, such as personal schedulers, notetakers, and small spreadsheets. Virtually all palmtop computers are designed around the Intel X86 processor architecture and can run DOS and DOS applications; some are powerful enough to run Windows applications as well.

PCMCIA
: *Personal Computer Memory Card Industry Association.*

PDA
: *personal digital assistant.*

peer-to-peer networking
: A network operating environment that allows any computer on the network to share its data and peripherals with any other connected computer, eliminating the need for dedicated servers. Peer-to-peer

A • Glossary

networks tend to be less expensive and easier to install than *client/server networks*, but they are also less secure, support fewer users, and present more file management problems than client/server systems.

Personal Computer Memory Card Industry Association (PCMCIA)
An international nonprofit group that establishes hardware, software, and interface standards for credit card-sized memory and I/O peripheral cards for portable computers.

personal digital assistant (PDA)
A device that integrates the functions of a computer and communications device, such as a modem and cellular telephone, into a single handheld package. Unlike a palmtop computer, a PDA is not a general-purpose PC and often does not use an X86-compatible processor. PDAs run customized versions of DOS and Windows, or specialized operating systems such as PenGEOS and Go PenPoint. Applications are usually written specifically for PDAs.

platform-independent
The capability of an operating system or application program to run on otherwise incompatible computers.

portable
Capable of working on a variety of hardware platforms. UNIX is a portable operating system, as is Windows NT.

preemptive multitasking
A form of multitasking in which the operating system can suspend execution of one thread to allow another thread to execute (see *nonpreemptive multitasking* for comparison).

process
An executable object consisting of a program, one or more threads, a virtual address space, and system resources dedicated to the threads.

protected mode
A memory addressing mode that uses linear addressing, instead of segments and offsets, to access any byte within memory. Protected mode also implements hardware memory protection features used by Windows and Windows NT.

Windows NT: The Next Generation

protected subsystem
    A user mode server process that performs operating system functions and provides applications with access to the operating system.

protocol
    A standardized set of rules that specify how a conversation between two computers is to take place, including the format, timing, sequencing, and error checking.

protocol stack
    The set of network protocols (following the OSI model) used to transmit a network request or response from one computer to another.

provider
    Software that allows NT to act as a client to a remote server.

RAM
    random-access memory.

random-access memory (RAM)
    The high-speed semiconductor memory used by computers for program execution. In general, RAM is short-term, or volatile, storage. When the computer's power is turned off, all data and programs stored in RAM are lost.

read-only memory (ROM)
    A form of memory that can be read from but not written to or otherwise modified by the computer.

real mode
    A memory addressing mode that uses the same memory segmentation model (segment:offset addresses) as the original Intel 8086 processor.

redirector
    Networking software that intercepts requests for remote devices, files, named pipes, and mailslots, and routes them to the targeted remote server.

reduced instruction set computer (RISC)
    A type of processor that uses a small set of machine-language instructions to perform its operations. Compared to CISC

A • *Glossary*

processors, RISC processors are more efficient and thus offer superior performance. The MIPS 4000, Digital Alpha, Hewlett-Packard HP-PA, and Sun SPARC processors are all RISC designs.

remote procedure call (RPC)
A mechanism that allows distributed applications (applications simultaneously running on more than one processor) to pass messages and access system services on processors locally or across the network without regard to each processor's actual physical location.

RISC
reduced instruction set computer.

ROM
read-only memory.

RPC
remote procedure call.

SCO UNIX
UNIX variety, marketed by Santa Cruz Operation, based on UNIX System V Release 3.2.

server
A special-purpose computer or device controller that provides access to shared resources, such as files, printers, or applications.

SMP
symmetric multiprocessing.

Solaris
UNIX variety marketed by SunSoft, Inc., based on UNIX System V Release 4.

SOM
System Object Model.

streams
A standardized network transport protocol driver environment, originally developed for UNIX System V by AT&T and implemented in Windows NT to support non-NetBEUI transport protocols.

Windows NT: The Next Generation

striped disk set
> A data storage system in which data is spread out across all the hard disks in an array, or set, of drives. If a single striped disk fails, you can still reconstruct your original data from the remaining drives by using NT's error correction software.

swap file
> A section of a hard disk used by virtual memory managers to temporarily hold a portion of the RAM's contents in order to allow the system to run programs that are larger than the size of available RAM alone.

symmetric multiprocessing (SMP)
> A multiprocessing system that runs the computer's operating system on more than one processor. Compared to *asymmetric multiprocessor* systems that dedicate one processor to running the operating system, symmetric systems are more reliable because the failure of a single processor is unlikely to crash the entire system.

synchronization objects
> NT executive objects used to synchronize the execution of one or more threads.

System Object Model (SOM)
> An OS/2 feature that provides a common programming-language-independent method for controlling objects like files, printers, or spreadsheets.

Taligent
> A new, object-oriented operating system under development by IBM and Apple Computer. Taligent is based on the "Pink" operating system originally developed by Apple.

TCP/IP
> *Transport Control Protocol/Internet Protocol.*

thread
> The portion of a process that the operating system actually executes. All processes have at least one thread, but no thread can belong to more than one process. A multithreaded process has more than one

A • Glossary

thread and is designed so that more than one thread can be executed simultaneously.

thunking layer
A portion of the Win32s API that converts Win32s 32-bit system calls and parameters to 16-bit calls and values for processing by the Win16 16-bit API.

timesharing
The capability of enabling several users to simultaneously run programs on a computer, via multitasking.

token ring
A local area networking media standard introduced by IBM that sends data across the network by attaching the data to a token, which is passed from one station to the next.

Transport Control Protocol/Internet Protocol (TCP/IP)
The transport protocol used primarily by UNIX systems for local and wide area networking. NT supports TCP/IP as an alternative to NetBEUI for interoperability with UNIX-based systems.

Unicode
A standardized 16-bit format for character representation. All characters in all the world's languages used for computing can be represented with Unicode.

uninterruptible power supply (UPS)
A backup power supply for computers and peripherals, used when primary (AC) power fails. Usually battery-based (but sometimes based on gasoline or natural gas generators,) UPS systems are designed to provide temporary power until primary power is restored.

UNIX
A multitasking, multiuser operating system. Developed by Bell Laboratories and widely implemented in universities, UNIX is gaining popularity in corporate enterprise-wide networks. It is commercially available in a wide variety of versions from a wide variety of vendors.

Windows NT: The Next Generation

UnixWare
> Operating system developed by Univel, a joint venture between UNIX Systems Laboratories (USL) and Novell. UnixWare is based on USL's UNIX System V Release 4.2.

UPS
> *uninterruptible power supply.*

user mode
> The processor mode in which user applications and the protected subsystems run.

VCPI
> *Virtual Control Program Interface*

VDM
> *virtual DOS machine.*

virtual address space
> The 4G address space available for use by a process.

Virtual Control Program Interface (VCPI)
> A DOS extender specification for Intel 386 or greater processors that enables DOS extended programs to run together in a cooperative multitasking environment with DOS real mode programs.

virtual DOS machine (VDM)
> A protected subsystem consisting of a DOS emulator that runs unmodified DOS applications on top of Windows NT.

virtual memory
> A form of memory that substitutes hard disk or other mass storage for RAM in order to enable computers to run applications that require more memory than is physically installed.

Virtual Memory Manager (VMM)
> The portion of the NT executive that implements *virtual memory.*

VMM
> *Virtual Memory Manager.*

A • Glossary

WFW
Windows for Workgroups.

Win32
The standard 32-bit *application programming interface* (API) for Windows NT applications, Win32 extends the existing 16-bit Win16 API with support for NT's new features, including multithreading, multiprocessing, and advanced graphics. Variations on Win32 include Win32s, a subset designed to run 32-bit applications under 16-bit Windows, and Win32c (Chicago), a supposed subset rumored to provide support for most Win32 features except server networking capabilities.

Windows for Workgroups (WFW)
Enhanced version of 16-bit Windows 3.1 that incorporates built-in peer-to-peer networking features and applications.

Windows on Win32 (WOW)
A protected subsystem that runs within a VDM to enable most 16-bit Windows applications to run on top of Windows NT. WOW supports cooperative multitasking and runs any number of 16-bit Windows applications in a single virtual machine.

WOW
Windows on Win32.

Xenix
A UNIX variant originally developed by Microsoft and marketed by the Santa Cruz Operation (SCO).

XMS
extended memory specification.

Bibliography

Bachus, Kevin. "How Windows NT Stacks Up: Pros and Cons," *Corporate Computing*, January 1993, p. 49.

Bachus, Kevin. "Windows Power Play: Microsoft's NT Comes Into the World a Bruiser," *Corporate Computing*, January 1993, pp. 47-52.

Binstock, Andrew. "NT vs. UNIX," *UNIX Review*, December 1992, p. 5.

Chisholm, John. "Challenge of NT," *UNIX Review*, December 1992, p. 7.

Cortese, Amy. "IBM Blueprints OS Lineup for Desktops," *PC Week*, December 21, 1992, p. 49.

Cortese, Amy. "Microsoft Regroups for 'NT Generation'," *PC Week*, December 21, 1992, p. 1.

Custer, Helen. *Inside Windows NT*. Redmond, Wash.: Microsoft Press, 1993.

Davis, Dwight. "Microsoft's Walker: How Microsoft Will Roll Out Windows NT," *Datamation*, November 15, 1992, p. 80.

Davis, Fred. "Phillipe Kahn on NT and the Future of OLE," *Windows Sources*, February 1993, p. 107.

Davis, Frederic. "Bill Gates on CDs, PDAs, and Cable TV," *Windows Sources*, March 1993, pp. 95-97.

DeVoney, Chris, and Richard Summe, et. al. *IBM's Personal Computer*. Carmel, Ind.: Que Corporation, 1982.

Dortch, Michael, and Chris Roeckl. "LAN Man Gets a Boost: OS/2's Role to Diminish as NT Becomes Available," *Communications Week*, October 12, 1992, p. 1.

Duncan, Ray. "Exploring the Win16, Win32, and Win32s APIs," *PC Magazine*, October 13, 1992, p. 405.

Duncan, Ray. "Multitasking and Multithreading in Windows NT," *PC Magazine*, December 1992, p. 392.

Farrow, Rik. "Understanding Windows NT," *UnixWorld*, February 1993, pp. 47-50.

Girishankar, Saroja. "Microsoft Details SNA Links for Windows NT," *Communications Week*, p. 1.

B • Bibliography

Greenbaum, Joshua. "Windows NT Divides Europe," *UnixWorld*, February 1993, pp. 37-38.

Hayes, Frank. "Is There Life After NT?" *UnixWorld*, February 1993, pp. 42-45.

Jamsa, Kris. *Using OS/2*. Berkeley, Calif.: Osborne McGraw-Hill, 1988.

Jerney, John, and Elna Tymes. *Maximizing Novell NetWare*. Carmel, Ind.: New Riders Publishing, 1992.

Kent, Les. "Microsoft Opens a Window on the Future with NT," *Infoworld*, January 18, 1993, pp. 48-49.

Kernighan, Brian W., and Dennis M. Ritchie. *The C Programming Language*. Englewood Cliffs, N.J.: Prentice Hall, 1978.

Kernighan, Brian W., and Rob Pike. *The UNIX Programming Environment*. Englewood Cliffs, N.J.: Prentice Hall, 1984.

King, Richard Allen. *The IBM PC DOS Handbook*. Alameda, Calif.: Sybex, 1983.

Krohn, Nico. "NetWare Casts Shadow Over NT: Beta Testers Say Microsoft's OS Lacks Enterprise Features," *PC Week*, January 25, 1993, p. 1.

Krohn, Nico. "UnixWare Arrives on the OS Scene: Offering Challenges Win NT, OS/2 2.0," *PC Week*, December 21, 1992, p. 49.

Morrissey, Jane. "Novell Bets Big on Unix: USL Purchase Gives Networking Giant Alternative to NT," *PC Week*, December 28, p. 1.

Norton, Peter. *Inside the IBM PC: Access to Advanced Features and Programming*. New York: Robert J. Brady Co., 1983.

"Operating Systems: PC Week Special Report," *PC Week*, December 21, 1992, Supplement.

Poole, Gary Andrew. "And Now, Heeeeere's NT," *UnixWorld*, February 1993, pp. 53-56.

Poole, Gary Andrew. "The Brain Behind NT: Microsoft's David Cutler," *UnixWorld*, February 1993, pp. 59-60.

Singh, Jai, and Amy Cortese. "Microsoft's Gates Prepares for the NT Plunge," *PC Week*, January 18, 1993, p. 22.

Siyan, Karanjit. *NetWare: The Professional Reference*. Carmel, Ind.: New Riders Publishing, 1992.

Smith, Douglas K., and Robert C. Alexander. *Fumbling the Future: How Xerox Invented, Then Ignored, the First Personal Computer*. New York: William Morrow and Company, 1988.

Soat, John, and Anthony Vechione. "NT's Magical Mystery Tour," *InformationWeek*, February 15, 1993, pp. 34-40.

Spanbauer, Scott. "Windows NT: A DOS for the '90s," *PC World*, December 1992, p. 141.

"Sun Aiming Solaris at NT, Taligent," *Software Magazine*, November 15, 1992, p. 12.

Wallace, James, and Jim Erickson. *Hard Drive*. New York: John Wiley & Sons, 1992.

Wylie, Margie. "The OSes are Coming, The OSes are Coming," *Network World*, January 18, 1993, pp. 40-44.

Zaks, Rodnay. *The CP/M Handbook with MP/M*. Alameda, Calif.: Sybex, 1980.

Index

Symbols

8-bit processors, 15
16-bit Windows, 15
   API calls
      changing, 171
      dropped, 171-172
      widening, 170
   applications
      running under Windows NT, 96-97, 354
      UNIX compatibility, 343
   compatibility, 339-340
   contemporary/future uses, 50-55
   drag and drop capability, 54
   incorporation of third-party additions, 54-55
   memory, addressing, 65
   multiplatform support, 52
   running 32-bit programs, 231-232
   versus Win32, 161
   virtual memory support, 72
286-based PCs, 22-23
32-bit addressing
   program sizes, 67
   Windows NT, 64-68
32-bit operating systems, 272
   Chicago, 373
386-based PCs, 22-24
3Com company, 186
3D Graphics Kit, 300
486-based PCs, 54
4G virtual address space, 161-162
802.3 standard, 375

A

access control, 133
   objects, 146-147
   restricting, 165-166
   security, 88-91
access control entries, *see* ACEs
access control list, *see* ACL
Access Token object, 144, 165
accessing
   addresses, 65
   DOS, 221-222
accounts, user, listing, 119
ACE (advanced computing environment), 32-33
ACEs (access control entries), 147
ACL (access control list), 146-147, 165
adapters, video, OS/2 support, 254
add-ons, security, 331
adding users, 123
addresses, 65, 372
   accessing, 65
   spaces, 93, 162
addressing memory
   linear, 65-68
   more than 640K, 66
   OS/2 versus Windows NT, 251-253
Administrative Tools, 119-130
   Backup, 127-128
   Disk Manager, 124-126
   Event Viewer, 113, 128-129
   Performance Monitor, 126
   Registry Editor, 129-130
   User Manager, 119-124

Index

administrators
  access control, 90
  logging on, 108
Adobe Type Manager, *see* ATM
advanced computing
  environment, *see* ACE
AIX microkernel, 360
Allen, Paul, 12
Altair personal computer, 10-12
Alto personal computer, 16
ANDF (Application-Neutral
  Distribution Format), 342
API (application programming
  interface), 20, 372
    new calls, 172
    POSIX, 31
    UNIX, 288
    Win32, 168-173, 231-232, 389
APL programming language, 14
Apple networks, resource sharing,
  102
application layer (OSI model), 191
Application log, 128
application programming inter-
  face, *see* API
Application-Neutral Distribution
  Format (ANDF), 342
applications
  16-bit Windows
    running under Windows NT,
      96-97, 354
  availability, 350-354
    DOS versus Windows,
      350-351
    OS/2, 351
    UNIX, 351-353
    Windows, 51

character mode, 97, 327
compatibiliy, 253-256, 343-346
crashing, Windows 3.0, 92
debugging, Process Viewer,
  176-178
development, 353-354
DOS, Windows NT
  compatibility, 255
engineering, 350
horizontal/vertical, 256, 350
mission-critical, 37, 375, 379
multimedia computer, 41-42
Presentation Manager-based, 97
protection, OS/2 versus
  Windows NT, 260-262
scientific, 350
third-party compatibility, 341
UNIX, porting to Windows NT,
  353
Win32, 169-172
architecture
  client/server, 82-87
  master/slave, asymmetric
    multiprocessing, 80
  microkernel, 365
  multiprocessor standards, 167
  ring, 5-6
  system, 140-160
ASCII, sharing terminals under
  UNIX, 326
assigning
  trust, 333
  users to groups, 121
asymmetric multiprocessing,
  78-80, 372

397

Windows NT: The Next Generation

asynchronous I/O, 372
  I/O multitasking, 162-163
  multithreaded applications, 163-164
ATM (Adobe Type Manager), 256-257
Auditing command (Security menu), 134
authentication, 372

B

Backup administrative tool, 127-128
backward compatibility
  real mode, 66
  Windows and DOS, 95
bar diagrams (Disk Manager window), 124
BASIC programming language, 11
batch languages, REXX, 262-263
battery capacity, Mobile Windows, 48-49
Binary Compatibility Standard, 343
bootstrap loader, 12
bps (bits per second), 49, 372-373
Bravo personal computer, 16
BSD 4.3 operating system, 378
BSD UNIX, 281
bugs, 11
bundles, plug and play, 58
buttons
  Connect Printer/Disconnect Printer, 115
  Connect/Disconnect Network Drive, 131
  Copy/Move/Delete, 132
  Filename Sort/Extension Sort, 132
  Filesize Sort/Creation Sort, 132
  Name-Only/Full Information, 131-132
  New Window, 132
  Permissions, 118
  Printer Properties, 116
  Printer-Play/Printer-Pause, 115
  Security, 133
  Share/Stop Sharing, 132
  Stop Printing, 118
bypassing
  device drivers, 156
  security, 129

C

C programming language, 8
C2 (Controlled System Access) security, 4, 241, 332, 373
Cairo object-oriented operating system, 152, 365, 373
callbacks, 151
calls
  API, 170-172
  device driver-specific, 171
  local procedure, 378
  memory-management, 171
  multimedia, 171
  remote procedure, 378
  sleep, 286
  wake-up, 286
Cannavino, Jim, 26

Index

Carnegie-Mellon University
  Mach, 281
carrier sense multiple access/
  collision detection, *see* CSMA/
  CD
character mode, 97
character-based applications, 256
character-encoding standards,
  Unicode, 91
character-mode applications,
  Windows NT support, 327
Chat program (WFW), 233,
  236-237
Chicago version, Windows, 230
chips, Pentium (586), 244
CHKDSK program (DOS), 223
CISC (complex instruction set
  computer), 373-374
client/server computing, 38, 82-87
client/server networking, 56,
  204-208, 373
clients, 85
clipboard, 237-238
COBOL (Common Business-
  Oriented Language), 11
collisions, avoiding, 93-94
Color command (Control Panel),
  109
command languages
  REXX, 262-263
  Windows NT, 263
command prompt language, 122
commands
  Control Panel, 109-111
  Fault Tolerance, 126
  File menu, 135

LAN Manager, 224
NetWare, 224
Security menu, 134-135
User menu, 124
Common Business-Oriented
  Language, *see* COBOL
communication ports, 150
communications
  capabilities, Mobile Windows,
    48
  port-to-port, 150
compatibility, 338-339
  backward, 66
  DOS, 253-256
  DOS/Windows, 339-340
  LAN Manager, 344-345
  Modular Windows, 44
  NetWare with Windows NT, 345
  OS/2, 253-256, 340-341, 356
  UNIX, 341-343, 363
  upgrading from DOS-based
    Windows, 345
  WFW (Windows for
    Workgroups), 57-58
  Win32 API, 168
  Windows, 253-256
  Windows NT, 59, 343-346
  Windows NT and DOS, 95
  Windows NT and OS/2, 97
compilers, 7, 166, 374
complex instruction set computer,
  see CISC
computer industry, historical
  development, 13-14
  Apple, 19-22
  IBM, 14-16, 22-29
  Xerox, 16-25

computing
    client/server, 38
    pen, 39
Confirm Password field, 120
Connect Printer/Disconnect
    Printer buttons, 115
Connect to Printer dialog box, 115
Connect/Disconnect Network
    Drive buttons, 131
connection ports, 149
connectivity, OS/2, 266
Control Panel, 109-114
Controlled System Access
    security, *see* C2
cooperative multitasking, 75
    see also nonpreemptive
        multitasking
Copy/Move/Delete buttons, 132
corrupting files, 92
costs
    hard disks, 69
    operating systems, 349
    RAM, 69
CP/M operating system, 14
CP/M SoftCard, 14
CPU (central processing unit)
    redundancy, 244
    threads, executing, 76
CPUTherm utility, 179
Crash Protection, 323
crashes
    DOS, 329
    Windows 3.0, 92
    Windows 3.1, 329

CSMA/CD (carrier sense multiple
    access/ collision detection), 18
Ctrl+Alt+Del key combination, 107
customizing dialog boxes, 175-176

D

data link layer (OSI model), 190
Database Kit, 300
DDE (dynamic data exchange),
    226, 374
debugging, 11
    Process Viewer, 176-178
DEC (Digital Equipment
    Corporation), 6-7
dedicated threads, 150-151
Desktop command (Control
    Panel), 109
device drivers, 155
    bypassing, 156
    DOS compatibility, 222
    IRPs, controlling, 156
    UNIX, 285
    Windows, 227-228
device independence, 228
devices, multimedia control
    panels, 112
dialog boxes
    Connect to Printer, 115
    Directory Permissions, 134
    editing/creating, 175-176
    File Permissions, 133
    Group Memberships, 122
    Local Group Properties, 122
    Memory Details, 178

Index

Networks, 112-113
Networks Advanced options, 112
New Local Group, 124
New User, 123
Order/Group, 176
Owner, 135
Printer Details, 117
Printer Permissions, 118
Printer Properties, 116
Services, 114
Special Access, 133
Spy Options!, 179
Spy window, 179
System, 110
Time Zone, 111
User Environment Profile, 122
User Properties, 120-122
Virtual Memory, 111
Dialog Editor, 174-176
Digital Equipment Corporation, *see* DEC
directories
　home, 122
　protecting, 31-32
Directory Permissions dialog box, 134
Disk BASIC, 12
Disk Manager administrative tool, 124-126
Disk Manager window, 124-126
disks
　mirroring, 212, 268
　striping, 212
dispatching threads, 157
distributed processing, 213-214

DLLs (dynamic link libraries), 199, 232, 374
domains, 206-207, 374
　access control, 209
　local, 208
　trusted, 333
DOS, 55, 220-221, 379
　absorption into Windows, 52-54
　accessing from Windows NT, 221-222
　applications, availability, 350-351
　as mainframe terminals, 334
　challenges, 322
　compatibility, 253-256, 339-340
　　device drivers, 222
　　UNIX, 343
　　Windows NT, 95, 255
　contemporary/future uses, 50-55
　crashes, 329
　emulators for UNIX, 342
　features (Version 6.0), 52, 225
　file system integrity, 223
　functionality, 321-323
　hardware requirements, 223
　interoperability, 334-335
　networking, 224
　out of memory, 69
　platform independence, 98
　reliability, 329
　security, 223
　shell program, 221
　viruses, preventing, 223
　Windows NT, purchasing, 225

DPMI (DOS Protected Mode Interface), 252, 374
DR DOS, 52, 362
drag and drop capability, 54
drivers
  device, 155
    DOS, 222
    IRPs, controlling, 156
    Windows, 227-228
  network, installing, 101
Drivers control panel, 112
drives
  designating as FAT file system, 244
  designating as HPFS, 244
  tape, configuring, 127
dual boot capability, 340-343
dynamic data exchange, *see* DDE
dynamic link library, *see* DLL

E

EAs (extended attributes), 256, 374-375
editing
  dialog boxes, 175-176
  in HPFS, 258
  object properties, 129
EMS (Expanded Memory Specification), 252, 375
emulation, 342-343
  DOS, 95
  mainframe terminals, 334
engineering applications, 350
enterprise-wide network, 375

environments
  operating versus systems, 219, 229-230
  Win32 versus 16-bit, 161
Erickson, Jim, 26
EtherNet LAN, 375
EtherNet networking standard, 19
Event object, 144
Event Pair object, 144
Event Viewer administrative tool, 128-129
EventLog service, 113
exceptions, processing, 158
executive objects, 144-145
Expanded Memory Specification, *see* EMS
extended attributes, *see* EAs
Extended Memory Specification, *see* XMS
extensibility, 7, 375
  OS/2 versus Windows NT, 270-271

F

FAT (file allocation table), 91, 375-376
  designating drive as, 244
  OS/2 2.0 support, 257
fault tolerance, 4, 211-212, 375
  RAID, 103
  Windows NT, 332
Fault Tolerance menu, 126
fields
  Confirm Password, 120
  Password, 120

Index

file allocation table, *see* FAT
File Manager, 130-135
  toolbar, 131-135
  unification with Program Manager, 52
File Manager window, 130-135
File menu, 109, 135
File object, 144
File Permissions dialog box, 133
file servers, 84-85, 376
  NetWare network operating system, 56
file synchronization, 49-50
file systems
  FAT, 91, 257-258, 376
  HPFS, 91, 257-259
  NTFS, 91
Filename Sort/Extension Sort buttons, 132
files
  corrupting, 92
  overwriting, 50
  paging, 110
  random-access, 284
  security, 88
  sequential, 284
  swap, 70-72
  system integrity, DOS, 223
  virtual, 155
Filesize Sort/Creation Sort buttons, 132
first versions, purchasing, 349
flags, page, 93
fonts, Postscript (ATM), 257
Fonts command (Control Panel), 109
forecasts
  longevity
    OS/2, 356-357
    UNIX operating system, 355-356
    Windows, 357-358
  Microsoft, Inc., 364-366
  sales, software applications, 367-368
  Windows NT, 366-368
formats, Unicode, 387
functionality, operating systems, 321
  DOS/Windows, 321-323
  OS/2, 323-325
  UNIX, 325-326
  Windows NT, 326-328

G

Gates, Bill, 12, 20-25, 357
GDI (graphical device interface), 96
global permissions, 166
graphical development tools, SDK, 173-180
graphical device interface, *see* GDI
graphical user interfaces, *see* GUIs
graphics, 226-227
Group Memberships dialog box, 122
groups, describing, 123

403

guard pages, 154
GUIs (graphical user interfaces), 16-18, 376
　historical development, 19-22
　Interface Manager, 20
　VisiOn (VisiCorp), 21-22

H

HAL (hardware abstraction layer), 159-160, 376
handprint recognition software, 47
hard disks
　contents, restoring, 127
　costs, 69
　management, 124-126
Hard Drive, 26
Hard Error Popup, 260
hardware
　memory protection, 154
　requirements
　　DOS, 223
　　Windows, 229
　　Windows NT, 243
hardware abstraction layer, *see* HAL
high performance file system, *see* HPFS
high-level languages, 7-8, 376
home directories, specifying, 122
horizontal applications, 256, 350
　OS/2, 351
　UNIX, 352
　Windows, 350
host (mainframe) network SNA connectivity, 100

HPFS (high performance file system), 91, 376
　access security, 330
　designating drives as, 244
　features, 257-259
　versus NTFS, 272

I

I/O
　asynchronous, 372
　system, 155-157
I/O manager, 155-157
I/O request packet, *see* IRP
iBCS2 (Intel Binary Compatibility Standard 2), 342-343
IBM operating systems, 359-361
icons, 17-18, 377
IDE (Integrated Drive Electronics), 230
IFS (Installable File System), 244
independence, device, 228
input messages, OS/2 versus Windows NT, 250-251
Installable File System, *see* IFS
installation protocols, 101
installing network drivers, 101
Integrated Drive Electronics, *see* IDE
integrity
　ensuring, shared memory, 154
　file system, DOS, 223
　Windows NT, 332
Intel Binary Compatibility Standard 2 (iBCS2), 342-343
Interface Builder, 300
Interface Manager GUI, 20

Index

Internet network
  DOS/Windows link, 334
  TCP/IP protocol, 336
Internetwork packet exchange/ sequenced packet exchange, *see* IPX/SPX
internetworking, 377
interoperability, 334
  LAN Server network operating system, 336
  NetWare 4.0 for OS/2, 335
  OS/2, 335-336
  UNIX, 336-337
  Windows NT, 100-101, 337-338
interrupts, 158, 377
IPX/SPX (Internetwork packet exchange/sequenced packet exchange, 377
  UnixWare support, 336
IRP (I/O request packet), 155-157
isolation, memory, 323

J-K

Jobs, Steve, 19-22

kernel mode, 85, 93, 141, 377
kernels, 7, 157-159, 377
  interrupts, handling, 158
  multiprocessor synchronization, 158
  objects, 144
  system recovery, 159
  threads, scheduling/dispatching, 157
Key object, 145
Keyboard command (Control Panel), 110

L

LAN Manager, 100, 186-187, 377
  compatibility, 344-345
  OS/2 1.3, 268-269
  Windows NT as client/server, 338
LAN Manager for Windows NT, 102-103
LAN Server (IBM), 377
  interoperability, 336
  OS/2 support, 268
  Windows NT as client/server, 338
landscapes, Microsoft, 42
languages
  command prompt, 122
  high-level, 7-8, 376
  low-level, 7-8
  machine, 378
  REXX, 262-263
LANs (local area networks), 83, 377
  EtherNet, 19, 375
  historical development, 18-19
  operating systems, 38
  OS/2 platform, 266-267
LANtastic peer-to-peer network, 57
layers, thunking, 387
lazy write caching, 258
LeTocq, Chris, 366
libraries
  DLLs, 199
  X Windows, 337
linear
  address space, 162
  memory, addressing, 65-68

load balancing, 77
local area networks, *see* LANs
local domains, 208
Local Group Properties dialog box, 122
local procedure calls, *see* LPCs
locking workstations, 136
logging off, 135-136
logging on, 106-109, 378
  executing scripts, 122
Logoff command (File menu), 135
longevity, operating systems, 354-358
low-level languages, 7-8
LPC facility, 149-152
LPCs (Local procedure calls), 149-152

M

Mach operating system, 378
machine language, *see* low-level languages
Macintosh computer, 19-22
macro languages, REXX, 262-263
macro recorder, 263
mailboxes, 378
mainframe-based systems
  terminals, DOS/Windows emulation, 334
  Windows NT support, 102
maintenance mode, 339
managers
  I/O, 155-157
  object, 144-146
  process, 148-149

MAP command (NetWare), 224
marketing strategies, 348-368
master/slave architectures, 80
memory
  addressing
    linear, 65-68
    more than 640K, 66
    OS/2 versus Windows NT, 251-253
  collisions, avoiding, 93-94
  isolation, 323
  management, VMM, 152-153
  protection
    hardware, 154
    mechanisms, 93
    VMM, 153-154
  segmentation, 65, 378
  shared, 286
    ensuring integrity, 154
  virtual, 23, 253, 388
    paging files, 110
    sharing, 153
    swap files, 70-72
    VMM, 152
    Windows NT, 70-72
Memory Details dialog box, 178
memory-management calls, 171
menus
  Fault Tolerance, 126
  File, 109, 135
  Operations, 127
  Options, 175
  Partition, 125
  Policies, 124
message queues, 286

Index

messages
  input, OS/2 versus Windows NT, 250-251
  monitoring, Spy, 178-181
Micro Instrumentation & Telemetry Systems (MITS), 10
microkernel architecture, 359, 365, 378
  OS (IBM), 359-361
Microsoft, Inc.
  forecasts, 364-366
  history, 12
  importance of DOS, 51-52
  marketing strategies, 348-368
  networking, 365
  support, 365-366
  Windows historical development, 21-25
MIDI Mapper control panel, 112
minicomputer-based systems, 102
mirrored disk sets, 126, 378
mirroring disks, 212, 268
mission-critical applications, 37, 59, 375, 379
MITS (Micro Instrumentation & Telemetry Systems), 10
Mobile Windows
  communications capabilities, 48
  features, 46-50
  file synchronization, 49-50
  power consumption, 47-49
  storage space management, 50
modems, 49, 379
modes
  character, 97
  kernel, 85, 93, 141, 377
  maintenance, 339

  Privileged, 126
  protected, 22, 67, 383
  real, 22, 66, 384
  standard, 238
  UNIX, 287-288
  User, 85, 93, 126, 388
  virtual 86, *see* VDM
Modular Windows, 44-45
modulator/demodulator, *see* modem
monitoring system logs, 128
  messages, Spy, 178-180
  processes, 177-178
  threads, 177-178
monitors, security reference, 146-147
mouse, 17
Mouse command (Control Panel), 109
MS Mail (WFW), 233-236
MS-NET, 185-186
MULTICS operating system, 5-6
multimedia
  calls, 171
  control panels, 112
multimedia computers, 41-42
  applications, 41-42
  operating systems, 42-45
  processors, 45
multiplatform support
  16-bit Windows, 52
  Windows NT, 60
multiprocessing, 31, 76-77, 284, 379
  asymmetric, 372
  symmetric, 243-244, 268
  UNIX, 31

407

multiprocessors, 77-78
  architecture standards, 167
  support, 166-167
  synchronization, 158
multitasking, 5, 72-74, 379
  asynchronous I/O, 162-163
  cooperative, 75
  nonpreemptive, 381
  OS/2, 250-251, 323
  preemptive, 74-75, 383
  support, 162-164
  UNIX, 31
multithreading, 80-82, 379
  asynchronous I/O, 163-164
  processes, creating, 148
Mutant object, 145

N

Name-Only/Full Information buttons, 131-132
named pipes, 198, 378-379
National Security Agency, see NSA
Nbt process, 113
NDIS (Network Driver Interface Specification), 191-192, 379-380
  mailslots, 198
  named pipes, 198
  OSI layers
    application, 198-200
    network, 192-194
    presentation, 196-197
    session, 195-196
    transport, 192-194
  providers, 196-197
  redirectors, 195-196

  RPCs, 199-200
  support, 337
  transport protocols, 192-194
  Win32 I/O API, 198
Net Use command (LAN Manager), 224
NetBEUI (NetBIOS Extended User Interface), 192, 379
NetBIOS API, 380
NetWare, 55-57, 185, 380
  interoperability, 335
  OS/2 support, 267
  support, 337-338
  Windows NT compatibility, 345
NetWare Lite peer-to-peer network, 57
Network Driver Interface Specification, see NDIS
network drivers, installing, 101
network interface card, see NIC
network layer (OSI model), 190
network operating systems, see NOS
networking, 184
  client/server, 204-208, 373
  distributed processing, 213-214
  domains, 206-209
  DOS, 224
  fault tolerance, 211-212
  history, 184-187
  interoperability, 334-338
  Microsoft, 365
  NDIS, 191-192
    mailslots, 198
    named pipes, 198
    providers, 196-197
    redirectors, 195-196

Index

RPCs, 199-200
transport protocols, 192-194
Win32 I/O API, 198
NeXTSTEP, 299
operating systems, 187-188
OS/2, 266-267
OSI model, 188-191
peer-to-peer, 57-58, 101, 200-204, 382
RPCs, 213-214
SCO UNIX, 303
security, 208-211
SunSoft Solaris, 307-308
UNIX, 290-292
UnixWare, 311-312
Windows, 228-229
networks, 38, 380
client/server, 56
enterprise-wide, 375
peer-to-peer, 83
support, 99-102
tools, WFW, 233
Networks Advanced options dialog box, 112
Networks dialog box, 112-113
new calls, API, 172
New Local Group command (User menu), 124
New Local Group dialog box, 124
New User dialog box, 123
New Window button, 132
NeXTlinks, 300
NeXTSTEP, 296-298, 380
3d Graphics Kit, 300
architecture, 298
Database Kit, 300

distributed objects, 300
graphics, 298-299
GUIs, 298-299
Interface Builder, 300
languages, 301
networking, 299
NeXTlinks, 300
object libraries, 301
NFS, 380
UNIX support, 336
NIC (network interface card), 191, 380
nonpreemptive multitasking, 74-75, 381
nonvolatile storage, 69
NOS (network operating systems), 55-57, 380-381
interoperability with Windows NT, 101-103
notebook computers, 46
Novell
NetWare, *see* NetWare
operating systems, 361-364
UNIX acquisition, 355-356, 362
NSA (National Security Agency), 373
NT compilers, 166
NT executive, 141-142, 377, 381
executive components, 143-157
system services, 142-143
NT File System, *see* NTFS
NT kernel, 381
NT Lite, 365
NTFS (NT File System), 91, 244, 259, 381
versus HPFS, 272

409

O

Object Directory object, 145
object linking and embedding, *see* OLE
object manager, 144-146
object-oriented operating systems, 144
    Cairo, 373
    Taligent, 360-361, 386
objects, 381
    access control, 146-147
    access token, 165
    editing properties, 129
    executive, 144
    kernel, 144
    power notify, 159
    section, 150
    security, 93, 165-166
    synchronization, 164-170
    Timer, 145
    viewing properties, 129
OLE (object linking and embedding), 235, 381
Open Systems Interconnection, *see* OSI, 188
operating systems, 2-3, 382
    16-bit, 15
    32-bit, 272
        Chicago, 373
    adopting, costs, 349
    applications/choices, 37-42
    BSD 4.3 (U. of C.), 378
    compatibility
        DOS/Windows, 339-340
        OS/2, 340-341
        UNIX, 341-343
        Windows NT, 343-346
    CP/M, 14
    DOS, *see* DOS
    forecasts, 364-366
    forthcoming
        IBM, 359-361
        Novell, 361-364
    functionality, 321
        DOS/Windows, 321-323
        OS/2 operating system, 323-325
        UNIX, 325-326
        Windows NT, 326-328
    historical development, 12-16
    interoperability
        DOS/Windows, 334-335
        OS/2, 335-336
        UNIX, 336-337
        Windows NT, 337-338
    LAN, 38
    landscapes, 42
    longevity, 354-358
    Mach, 378
    mission-critical, 59
    MULTICS, 5-6
    multiple installations, 110
    network, *see* NOS
    NeXTSTEP, *see* NeXTSTEP
    object-oriented, 144
        Cairo, 373
        Taligent, 360-361, 386
    OS/2, *see* OS/2
    OS/9, 41
    paths, 40-41
    PenDOS, 39
    PenPoint, 39
    platform-independency, 10
    portability, 269-270

Index

portable, 243
QDOS, 15-16
reliability, 328
    DOS/Windows, 329
    OS/2, 330
    UNIX, 331-332
    Windows NT, 332-334
selecting, 320-345
single-user, 55
UNIX, *see* UNIX
UnixWare, 388
vendors, competitive needs, 358-359
versus environments, 219, 229-230
Windows NT, 29-32, 58-60
XENIX, 30
Operations menu, 127
Options menu, customizing dialog boxes, 175
Order/Group dialog box, 176
OS Loader, 222
OS/2, 382
  access security, 330
  applications
    availability, 351
    protection, 260-262
    UNIX compatibility, 343
  as platform for LAN, 266-267
  ATM support, 256-257
  compatibility, 97, 253-256, 340-346
  connectivity, 266
  described, 248-249
  dual boot capability, 340
  FAT system support, 257
  features, 249-250

forecasts, 356-357
functionality, 323-325
historical development, 24-26
HPFS features, 257-259
interoperability, 335-336
LAN Manager, 102
limitations, 324-325
moving to Windows NT, 345
multitasking support, 250-251, 323
networking, 266-267
reliability, 330
REXX programming language, 262-263
support
    file system, 258
    LAN Manager 2.1, 268-269
    LAN Server 3.0, 268
    NetWare, 267
    video adapters, 254
usability, 324
VDD (virtual device driver), 261-262
VDM protection, 260-262
versus Windows NT, 269-272
    input messages, 250-251
    memory addressing, 251-253
vertical applications, 352-353
Windows compatibility, 356
Workplace Shell, 248-249, 258-259, 263-266, 324
OSI (Open Systems Interconnection) reference model, 188, 381-382
  application layer, 191
  data link layer, 190

411

Windows NT: The Next Generation

network layer, 190
physical layer, 189
presentation layer, 191
session layer, 191
transport layer, 190
overwriting files, 49-50
Owner dialog box, 135
Ownership command (Security menu), 134-135

P

page flags, 93
pages, 382
 guard, 154
paging files, 110
palmtop computers, 36, 46, 382
PARC (Palo Alto Research Center), 16
parity, striping, 103
Partition menu, 125
partitions, creating, 125
Password field, 120
passwords, 107
 creating, 120
 validity period, 124
Paterson, Tim, 15
PC DOS, *see* DOS
PC/AT computer, 22-24
PCMCIA (Personal Computer Memory Card Industry Association), 250, 382-383
PDAs (Personal Digital Assistant), 36, 40-45, 382-383
 operating system paths, 40-41

peer-to-peer networking, 57-58, 83, 99-101, 200-204, 382
pen computing, 39, 46-47
Pen Windows API, 46-47
PenDOS operating system, 39
PenPoint operating system, 39, 47
Pentium (586) chip, 244
performance
 resources, sharing, 83
 Win32s API, 231
Performance Monitor administrative tool, 126
Performance Monitor window, 126
permanent section objects, 150
permissions, global, 166
Permissions button, 118
Personal Computer Memory Card Industry Association, *see* PCMCIA
Personal Digital Assistant, *see* PDA
physical addresses, 65
physical layer (OSI model), 189
pipes, named, 378-379
platform independence, 10, 98-99, 383
 DOS, 98
 UNIX, 30-31, 98
platforms, multimedia computer, 41-42
plug and play bundles, 58
Policies menu, 124
Popular Electronics magazine, 10
Port object, 145
port-to-port communications, 150

412

Index

portability
  POSIX API source code, 97
  Windows NT, 269-270
portable computers, 46
portable operating systems, 243
ports
  communication, 150
  connection, 149
Ports command (Control Panel), 109
PORTTOOL utility, 169
POSIX API, 31, 97, 327
  compatibility, 343-346
PostScript fonts (ATM), 257
power
  failures, recovery, 159, 332
    consumption, Mobile Windows, 47-49
power notify objects, 159
preemptive multitasking, 74-75, 383
presentation layer, 191
Presentation Manager (Windows), 24, 97
Print Manager, 114-118
Print Manager window, 115
Printer Details dialog box, 117
Printer Permissions dialog box, 118
Printer Properties button, 116
Printer Properties dialog box, 116
Printer-Play/Printer-Pause buttons, 115
Privileged Mode, 126
process manager, 148-149

Process object, 145
Process Scheduler (UNIX), 283
Process Viewer, 176-178
processes, 383
  creating/terminating, 148
  logon, 378
  memory usage, 178
  monitoring, 177-178
  multithreaded, creating, 148
  Nbt, 113
  Tcpip, 113
  Telnet, 113
  Ups, 113
processors
  8-bit, 15
  16-bit, 15, 65
  80286, 22-23
  80386, 22-23
  80486, 54
  multimedia computers, 45
  RISC, 45, 98
  X86, 45
Profile object, 145
Program Manager, 52, 108
programming languages
  APL, 14
  BASIC, 11
  C, 8
  REXX, 262-263
programs
  platform-independency, 10
  sizes, 32-bit addressing, 67
Project DOE, 306
properties, object, 129
proprietary transport protocols, installation, 101

protected mode, 22, 67, 383
protected subsystems, 86-87, 378, 384
protection
  application, OS/2 versus Windows NT, 260-262
  directories, 31-32
  memory, 93, 153-154
  resource access, 93-94
protocols, 384
  IPX/SPX, UnixWare support, 336
  NDIS, Windows NT support, 337
  proprietary transport, installation, 101
  stacks, 384
  TCP/IP, 336-337, 386-387
providers, 196-197, 384
purchasing Windows NT, 349

Q-R

QDOS operating system, 15-16
queues, message, 286
Quick LPCs, 150-151

RAIDs (redundant array of independent drives), 103, 212
RAM (random-access memory), 44, 384
  costs, 69
  features, 68-69
  speeds, 68
  storage, swap files, 71-72
random-access files, 284
random-access memory, *see* RAM

Raskin, Jef, 19
read-only memory, *see* ROM
real mode, 22, 66, 384
rebooting, 107
recorders, macro, 263
recovery
  system, 159
  UNIX, 332
redirectors, 195-196, 384
Reduced Instruction Set Computer, *see* RISC
redundancy, CPU, 244
redundant array of independent drives, *see* RAIDs
Regenerate command (Fault Tolerance menu), 126
Registry Editor administrative tool, 129-130, 333
Registry Editor window, 130
reliability
  operating systems, 328-329
  OS/2, 330
  UNIX, 331-332
  Windows NT, 332-334
remote procedure calls, *see* RPCs
Replace Permissions on Existing Files/Subdirectories command, 134
resource sharing
resources
  access protection, 93-94
  sharing
    Apple networks and Windows NT, 102
    historical development, 18-19

Index

REXX programming language, 262-263
ring architecture, 5-6
RISC (Reduced Instruction Set Computer), 30, 384-385
　processors, 45, 98
risk factors, purchasing Windows NT, 349
Ritchie, Dennis, 6-8
Roberts, Ed, 12
ROM (read-only memory), 44, 384-385
RPCs (remote procedure calls), 199-200, 213-214, 378, 385

S

sales forecast, software applications, 367-368
Schedule+ application (WFW), 233-234
scheduling threads, 157
SCI (System Call Interface), 288
scientific applications, 350
SCO UNIX, 301-303, 385
scripts, logon, 122
SCSI (Small Computer System Interface), 230
SDK (Software Development Kit), 140
　graphical development tools, 173
　　Dialog Editor, 173-176
　　Process Viewer, 176-178
　　Spy, 178-181
seamless windows, 254

section objects, 145, 150
security
　access control, 88-91, 330
　add-ons, 331
　bypassing, 129
　DOS, 223
　files, 88
　LAN Manager for Windows NT, 103
　MULTICS operating system, 5
　network operating systems, 89
　networks, 208-211
　object, 93, 165-166
　OS/2 versus Windows NT, 271-272
　reference monitor, 146-147
　single-user operating systems, 89
　subdirectories, 88
　UNIX, 31-32, 289-290, 331-332
　VDMs, 87
　Welcome message, 107
　Windows 3.1, 241
　Windows NT, 88-89, 241-242, 332
Security button, 133
Security log, 128
segmentation, memory, 65, 378
selecting operating systems, 320-345
Semaphore counter, 145
semaphores, 286
sequential files, 284
Server control panel, 112
servers, 84-85, 376, 385
Services control panel, 112

415

Windows NT: The Next Generation

Services dialog box, 114
session layer (OSI model), 191
Share program (DOS), 224
Share/Stop Sharing buttons, 132
shared memory, 286
  ensuring integrity, 154
sharing
  resources, historical
    development, 18-19
  virtual memory, 153
shell program, 221
Shutdown command (File menu), 135
sidegrades, 351
signaling synchronization, 164
signals, 286
single threading, 80-82
Single-Line Internet Protocol,
  see SLIP
single-user operating systems, 55
  security, 89
sizes, program, 67
sleep calls, 286
SLIP (Single-Line Internet
  Protocol), 334
Small Computer System Interface,
  see SCSI
SMP (symmetric multiprocessing), 270, 385-386
SNA (Systems Network
  Architecture), 266
    Windows NT as client/terminal,
      338
sneakernet, 83
SoftPC DOS emulator, 342

software
  applications, sales forecast,
    367-368
  development
    multiprocessor support,
      166-167
    multitasking support,
      162-164
    Windows NT, 161-167
  handprint recognition, 47
Software Development Kit,
  see SDK
Solaris, 385
  security add-ons (Sun), 331
SOM (System Object Model), 265,
  385-386
Sound control panel, 112
source codes, POSIX API, 97
spaces
  address, 93
  UNIX, 287-288
Special Access dialog box, 133
speeds
  RAM, 68
  Windows NT, 327
spin locks, 158
Spy messages, monitoring,
  178-181
Spy Options! dialog box, 179
Spy window dialog box, 179
stacks, protocol, 384
standard mode, 238
standards
  802.3, 375
  ACE (advanced computing
    environment), 32-33

Index

Binary Compatibility, 343
EtherNet, 19
multiprocessor architectures, 167
PCMCIA, 250
POSIX, 327
token ring, 387
Unicode character-encoding, 91
Stop Printing button, 118
storage
  nonvolatile, 69
  RAM swap files, 71-72
  space management, Mobile Windows, 50
  volatile, 68
streams, 385
striped disk sets, 126, 386
striping disks, 103, 212
subdirectories, security, 88
subnetworks, 207
subnotebook computers, 46
subsystems, 241
  protected, 86-87, 242-243, 378, 384
  security, *see* security
SunSoft Solaris, 304
  architecture, 305-306
  development tools, 308
  graphics and GUIs, 307
  networking, 307-308
  Project DOE, 306
swap files, 70-72, 386
Symbolic Link, 145
symmetric multiprocessing, 78-80, 243-244, 268

synchronization
  multiprocessor, 158
  objects, 164-170, 386
  signaling, 164
synchronous I/O processing, 162-163
system administrators, access control, 90
System Call Interface (SCI), 288
System command (Control Panel), 110
System dialog box, 110
System log, 128
System Object Model, *see* SOM
systems
  integrity, 88-93
  I/O, 155-157
  logs, monitoring, 128
  recovery, 159
Systems Network Architecture, *see* SNA

T

Taligent object-oriented operating system, 360-361, 386
Tape Backup window, 127
tape drives, configuring, 127
TCP/IP (Transport Control Protocol/Internet Protocol), 336, 386-387
  connecting to, 113
  Windows NT interoperability, 338
  Windows NT support, 337

Telnet process, 113
temporary section objects, 150
terminals, DOS/Windows
　emulation, 334
terminate-and-stay-resident
　programs (TSRs), 329
third-party
　applications, 341
　developers, 28-29
　vendors, 337
Thompson, Ken, 6-8
Thread object, 145
threads, 72-73, 386
　creating, 148
　dedicated, 150-151
　monitoring, 177-178
　scheduling/dispatching, 157
　single versus multiple, 80-82
thunking layers, 387
tiling, 25
time slices, 74
Time Zone command (Control
　Panel), 111
Time Zone dialog box, 111
Timer object, 145
timesharing, 5, 387
token rings, 387
toolbar, File Manager, 131-135
tools
　Administrative, 119-130
　graphical development, SDK,
　　173-180
　network, WFW, 233
Transport Control Protocol/
　Internet Protocol,
　see TCP/IP

transport layer (OSI model), 190
trap handler, 158
trust, assigning, 333
trusted domains, 333
TSR (terminate-and-stay-
　resident) programs, 329

U

U.S. Government C2 security, 4,
　241, 332, 373
UAE (unrecoverable application
　error), 92-93
Unicode character-encoding
　standard, 91, 387
uninterruptible power supplies,
　see UPSs
UNIX, 280, 387
　acquisition by Novell, 362
　APIs, 288
　applications
　　availability, 351-353
　　porting to Windows NT, 353
　ASCII terminals, sharing, 326
　capabilities, 282-283
　compared to Windows NT,
　　278-279, 292
　　NT advantages, 294-295
　　NT disadvantages, 295
　　UNIX advantages, 292-293
　　UNIX disadvantages,
　　　293-294
　　UNIX variants, 313-317
　compatibility, 341-343
　　variants, 363
　connecting to, 113
　device drivers, 285

Index

DOS emulators, 342
features, 6-8, 30-32
file system, 284-285
forecast, 355-356, 361-364
functionality, 325-326
horizontal applications, 352
interoperability, 336-337
interprocess communications, 286
memory, 287
modes, 287-288
moving to Windows NT, 346
multiprocessing, 31, 284
multitasking, 31
networking, 290-292
    DOS/Windows link, 334
Novell acquisition of, 355-356
platform independence, 98
power-fail recovery, 332
Process Scheduler, 283
reliability, 331-332
SCI, 288
security, 31-32, 289-290, 331-332
shells, 288
spaces, 287-288
System V Release 4, 341
unification, 341
universal appeal, 8-10
usability, 325-326
USL version compatibility, 341
versions, 280-282
versus Windows NT, 59
vertical applications, 352-353
X Window, 288
UnixWare, 308-312, 362, 388
  architecture, 310
  development tools, 312
  graphics and GUIs, 310
  networking, 311-312
  support, IPX/SPX protocols, 336
unrecoverable application error, *see* UAE
upgrading from DOS-based Windows, 345
UPS control panel, 113
Ups process, 113
UPSs (uninterruptible power supplies), 159, 387-388
  for UNIX systems, 332
usability
  OS/2, 324
  UNIX, 325-326
user accounts, 90, 119
User Environment Profile dialog box, 122
User Manager administrative tool, 119-124
User Manager window, 119-124
User Mode, 85, 93, 126, 388
User Must Change Password at Next Logon command, 121
User Properties dialog box, 120-122
user rights policy, 90
users
  adding, 123
  assigning to groups, 121
  needs, evaluating, 218-219
  passwords, 107
USL System V, 280
utilities
  CPUTherm, 179
  PORTTOOL, 169

419

V

validity period, passwords, 124
value-added resellers (VARs), 185
variants
   UNIX compatibility, 363
   Windows, 357
VARs (value-added resellers), 185
VCPI (Virtual Control Program Interface), 253, 388
VDD (virtual device driver), 261-262
VDMs (virtual DOS machines), 67, 95, 388
   emulators, 343
   DOS applications, running, 222
   WOW (Windows on Win32), 96
vendors, operating system, 358-359
vertical applications, 256, 350-353
   OS/2, 352-353
   UNIX, 352-353
video adapters, OS/2 support, 254
views, virtual memory, 153
virtual
   addresses, 65, 388
   files, 155
   memory, 23, 253, 388
      paging files, 110
      sharing, 153
      swap files, 70-72
      views, 153
      VMM, 152
      Windows NT, 70-72
virtual 86 mode, *see* VDM
Virtual Control Program Interface, *see* VCPI
virtual device driver, *see* VDD
virtual DOS machines, *see* VDMs
Virtual Memory dialog box, 111
viruses, 223
VisiOn GUI (VisiCorp), 21-22
VMM (virtual memory manager), 143, 152-154, 388
   managing memory, 152-153
   protecting memory, 153-154
   sharing memory, 153
volatile storage, 68

W

wake-up calls, 286
Wallace, James, 26
WFW (Windows for Workgroups), 232-233, 389
   Chat program, 236-237
   clipboard, 237-238
   features, 57-58
   limitations, 238
   MS Mail e-mail system, 234-236
   network tools, 233
   OS/2 compatibility , 255
   peer-to-peer workgroups, 334
   Schedule+ application, 233-234
   Windows NT as client/server, 338
what-you-see-is-what-you-get, *see* WYSIWYG
Win32 API, 86, 168-172, 389
   4G virtual address space, 161-162
   developing applications, 169-170
   functuality, 170-173
   versus 16-bit environment, 161

Index

Win32-specific applications, 172
Win32/NT, 367
Win32c *see* Chicago version, Windows
Win32s API, 168, 172, 231-232, 367
  compatibility, 339
  limitations, 232
  OS/2 compatibility, 255
Window Manager, 45
Windows
  16-bit
    contemporary/future uses, 50-55
    drag and drop capability, 54
    incorporation of third-party additions, 54-55
    multiplatform support, 52
  absorption of DOS, 52-54
  applications, availability, 51, 350-351
  Chicago version, 230
  compatibility, 253-256, 339-340
  costs (version 3.1), 226
  crashes, 92, 329
  device drivers, 227-228
  DOS-based, future of, 230-231
  features (version 3.0), 27-29
  forecasts, 357-358
  functionality, 321-323
  graphics, 226-227
  hardware requirements, 229
  historical development, 21-26
  interoperability, 334-335
  Mobile, *see* Mobile Windows
  networking, 228-229
  OS/2 compatibility, 254
  Presentation Manager, 24

reliability, 329
security, 241
variants, 357
windows
  Disk Manager, 124-126
  Event Viewer, 128
  File Manager, 130-135
  Performance Monitor, 126
  Print Manager, 115
  Registry Editor, 130
  seamless, 254
  tiling, 25
  User Manager, 119-124
Windows for Pen Computing, *see* Pen Windows
Windows for Workgroups, *see* WFW
Windows NT
  16-bit Windows applications, running, 96-97
  32-bit addressing, 64-68
  Administrative Tools, 119-130
  applications
    protection, 260-262
    development, 353-354
  backward compatibility, 95
  client/server, 87, 267
  clipboard, 237-238
  command language, 263
  compared to UNIX, 59, 278-279, 292
    NT advantages, 294-295
    NT disadvantages, 295
    UNIX advantages, 292-293
    UNIX disadvantages, 293-294
    UNIX variants, 313-317

421

Windows NT: The Next Generation

compatibility, 59, 343-346
   OS/2, 97, 255
Control Panel, 109-114
costs, 226
device driver requirements, 228
DOS
   accessing, 221-222
   applications, running, 262
extensibility, 270-271
fault tolerance, 332
features, 3-4, 58-60
   comparison with Windows family, 239-240
   not shared by OS/2, 269-272
File Manager, 130-135
forecasts, 366-368
functionality, 326-328
hard disk management, 124-126
hardware, 243
historical development, 29-32
host (mainframe) network SNA connectivity, 100
interoperability, 101-103, 337-338
kernel, 157-159
   interrupts, handling, 158
   multiprocessor synchronization, 158
   system recovery, 159
   threads, scheduling/dispatching, 157
LAN Manager network operating system, 100
logging off, 135-136
logging on, 90, 106-109
macro recorder, 263

marketing strategies, 348-368
memory protection mechanisms, 93
MS Mail e-mail system, 234-236
multiplatform support, 60
multiprocessing, symmetric, 243-244
networking, 184
   history, 184-187
   operating system in, 187-188
   peer-to-peer, 99-101
   support, 99-102
NT executive, 142
   executive components, 143-157
   system services, 142-143
NTFS, 272
operating systems, 272
OS Loader, 222
platform independence, 10, 98-99
portability, 269-270
Print Manager, 114-118
Program Manager, 108
protected subsystems, 242-243
protection, resource access, 93-94
purchasing, risk factors, 349
Registry Editor, 333
reliability, 332-334
resource sharing, Apple networks, 102
SDK, 173-180
security, 88-89, 241-242, 271-272
SMP, 270
software development, 161-167

Index

speed, 327
subsystems, 241
support
   character-mode
     applications, 327
   mainframe-based systems,
     102
   minicomputer-based
     systems, 102
   NetWare, 337-338
   third-party vendors, 337
system architecture, 140-160
system integrity, 88-89, 92-93
technical support, 60
TrueType font support, 256-257
user needs, evaluating, 218-219
VDD, 261-262
VDM protection, 260-262
versus OS/2
   input messages, 250-251
   memory addressing, 251-253
virtual memory, 70-72
virus protection, 223
Windows on Win32, *see* WOW
Windows Open Systems
 Architecture (WOSA), 99

WNet API, 196
Workgroup Connection package,
  224
Workgroup Postoffice, 235
workgroups, peer-to-peer, 334
Workplace Shell (OS/2), 248-249,
  258-259, 263-266, 324
workstations, 29-30, 136
WOSA (Windows Open Systems
  Architecture), 99
WOW (Windows on Win32), 96,
  343, 389
WYSIWYG (what-you-see-is-what-
  you-get), 16, 256

X-Z

X Terminals, 334
X Window, 288
X Windows library, 337
X86 processors, 45
XENIX operating system, 30, 98,
  279, 389
XMS (Extended Memory
  Specification), 252, 375, 389